THE KATALAN COLLECTION OF ITALIAN DRAWINGS

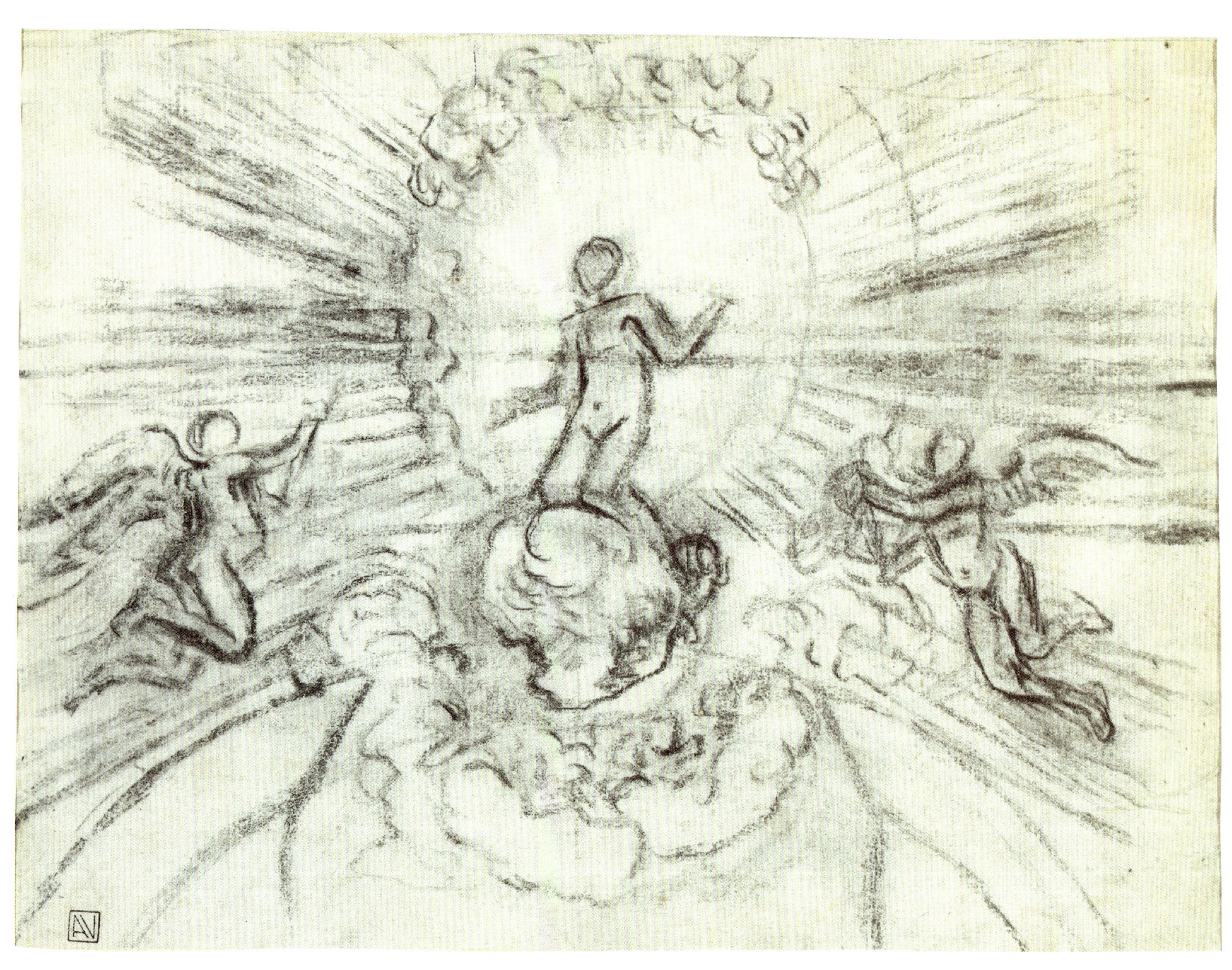

Gian Lorenzo Bernini (1599–1680), *Virgin in Glory with Two Angels (1636–39),* black chalk on buff paper

THE KATALAN COLLECTION OF ITALIAN DRAWINGS

The Frances Lehman Loeb Art Center

Vassar College

Poughkeepsie, New York

Exhibition Schedule

The Frances Lehman Loeb Art Center, Vassar College, Poughkeepsie, New York
14 April–18 June 1995

The Minneapolis Institute of Arts, Minneapolis, Minnesota
16 July–10 September 1995

The Frick Art Museum, Pittsburgh, Pennsylvania
3 November 1995–7 January 1996

The Ackland Art Museum, University of North Carolina, Chapel Hill, North Carolina
2 February–2 April 1996

The Hood Museum of Art, Dartmouth College, Hanover, New Hampshire
17 April–16 June 1996

The Frances Lehman Loeb Art Center,
Vassar College, Poughkeepsie, New York 12601

Library of Congress Catalogue Card Number
94-061746
ISBN 0-9644263-1-5

This book has been published in conjunction with an exhibition entitled *The Katalan Collection of Italian Drawings,* organized by the Frances Lehman Loeb Art Center.

Design: **Lazin & Katalan,** New York, NY
Editing: **Kelli Peduzzi,** Poughkeepsie, NY
Printing: **Balding & Mansell,** Peterborough, UK

Cover Illustration:
Giovanni Battista Naldini (1537–91)
Hercules and the Nemean Lion;
Hercules and the Cretan Bull, (ca. 1565)
Pen and brown ink over black chalk

This publication has been supported by a grant from the **Smart Family Foundation, Inc.**

Contents

Foreword and Acknowledgments

Jak Katalan has come to the world of collecting Old Master drawings equipped with the six primary prerequisites—an eye for quality, passion, intelligence, a prodigious memory, patience, and diplomacy. While some of these attributes can be improved through hard work, they are for the most part gifts bestowed upon the individual spirit. Like so many of the great collectors in history, Giorgio Vasari, Peter Lely, Joshua Reynolds, Benjamin West, and Herbert List, to name a few, Jak Katalan also came to the collecting of drawings having been trained as an artist in his own right. Since receiving his MFA degree from Yale he has worked as a successful painter and graphic designer for almost twenty years.

Jak Katalan's well-informed initial forays into art collecting centered on twentieth-century art. This collection was eventually converted into funds that were applied to assembling a still relatively small but distinguished group of Italian sixteenth- and seventeenth-century drawings. The first drawing was purchased in 1985, and the collection is still in formation, ever increasing in range and quality. We are very happy to be able to present a large portion of this collection to a broader public at the Frances Lehman Loeb Art Center. My gratitude goes to the collector for sharing his superb collection with the various campus and public communities where the exhibition will travel.

Though valuable in a commercial sense, the Katalan Collection is not about money and what it can buy. The drawings in this collection are not mere trophies from the battlefield of the art market. The collection is, rather, about erudition, dedication, and the "sweat equity" of hard work that yields important discoveries—of which there are many in his collection. The Sodoma (cat. no. 1), Polidoro da Caravaggio (cat. no. 7), Lelio Orsi (cat. no. 12), Niccolò Circignani (cat. no. 15), Agostino Carracci (cat. no. 32), and Francesco Maffei (cat. no. 46), to name just a few, were all acquired as unattributed or wrongly attributed drawings, for example. Katalan's practical art history training is self-taught and highly specialized, and he is growing into a respected connoisseur and scholar in his own right, having published drawings from the Lugt Collection, Paris and the British Museum in the periodical, *Master Drawings*. Presently he is involved in a book-length edition of *corrigenda* to the catalogue of Italian drawings in the collection of the Art Museum, Princeton University.

As a collector, Jak Katalan has also been wise in knowing the limits of his general expertise and when the assistance of the career specialist becomes desirable. It is a testimonial to the high regard in which they hold the collector that a team of such premier experts in the field of Old Master drawings has generously compiled and written the entries for this catalogue. It is thus with great thanks that I acknowledge the learned contributions of Professor Babette Bohn, Texas Christian University; Peter Dreyer, former Curator of Drawings, The Pierpont Morgan Library; Professor Mario Di Giampaolo,

Florence; Madame Catherine Monbeig Goguel, Directeur de Recherche au C.N.R.S. Chargée de Mission au Cabinet des Dessins, Musée du Louvre; George Goldner, Drue Heinz Chair, Department of Drawings and Prints, The Metropolitan Museum of Art; Professor Ann Sutherland Harris, University of Pittsburgh; Nancy Ward Neilson, Sotheby's; Professor Emeritus W. Roger Rearick, University of Maryland; and Nicholas Turner, Curator of Drawings, The J. Paul Getty Museum. Vassar College and the Frances Lehman Loeb Art Center are indeed grateful for the opportunity to publish the fruits of their research. It is also a pleasure to acknowledge the hard work of Kelli Peduzzi, the editor of this publication; and the staff of the Frances Lehman Loeb Art Center, particularly Joann Potter, registrar, and Laura Morace, assistant registrar; Bruce Bundock, preparator; and Carol Jarvis, departmental secretary. The entries by Mario Di Giampaolo were translated by Marietta Cambareri and those by Catherine Monbeig Goguel were translated by Varena Forcione and Alberto Rosa.

Since the world of Old Master drawings has a delicate environment and synergism all its own, composed of many individuals, scholars, collectors, *marchands amateurs,* and dealers, it is important to acknowledge further the contributions and assistance of a number of colleagues. The collector has asked that the following individuals be thanked in particular: Morton Abromson, Marcello Aldega, Peggy Auchincloss, Fred Bancroft, Therèse and Bruno de Bayser, Katrin Bellinger, François Borne, Hugo Chapman, Keith Christiansen, Philippe Costamagna, Diane DeGrazia, Annamaria Edelstein, David Ekserdjian, Chris Fischer, Kate Ganz, Margot Gordon, Dieter Graf, William Griswold, Marion Hirschler, Nicholas Joly, Elizabeth Llewellyn, John Morton Morris, Joan Nissman, D. Stephen Pepper, the late Jacques Petit Hory, Michèle and Hubert Prouté, Crispian Riley-Smith, Christiana Romalli, David Rosand, Paola Rossi, Scott Schaefer, Marjorie Shelley, Yvonne Tan Bunzl, Françoise Viatte, Mia Weiner, Thomas Williams, and Linda Wolk-Simon.

After its viewing at Vassar College, the Katalan Collection will travel to four additional museums. It gives me great pleasure to cite the enthusiasm and cooperation of the following individuals for this project: Evan M. Maurer, Director, and Richard Campbell, Curator of Prints and Drawings, Minneapolis Institute of Arts; DeCourcy E. MacIntosh, Chief Executive Officer, and Nadine Grabania, Assistant Curator, The Frick Art Museum; Charles W. Millard, former Director, Gerald Bolas, Director, and Sarah Schroth, Curator, The Ackland Art Museum; and Timothy Rub, Director, and Richard Rand, Curator, The Hood Museum of Art.

James Mundy

Anne Hendricks Bass Director

The Frances Lehman Loeb Art Center, Vassar College

Contributors to the Catalogue

Babette Bohn (BB)
Numbers: 30a, 30b, 32, 38

Peter Dreyer (PD)
Numbers: 16, 28, 48, 49a, 49b, 55

Mario Di Giampaolo (MDG)
Numbers: 8, 13, 15, 24, 31, 33, 35, 39, 41

Catherine Monbeig Goguel (CMG)
Numbers: 3, 4, 5, 10, 11, 12, 17, 25, 26, 43, 47

George Goldner (GG)
Numbers: 1, 2

Ann Sutherland Harris (ASH)
Numbers: 27, 29, 34, 36, 44, 45, 50, 54

James Mundy (JM)
Numbers: 6, 7, 14

Nancy Ward Neilson (NWN)
Number: 23

W. Roger Rearick (WRR)
Numbers: 9, 18, 19, 20, 21, 22, 46

Nicholas Turner (NT)
Numbers: 37, 40, 42, 51, 52, 53

Index of Artists

Giovanni Antonio Bazzi, called Il Sodoma

Vercelli (Piedmont), 1477–Siena, 1549

1 ### *St. Jerome in the Wilderness* (ca. 1535)

Pen and brown ink over black chalk (recto); black chalk (verso)

200 x 280 mm (7 7/8 x 11 in)

PROVENANCE: Matthiesen Gallery, London, June 1963, *Old Master Drawings,* as Campagnola; C. R. Rudolph, London; Sotheby's, London, 19 May 1977, lot 148; Pietro Scarpa, Venice; [Phillips, London, 7 July 1993, lot 142, as D. Campagnola]

LITERATURE: photograph of drawing in Witt Library, Courtauld Institute, apparently from a catalogue of the 1963 exhibition; Scarpa 1978, cat. no. 3

EXHIBITIONS: *Old Master Drawings,* Matthiesen Gallery, London, June 1963, cat. no. 8

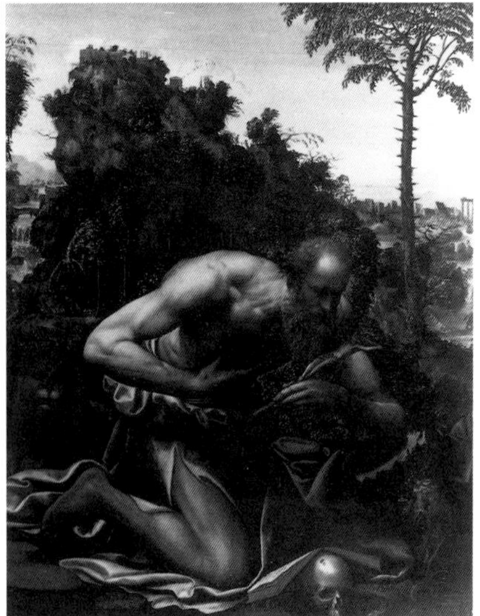

Fig. 1: Giovanni Antonio Bazzi, called Il Sodoma, *St. Jerome*, National Gallery, London

The drawing was attributed to the circle of Beccafumi in the Rudolph sale, to Lotto by Scarpa, and to Domenico Campagnola when it was recently sold at Phillips (see above). The attribution to Sodoma is, however, surely correct.

Both recto and verso show studies of St. Jerome that relate quite closely to a Sodoma painting of the same subject in the National Gallery, London, which seems to date from 1535 (Fig. 1). The drawing appears to be an early study for the painting, laying out the basic components of the scene. There are several adjustments made from verso to recto, notably the placement of a large tree in front of St. Jerome, in place of the rocks and base of a tree trunk that are found on the verso. In the painting, the tree is both in front and in back of the saint, but is given much less prominence. Equally, an extensive landscape appears in the background. Lastly, St. Jerome leans forward and has become a taller figure with a relatively smaller head. Despite these differences, the sheet seems surely to be an early effort to formulate the composition of this painting.

The graphic handling of the sheet is also typical of Sodoma. The faint chalk sketch on the verso compares well with the more fully evolved study for the *Madonna del Corvo* in the Uffizi Gallery, Florence. Moreover, the recto is very similar to several of the surviving pen studies by Sodoma. The manner of cross-hatching and modeling the figure compare closely to the earlier study for an old man at the right of the *Coronation of the Virgin* in the Oratorio of S. Bernardino, Siena, now in the British Museum, London. On the other hand, the heavily worked outlines and the drapery style are very similar to those in a study for the *Resurrection* in the Palazzo Pubblico, Siena, of 1535, now in the J. Paul Getty Museum, Malibu.

GG

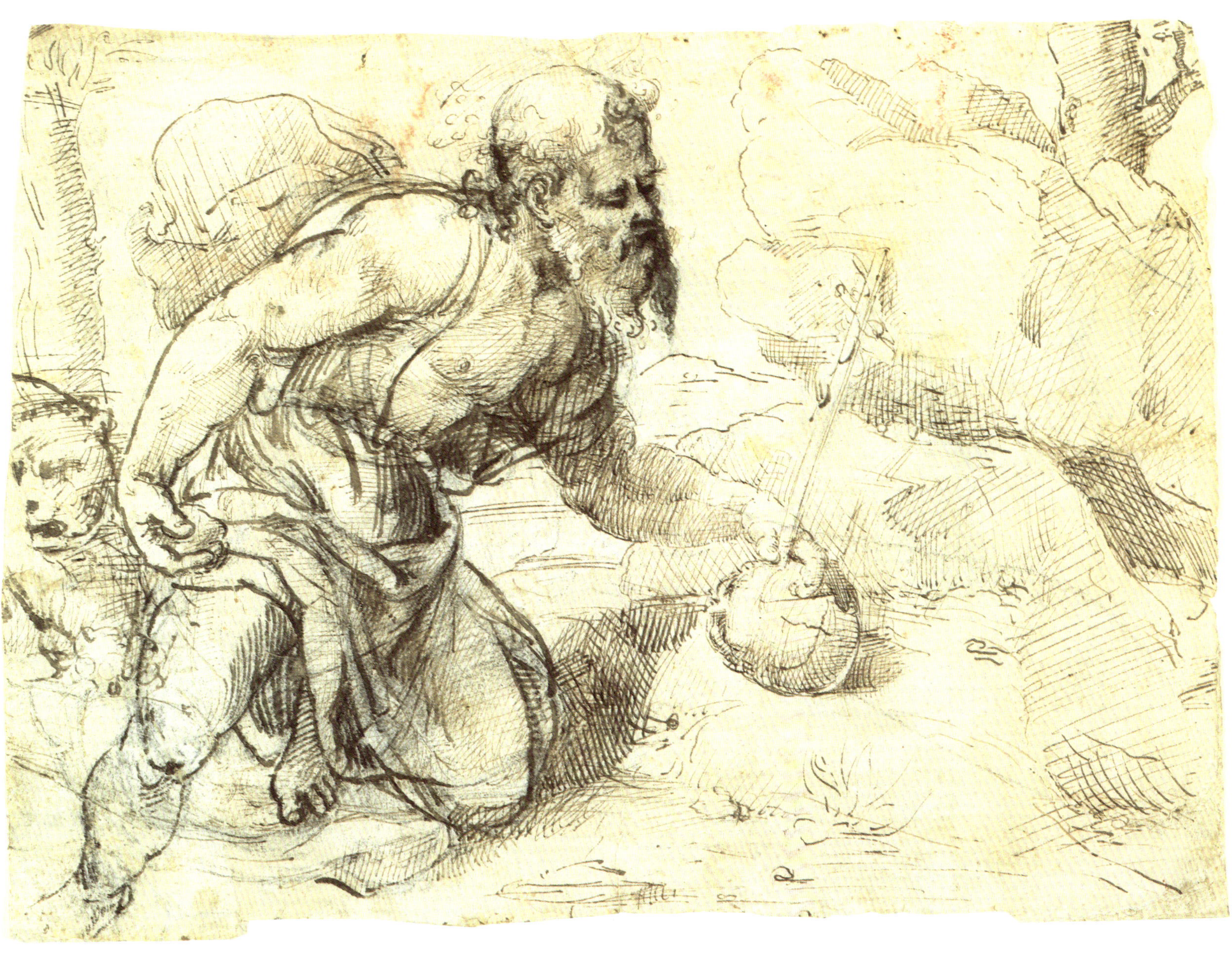

Baldassare Peruzzi

Siena, 1481–Rome, 1536

2 *The Madonna and Child* (ca. 1516)

Pen and brown ink; inscribed *Ano* in the lower right corner; the lower left corner made up

148 x 104 mm (5 3/4 x 4 in)

Provenance: Christie's, London, 2 July 1991, lot 237; [Christie's, London, 15 December 1992, lot 50]

Literature: Frommel 1990, 72; Goldner and Hendrix 1992, 86, cat. no. 31

It is likely that this is a preparatory study for the fresco by Peruzzi of the *Sacra Conversazione* of 1516 in the Cappella Ponzetti, Santa Maria della Pace, Rome. The pose and blessing gesture of the Christ Child are similar, as is the position of the right arm of the Virgin. On the other hand, she is shown looking directly outward in the drawing, whereas in the fresco, her head and gaze are turned toward a kneeling donor below. Despite this difference, the connection between drawing and fresco is strong.

More problematical is the relationship between these and two further drawings, one in the Getty Museum, Malibu and the other in the collection of Juan de Beistegui, Paris. The graphic style of these two sheets is closely comparable to that of the Katalan drawing, but they are iconographically different, with the figure of Joseph included alongside the Virgin and Child. However, the Getty drawing shows the Virgin looking downward, as in the fresco, and the pose of the Christ Child is close to the way he is shown in the Katalan drawing.

Lastly, the Beistegui sheet is furthest from both the fresco and the Katalan drawing, but contains sufficient similarity to the study in the Getty Museum to warrant its inclusion in this hypothetical group. Since the relationship of the Beistegui and Getty drawings to the fresco and the Katalan sheet is not secure, one cannot go further than to suggest that they may either represent rejected schemes for the fresco or studies for a contemporaneous project of similar type.

A copy of the Katalan drawing is in the Taccuino Senese IV 7, as has been noted by David Lachenmann, when he first proposed the attribution to Peruzzi for the present drawing.

GG

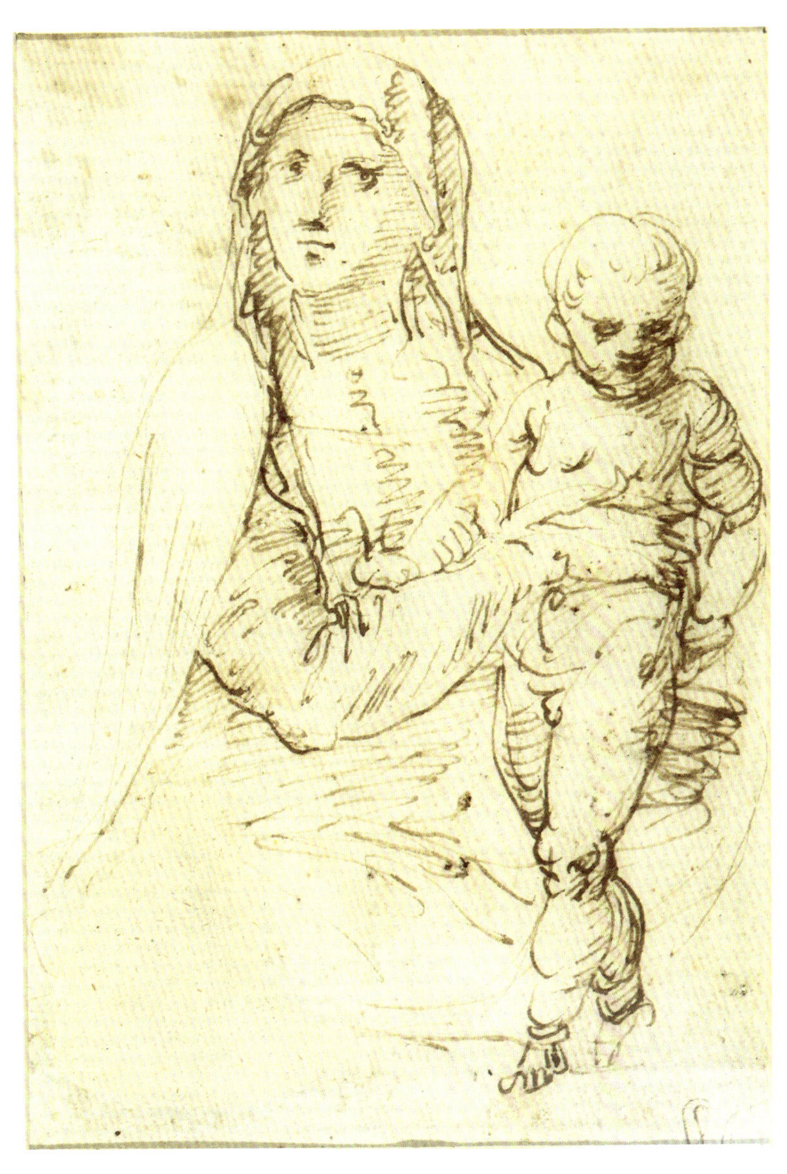

Domenico Beccafumi

Siena, 1484–Siena, 1551

3 ### Recto: *Head of an Old Man* Verso: *Putti in Various Positions* (1512–18)

Pen and brown ink and wash over black chalk; lines in black chalk on the right; annotated *u.p.*, in brown ink: *S R* (recto); red chalk (verso)

220 x 147 mm (8 5/8 x 5 1/2 in)

Provenance: George (?) Hibbert, London; Coghlan Briscoe, Dublin, 1928; Dr. W. M. Crofton; Christie's, London, 7 July 1959, lot 95; *Domenico Beccafumi, Drawings from a Sketchbook*, Thomas Agnew and Sons, London, November 1965, lot 9; Sotheby's, London, 1979, lot 28; [Sotheby's, London, 6 July 1987, lot 21]

Literature: Liphart Rathshoff 1935, 33–70, 162–200, fig. 28 (recto and verso); Sanminiatelli 1957, 405 n. 9 (for the verso); Nicholson 1965, 641, fig. 31

Exhibitions: *Domenico Beccafumi, Drawings from a Sketchbook*, Thomas Agnew and Sons, London, 1965

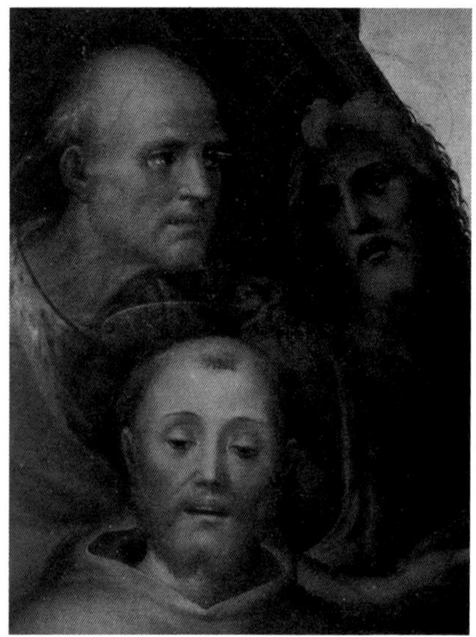

Fig. 2: Domenico Beccafumi, *The Mystical Marriage of St. Catherine of Alexandria and Eight Other Saints* (detail), The Hermitage, Moscow

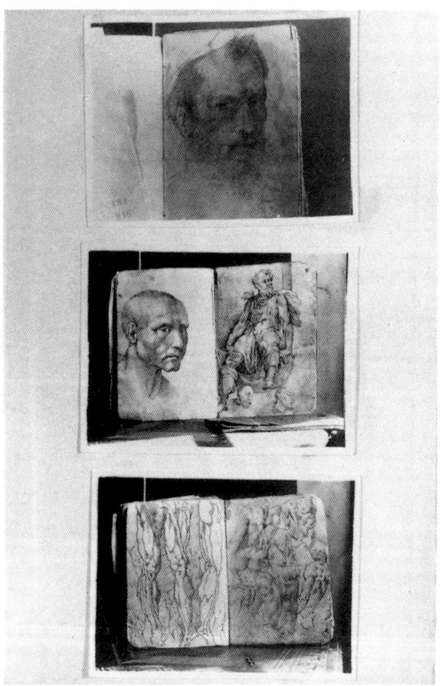

Fig. 3: Detail from a page of a book belonging to Coghlan Briscoe, private collection, Paris

The expressive power of this sheet stems from the type of model, an old man, bald, with ascetic features marked by age and defined by strong backlighting. The tragic physiognomy corresponds with Beccafumi's paintings. A striking relationship can be established with the head of St. Jerome, located in the left background of the altarpiece, *The Mystical Marriage of St. Catherine of Alexandria and Eight Other Saints* (The Hermitage, Moscow, Fig. 2).[1] The date of this painting, whose importance was underlined at the Siena exhibition of 1990, has been set at about 1518. The connection is more revealing than the one suggested in the past with the figure of Postumius Tiburtius, represented on the ceiling of the Sala del Concistorio (Palazzo Pubblico, Siena).[2]

Benedict Nicholson, underlining the play of light in this work, has said it is "a remarkably vigourous head of an old man which is already beginning to take on the character of Beccafumi's mature style... in distortions which convey a sense of real life far more vivid than he could ever have achieved, had he stuck dutifully to the great pictorial inventions around him."[3] Nicholson probably saw in it an anticipation of Caravaggesque realism's preoccupation with light. The putto in profile on the verso seems to be drawing a bow; he could represent a small cherub, rather than the Holy Child.

This sheet cannot be isolated from the problem presented by the ensemble of the Briscoe sketchbook to which it belonged, which was published in 1935 by Liphart Rathshoff. (The sketchbook was dispersed when it was presented at Agnew's in 1965.) Donato Sanminiatelli, who wrote the monograph that was the main source of information on the drawings of Beccafumi until the Siena exhibition of 1990, at first was in favor of an attribution to the artist himself, dating the sheet just after 1512. Subsequently he proposed an attribution to Marco Pino.[4]

A good analysis of the controversy, which involves all thirty-seven sheets of the sketchbook (almost all drawn on both the recto and verso), can be found in the catalogue entry by James Byam Shaw on the drawing acquired by Frits Lugt.[5] The question has been reexamined by De Marchi, and in his opinion not one of the drawings, dispersed in museums "dall'Australia al Massachusetts," is by Beccafumi.[6] He believes that they might have been executed in Siena during the 1580s, by artists such as Prospero Antichi, Cristoforo Roncalli, and Alessandro Casolani, in the circle of the academy of drawing promoted by Ippolito Agostini, notable protector of the arts in Siena.[7]

The problems of the Briscoe sketchbook are not isolated ones; the question of the plurality of hands can also be examined in connection with the drawings of the Biblioteca Comunale of Siena. In the Siena collections, one finds several old copies after other drawings by Beccafumi and some that are contemporary with the original drawings.[8] Despite these copies, Beccafumi did not have what could properly be called a school. One of the sheets quotes from Michelangelo's *Last Judgment* (1541). Indeed, some photographs inserted between the pages of a book belonging to Coghlan Briscoe (Fig. 3) indicate that he believed the drawings to be by Michelangelo.[9] The photographs show the original state of the sketchbook. The *Head of an Old Man* exhibited here was placed on the left-hand side of the sketchbook, facing

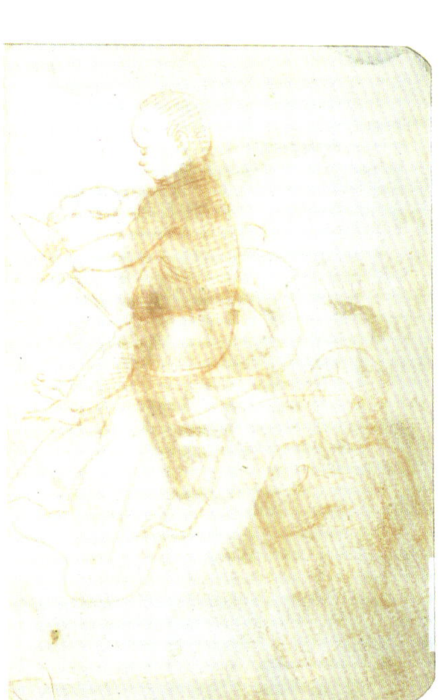

Verso

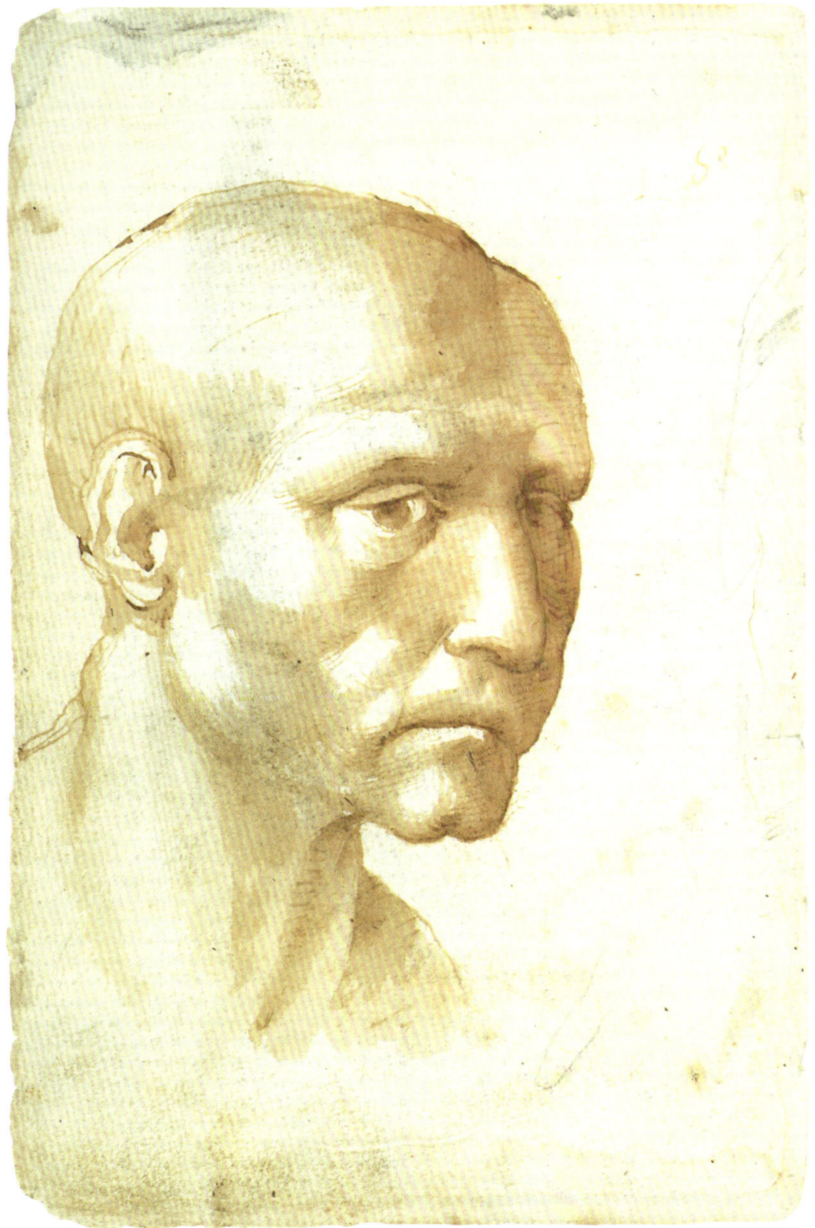

Recto

the drawing with the figure of *Lucius Junius Brutus* (Fitzwilliam Museum, Cambridge), painted by Beccafumi (tondo, Sala del Concistorio, Palazzo Pubblico, Siena). Michael Jaffé believes the Cambridge drawing to be an original preparatory study for the tondo of the ceiling of the Sala del Concistorio.[10] This author considers it a copy, mainly because of the dryness of the pen and the general arrangement.

Briscoe had also inserted the photograph of a delicate portrait, which he believed to be by Michelangelo, with a note dated June 1924, indicating that he had left the drawing on long-term loan at the Fitzwilliam Museum, Cambridge. In 1965 it entered the permanent collection as an original work by Domenico Beccafumi (PD. 7–1965, gift of the Friends of the Museum). David Scrase sees in this portrait the features of the artist himself, but does not express a definite opinion on its authorship.[11] The complexity of the problem posed by the ensemble of the drawings suggests that one should not be too quick to place some of these sheets outside Beccafumi's *oeuvre* or his immediate circle without serious consideration, since they could be by his hand.

The birth and death dates indicated here for Beccafumi are based on a recently published document.[12]

CMG

1. *Angelini (1990; 124–25, cat. no. 13).*

2. *Baccheschi (1977; 103, cat. no. 108, fig. 37A).*

3. *Nicholson (1965, 641).*

4. *Sanminiatelli (1967; 186, 189, cat. no. 8).*

5. *Byam Shaw (1983; 102–5, cat. nos. 94–96).*

6. *De Marchi (1990, 412–15).*

7. *De Marchi (1990, 415).*

8. *Bisogni (1981, 25–47).*

9. *Knackfuss (1896); Phillips, London, 7 July 1993, lot 19; private collection, Paris.*

10. *Jaffé (1977; cat. no. 8, ill.).*

11. *Scrase, by letter.*

12. *Certificate of baptism dated 2 October 1484, in Moscadelli and Zarrilli (1990, 680); the dates coincide with those given in Vasari (1963–64, 5:402).*

Giovanni Antonio Sogliani

Florence, 1492–Florence, 1544

4 ### Recto: *Two Studies of a Male Nude* Verso: *Four Studies of an Infant*

Black chalk, heightened with white, on beige paper (recto); black chalk (verso); inscribed on recto in pen and brown ink at lower margin, *dice Ciro Ferri una volta / del Frate di S. Marco / ma a' me non pare, and l' hebbi da Gasparo Mola / che in parere di Ciro Ferri / me li diede e del frate / ma Ciro un' altra volta...*

338 x 198 mm (13 1/4 x 7 3/4 in)

Provenance: Gasparo Mola; Padre Sebastiano Resta (L. Sup. 2992a); Edward Clive, first earl of Powis; by descent; the earl of Plymouth;[Christie's, London, 1 July 1986, lot 109, ill. (recto)]

Literature: Monbeig Goguel 1991, 453; Griswold and Wolk-Simon 1994, 26, cat. no. 20; Fischer 1994, 148–49, cat. no. 97

Exhibitions: *Sixteenth-Century Italian Drawings in New York Collections,* Metropolitan Museum of Art, New York, 1994, cat. no. 20

Vasari described Sogliani's melancholic and scrupulous disposition as totally possessed by the desire to represent the expression of outward piety, but he did not place the artist among the greatest Florentine painters. In the first edition of *Le Vite* (1550), he wrote rather unkindly: "La maniera sua molto piacque allo universale facendo egli arie pietose e devote, secondo l'uso degli ipocriti" [His style was universally liked as he executed demure and pious expressions, following the manner of hypocrites] (4:761). He also stated that Sogliani worked twenty-four years with Lorenzo di Credi. It seems that he did not have an independent career before 1515.

Fra Bartolommeo is an essential reference point for Sogliani, and the Katalan drawing can be placed among those imitating him. This can be seen in the use of black chalk, sometimes on colored paper, either gray or beige; in the stumping (*sfumato*) of contours, which gives a softer result; and finally in the successful treatment of the figure in its entire volume, filling the height of the sheet. The way in which the main figure study is repeated in a secondary smaller sketch, suggesting an alternative solution (note here the right leg), is a characteristic of Florentine drawing. Judging from the surviving drawings by Sogliani, often still placed among the school of Fra Bartolommeo, the study of completely nude figures is rather rare, even if the artist did use a naked model, following the teachings of Fra Bartolommeo and Andrea del Sarto (for instance in the study for the *Sacra Conversazione* (inv. 17054 F, Uffizi).[1] Generally his studies of isolated figures are at least partially draped.

1. *Petrioli Tofani (1988, cat. no. 11).*

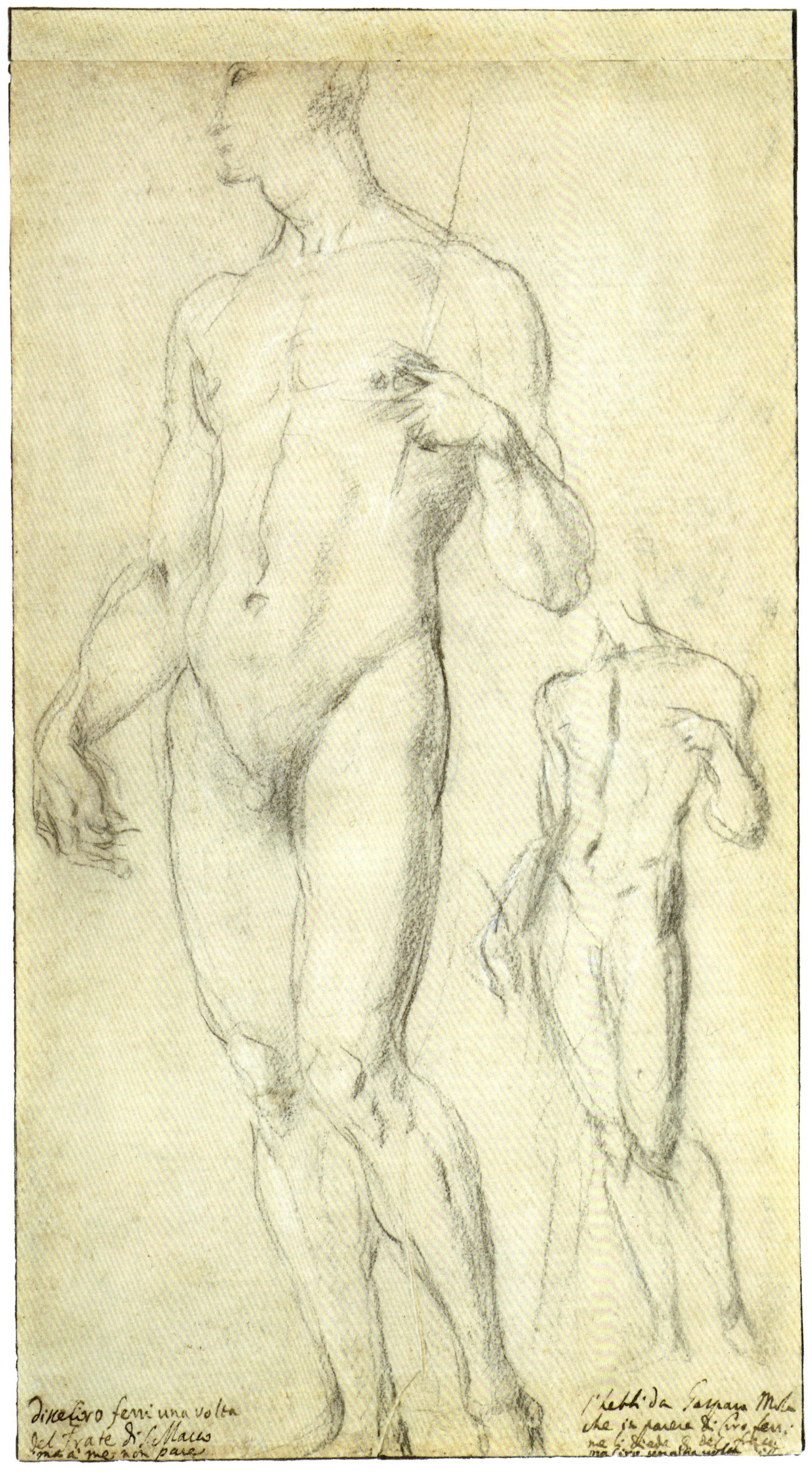

Recto

2. Fischer (1994, 148–49).

3. Monbeig Goguel (1991, 453); Griswold and Wolk-Simon (1994, 26).

4. Vasari (1963–64, 4:400).

The studies on the verso were associated by Chris Fischer with the recently uncovered verso of a sheet in the Louvre (inv. 216) and tentatively connected with the *Virgin and Child* in the Cathedral of Pisa.[2] They represent St. John the Baptist and the Holy Child and are typical of Sogliani. The annotation by Padre Resta (1635–1714), which has already been pointed out,[3] is interesting because it shows the role of the connoisseur played by Ciro Ferri, with whom Resta discussed whether the attribution should go to Fra Bartolommeo or Sogliani. The drawing appears to have belonged to Gaspare Mola (d. 1640), who was a famous medalist in the time of Grand Duke Cosimo II of Tuscany, and whom Filippo Baldinucci cites several times in association with Jacques Callot or Stefano della Bella. Resta recognized the hand of Sogliani, whose drawings were passed on by his widow to Bartolomeo Gondi, a close friend. The latter also owned "molti disegni e teste colorite dal vivo, sopra fogli mesticati" [many drawings and heads drawn from life, on colored paper].[4] Vasari also spoke of "alcuni disegni del medesimo nel nostro libro che sono belli affatto" [some drawings by the same artist that are in our *libro* and are very beautiful]. Nevertheless, none of the known drawings by Sogliani show traces of the mount of the *Libro de' Disegni*.

CMG

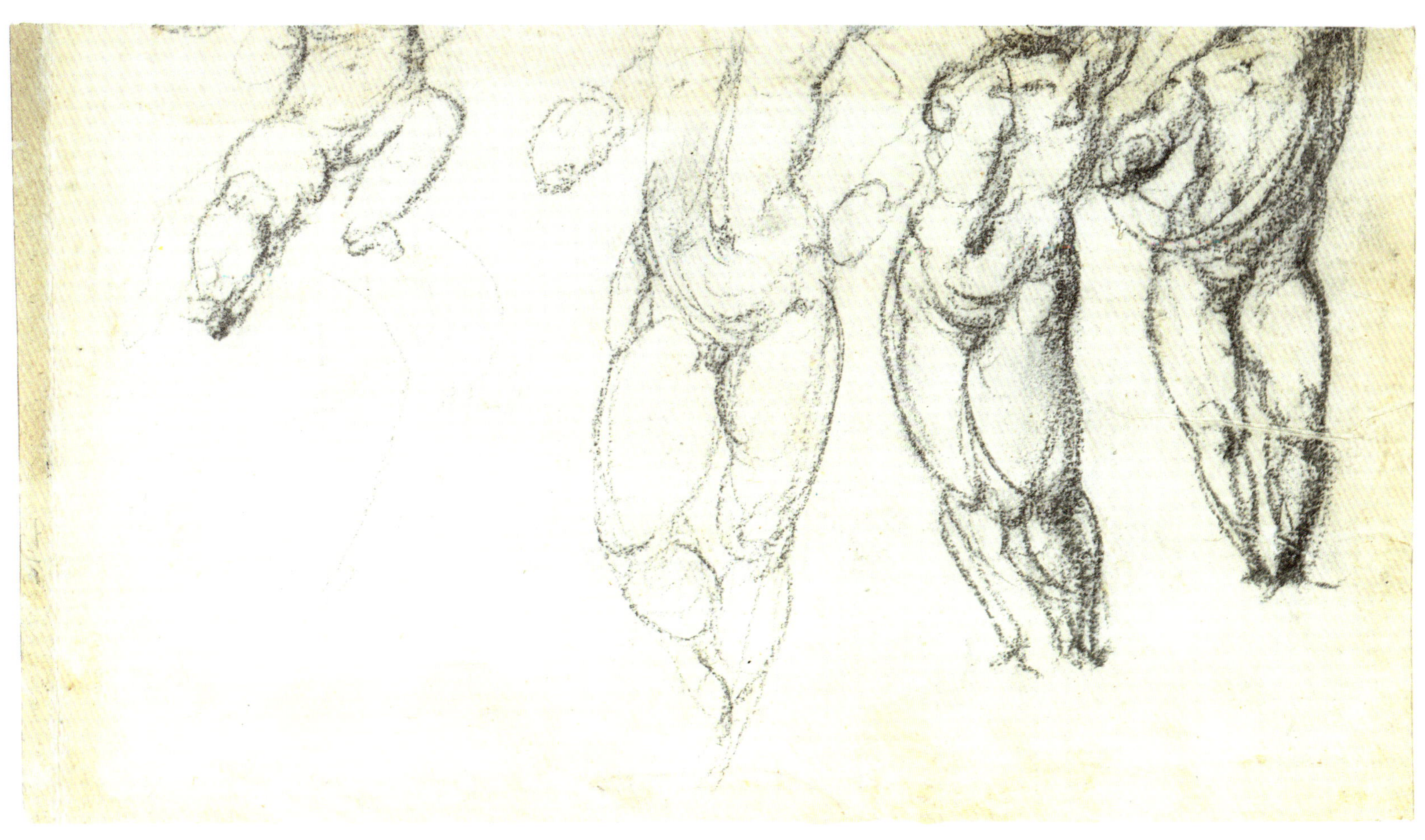

Verso

Jacopo di Giovanni di Francesco, called Jacone

Florence, 1495–Florence, 1553

5 *A Group of Three Figures*

Pen and brown ink

268 x 215 mm (10 1/2 x 8 3/8 in)

Provenance: Christie's, London, 23 November 1971, lot 204 (as attributed to Niccolò Tribolo); Feitelson collection, Los Angeles (collector's mark on the verso); [Marcello Aldega and Margot Gordon, 1987]

Literature: Aldega and Gordon 1987, cat. no. 3; Griswold and Wolk-Simon 1994, cat. no. 22; Ekserdjian 1994

Exhibitions: *Sixteenth-Century Italian Drawings in New York Collections,* Metropolitan Museum of Art, New York, 1994, cat. no. 22

Jacone is certainly one of the most interesting and, even today, least known of the circle of Florentine mannerists who were trained in Andrea del Sarto's workshop and remained close to both Bandinelli and Pontormo. Jacone had ties with Bacchiacca, with whom he is said to have traveled to Rome in 1524, the same year Parmigianino arrived there.[1]

The identification of subject matter presents consistent problems in the group of drawings that have been returned to Jacone based on Ulrich Middeldorf's oral opinion,[2] as in the typical example of his work exhibited here.[3] Indeed, this obscurity itself seems to have become a factor in the recognition of the powerfully sketched drawings characteristic of his style. Scattered examples of his work are to be found at the British Museum, London; Christ Church, Oxford; as well as the Uffizi Gallery and Casa Buonarrotti, Florence.[4] Other drawings remain unpublished (*Two Women*, inv. 1662 C, Musée des Beaux-Arts, Orleans).

Based on cross-hatching and monumentality in a very distinctive interpretation of Michelangelo's legacy, Jacone's technique is often close to that of Bandinelli, with whom he shared a strong penchant for very large figures grouped in unusual arrangements. This drawing can be related in more than one way to the latter's *Holy Family with St. John the Baptist*, which recently came on the art market. Vasari designated Jacone as the *discepolo, amico*, and *imitatore* of Andrea del Sarto.[5] However, nearly all the drawings that have been attributed to Jacone were done in pen and ink, a medium that is almost unknown in Andrea's extant work.

Jacone assisted Pontormo and Bronzino in the decoration of the Villa Medici at Carreggi. He was also a friend of the sculptor and cabinetmaker Antonio Particini. In "Life of Aristotile da San Gallo," Vasari says of Jacone: "Disegnò benissimo e con fierezza, e fu molto bizzarro e fantastico nella positura delle sue figure, stravolgendo e cercando di farle variate, differenziate dagl'altri in tutti i suoi componimenti; e nel vero ebbe assai disegno e quando volle, imito il buono" [He drew exceedingly well and forcefully, and was most bizarre and fantastical in the postures he gave his figures, distorting them and seeking to make them varied, differentiating each one from the others in all of its attitudes; and he was quite skilled in rendering true appearances and, when he wanted to, imitating good subjects].[6]

Recent studies have allowed us to dispel the confusion between Jacone's drawings and those of Tribolo, which originates in an otherwise instructive article by Lloyd, and to bring out his talents as a portraitist, comparable to Pontormo in the types of models he chose.[7] An unpublished drawing in pen over black chalk at the Louvre (inv. 11871), which presents studies of diverse male figures in unusual poses particularly reminiscent of those Pontormo painted at Poggio a Caiano, has been compared by Philip Pouncey to a group of drawings previously published under the name of Tribolo, but which is now generally considered to be Jacone's work. The importance of the Louvre sheet is that, unlike all of Jacone's other drawings, it does not include any grouped figures and reveals a much freer style, promising future attributions to unknown works by him. However, it poses the question of the relationship between

1. *Costamagna and Fabre (1991, 15–28).*

2. *Byam Shaw (1976; 1:61–62, under n. 102). For a more recent and complete study, see Pinelli (1988, 5–34).*

3. *David Ekserdjian (1994, 203) has recently expressed the opinion that the subject of the present drawing might represent Christ in the house of Mary and Martha.*

4. *Monbeig Goguel (1979, cat. nos. 13a and 13b).*

5. *Bellinger (1988, cat. no. 1); Vasari (1963–64, 4:328).*

6. *Vasari (1963–64; 6:179, 309).*

7. *Lloyd (1986, 243–46).*

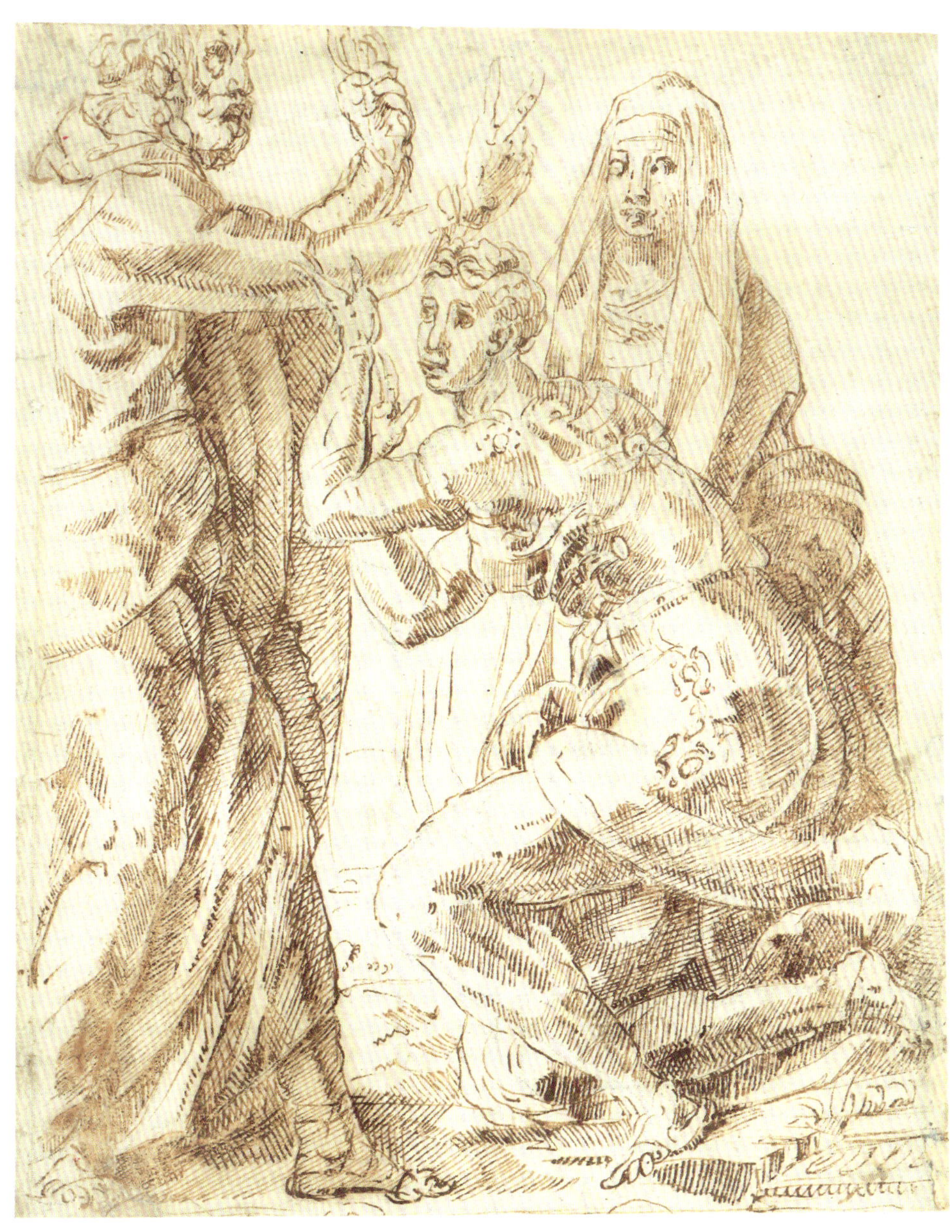

8. Pinelli (1988; 16, *fig.* 10); see also Angelini (1986; 85, *fig.* 1).

9. Vasari (1963–64, 6:311).

10. Carroll (1976; 2:470–71, cat. no. F.20, *figs.* 166–167).

11. Byam Shaw (1976; cat. no. 154, with mention, "Attributed to Francesco Salviati").

pen and ink, and red chalk drawings; indeed, at least one work in the latter medium had already been tentatively attributed to him (inv. 344F, Uffizi Gallery, Florence).[8]

Vasari, who disliked Jacone and was not inclined to give him much credit, recognized his talent in the construction of the triumphal arch for the *apparato* of the Feast of the Annunciation in 1525,[9] which he embellished with paintings on Old Testament themes alongside Bacchiacca, another major representative of Florentine mannerism. In this connection, the *Project for a Monument with Charity in a Frame, Surmounted by Two Caryatids* (inv. 1062 S, Uffizi Gallery, Florence), though credited to Bandinelli, was obviously drawn by Jacone. Another case of confusion with the latter can be found in the double-sided sheet rightly dismissed from Rosso's drawings by Carroll in 1976, nearly twenty years ago. This drawing, which has all the characteristics of Jacone's style, is now classified as Bandinelli at the Uffizi Gallery (inv. 6498F).[10] It has taken a long time before a better knowledge of the period allowed us to suggest the correct attribution to Jacone, a true consistent personality, in Pontormo's neighborhood more than in Rosso's. It is also tempting to recognize his hand in an elegant project for a fountain (perhaps a design for a goldsmith), formerly thought to be by Benvenuto Cellini (inv. 898, Christ Church, Oxford).[11]

CMG

POLIDORO CALDARA, called POLIDORO DA CARAVAGGIO

Caravaggio, 1490/1500–Messina, ca. 1536

6 Recto: *St. Jerome in the Wilderness* Verso: *Two Standing Men* (ca. 1520)

Red chalk (recto and verso)

208 x 134 mm (8 1/8 x 5 1/4 in)

PROVENANCE: [Sotheby's, London, 2 July 1990, lot 4]

LITERATURE: Griswold and Wolk-Simon 1994, 68–69, cat. no. 62

EXHIBITIONS: *Sixteenth-Century Italian Drawings in New York Collections,* Metropolitan Museum of Art, New York, 1994, cat. no. 62

Both sides of this sheet exhibit all the technical and stylistic hallmarks of the mature period of Polidoro during his time in Rome around 1520. The strong, faceted lighting on the figure of St. Jerome, created by broad strokes of the chalk, as well as his angular posture, suggest a mannerist aesthetic more akin to the drawings of Rosso Fiorentino than to Polidoro's assumed role model, Raphael.

Other drawings of a similar style are *A Death Bed Scene* (National Gallery of Art, Washington, D.C.), *Woman Seated with a Piece of Cloth* (also National Gallery of Art, Washington, D.C.), and the tightly composed *Deposition* (British Museum, London).[1] Polidoro is known to have executed only one other drawing of St. Jerome. It appears on a sheet of twelve studies (inv. NC270.G70932) in red chalk now at Christ Church, Oxford, thought by Marabottini to date from the artist's last period at Messina.[2] *The Death Bed Scene* was preparatory for the painting on one of the friezes in the Palazzo Melchiorre Baldassini, completed by 1520. In this commission Polidoro assisted the primary artist, Perino del Vaga. *The Woman Seated with a Piece of Cloth* is thought to be an alternative study for one of the Palazzo Baldassini paintings.[3] With the recent publication by Ravelli of the complete frieze done for the palazzo by Polidoro, the classical subject matter, the numerous figures seen from the rear, and the stylistic resemblance to other drawings for this commission all point to the plausible deduction that the Katalan drawing relates to this commission.[4]

Concerning the verso, it is extraordinary that, given the hundreds of laterally gesturing figures in the artist's collected drawings, only one includes a pair such as is found on the Katalan sheet. This drawing, *The Incredulity of St. Thomas* (Albertina, Vienna), while credited to Polidoro by Marabottini, was reattributed to Biagio Pupini by Ravelli.[5] Ravelli discovered that the identical composition is found in a drawing of a similar size (187 x 266 mm) attributed to Perino del Vaga in the Louvre.[6] The attribution to Perino is not accepted by Armani or Gere.[7]

Thus, however, we do have a relationship by implication to Perino del Vaga on both sides of this drawing. This relationship should come as no surprise given the somewhat homogenous atmosphere inhabited by Raphael's students at the time of his death.

JM

1. See illustrations in Marabottini (1969; 2:pl. lxxii, figs. 1 and 3; and 2:pl. xciv, fig. 2).

2. Byam Shaw (1976; 1:124, cat. no. 389); Marabottini (1969; 2:pl. cxix, fig. 3).

3. Armani (1986, 254–57).

4. All ten scenes to this frieze are published in Ravelli (1988).

5. Marabottini (1969; 2:pl. lxx, fig. 4); Ravelli (1978, fig. 966).

6. Ravelli (1978; 464, fig. 952). The Louvre drawing's inventory number is inv. 611 and measures 187 x 266 mm. The Polidoro/Pupini drawing measures 182 x 288 mm.

7. Armani (1986) leaves the drawing out of her study and Gere (1986, 71) definitively rejects it in his review of Ravelli (1978).

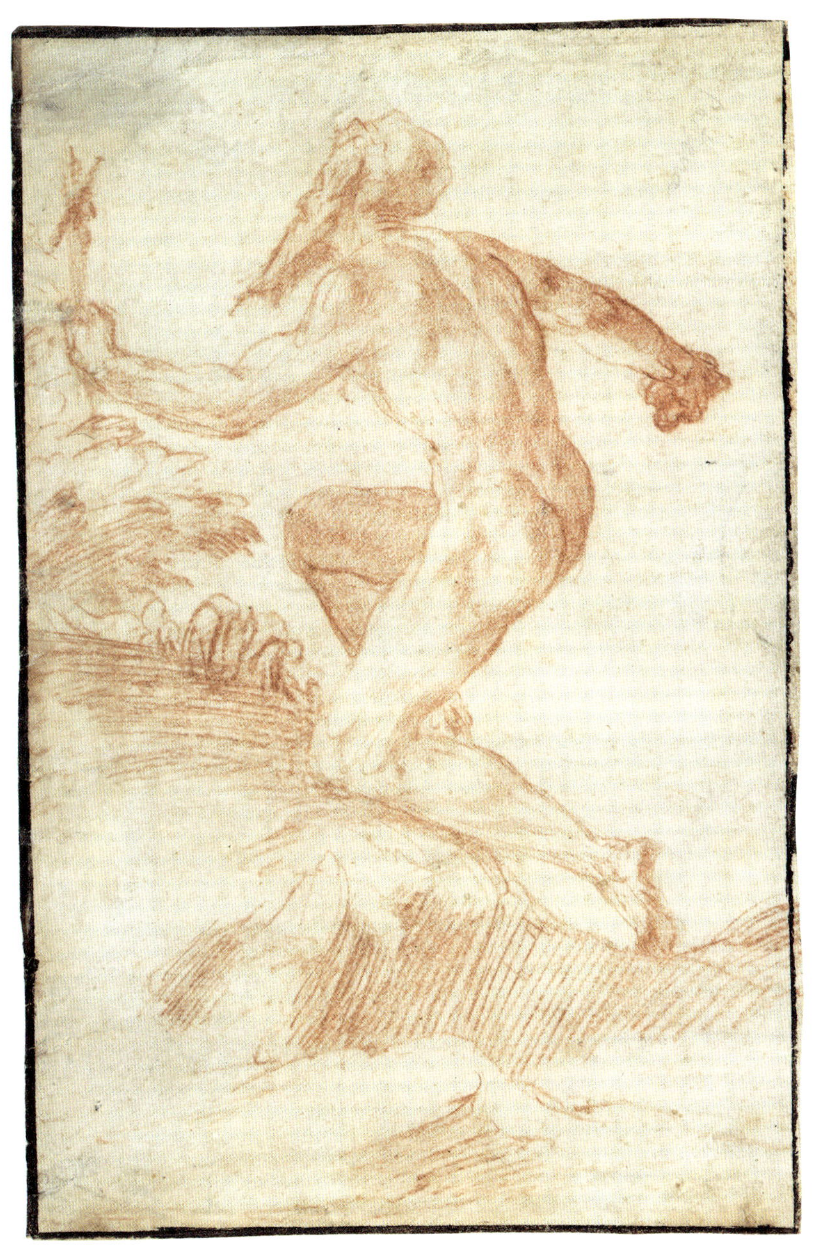

Recto

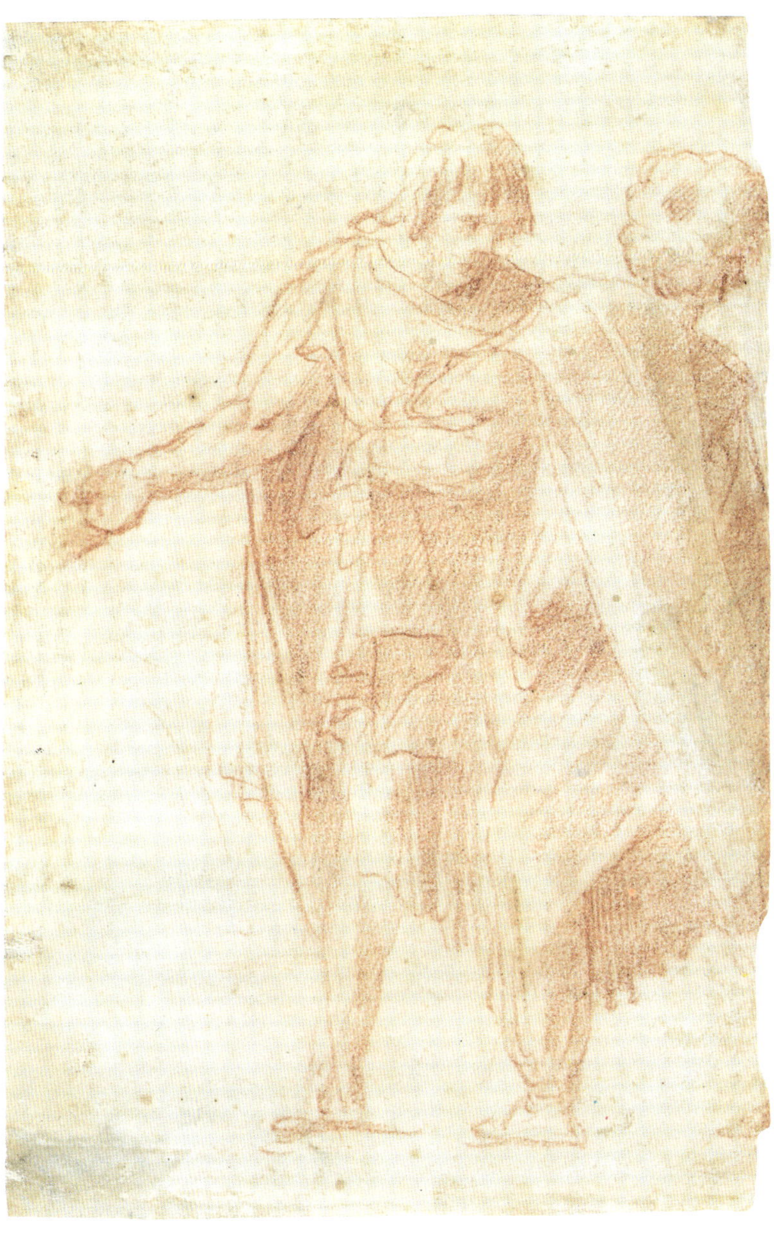

Verso

Polidoro Caldara, called Polidoro da Caravaggio

Caravaggio, 1490/1500–Messina, ca. 1536

7 *Christ or St. John the Baptist in a Niche* (ca. 1535)

Pen and brown ink

75 x 60 mm (3 x 2 3/8 in)

Provenance: [Christie's, London, 9 April 1990, lot 145, as Roman School ca. 1600]

Literature: unpublished

Previously unpublished, this small drawing must certainly stem from Polidoro's time in Messina, the city to which he fled following the Sack of Rome in 1527. A large number of comparable pen and ink drawings survive from this period, particularly those that once made up a sketchbook now in the Kunstgewerbemuseum of the Staatliche Museen, Berlin. These drawings and their history were first published by Cassirer.[1] These sketches record ideas for temporary decorations to celebrate the entry of Emperor Charles V into Messina in 1535.

The Katalan drawing depicts an elaborate niche with a broken pediment decorated with tendril-like and griffin volutes. In the niche is a striding figure, partially draped and carrying a tall, thin cross. The figure is at first understandable as that of the Risen Christ, but the slight proportions of the cross might lead one to the conclusion that it is the reed cross of St. John the Baptist. While there is no conclusive evidence that Polidoro designed sculpture, such a sketch as this and the sheet of studies of the Baptist in the British Museum add strength to the argument. The British Museum drawing was also associated with the entry of Charles V by Pouncey and Gere.[2]

During his period in Messina, Polidoro was given the opportunity to design architectural projects, as the Berlin sketchbook leaves amply demonstrate. Since there may be a number of missing sheets from it, the possibility cannot be ruled out that the present drawing was cut from a larger sheet that was once part of the sketchbook and should, in any event, date to the same year of 1535.

JM

1. Cassirer (1920, 344–58).

2. Pouncey and Gere (1962; 1:124–25, cat. no. 216; 2:pl. 186).

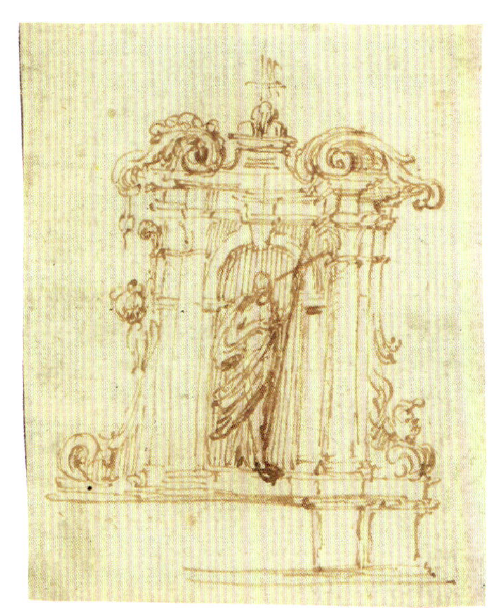

Francesco Mazzola, called Parmigianino

Parma, 1503–Casalmaggiore, 1540

8 *The Dead Christ in the Lap of the Virgin* (1526–27)

Red and white chalk, corners cut

222 x 244 mm (8 3/4 x 9 1/2 in)

Provenance: Sir Peter Lely (L. 2092); Jonathan Richardson, Sr. (L. 2184); Thomas Hudson (L. 2432); Timothy Clifford; [Sotheby's, London, 3 July 1989, lot 17]

Literature: Ekserdjian 1993

Exhibitions: *Sixteenth and Seventeenth-Century Italian Drawings*, Abbot Hall Art Gallery, Kendall, 2 May–21 June 1981, cat. no. 45

1. Popham (1971; 1:no. 311, pl. 213).

2. Ekserdjian (1993, 393–94).

3. Di Giampaolo (1991, no. 25).

The old inscription at the bottom of the sheet, *F. Parmigianino*, confirms the attribution of the drawing to the Parmese master. The composition showing a seated figure, with the head barely sketched in and leaning to the right, reasonably leads one to think that this is a study for a *Deposition*, although no painting of this subject by Parmigianino is known today. A drawing for a *Pietà*, in the Pierpont Morgan Library in New York,[1] executed, according to Popham, during the artist's Roman period, demonstrates an interest in Michelangelo's sculpture, particularly in the plastic definition of the formulation of the figure. The Morgan Library drawing reveals a monumentality that is not easily related to the graphic work of the painter, a point that has been reiterated in a recent publication.[2] The suggestion that the Katalan drawing might be an early idea for *S. Rocco in a Landscape* (private collection, Parma), recently added to Parmigianino's *oeuvre*,[3] should not be completely discounted: the position of the legs and the undefined atmosphere of the landscape in which the figure is placed appear to be identical.

MDG

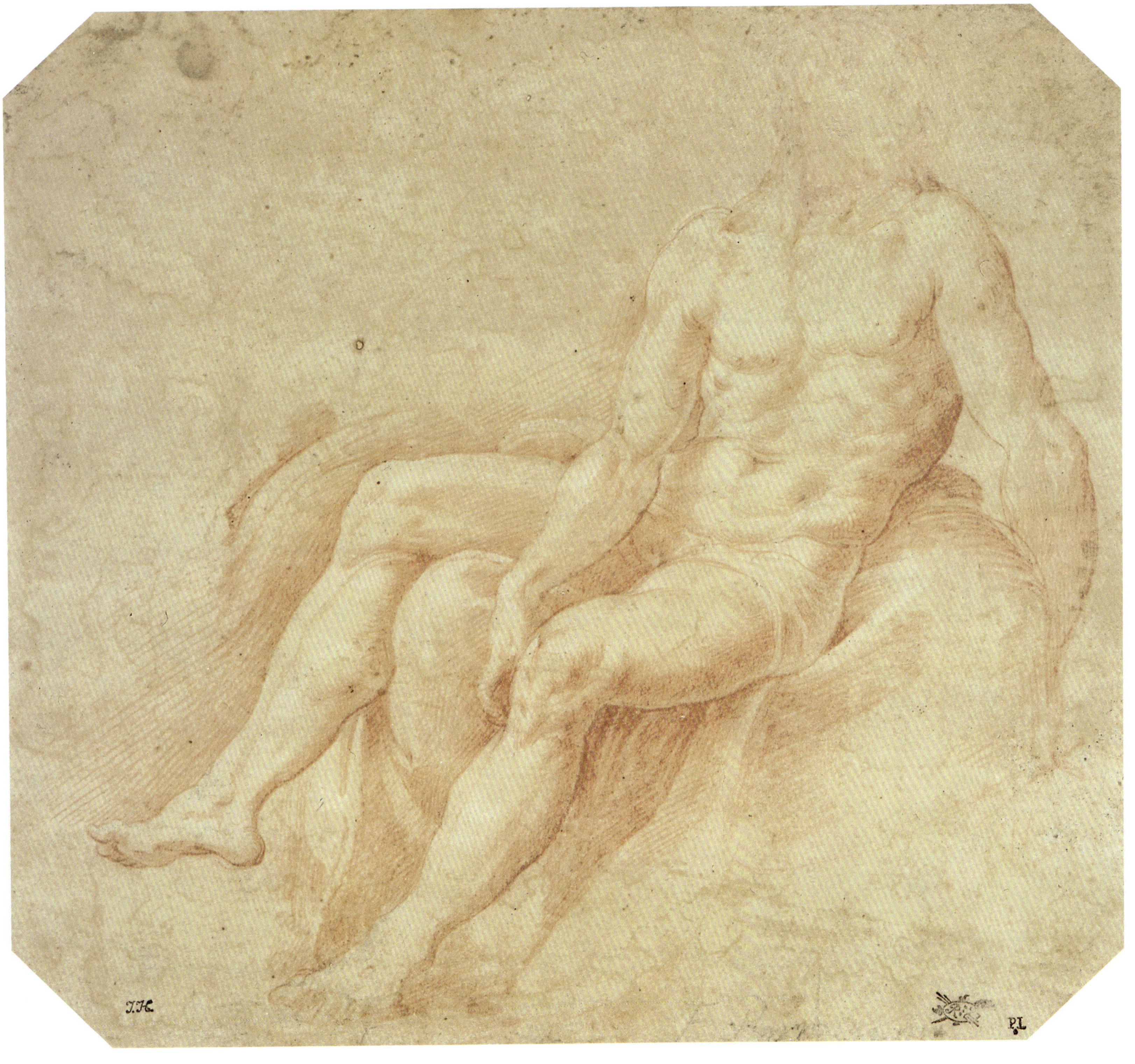
J.H.C.
P.L

ANDREA MELDOLLA, called SCHIAVONE

Zara, ca. 1510/15–Venice, 1563

9 ### *St. Andrew* (ca. 1559)

Pen and brown ink, bistre wash, heightened with white body color on ochre-prepared paper

132 x 91 mm (5 1/8 x 3 1/16 in)

PROVENANCE: VH collection; [Annamaria Edelstein, London, 1990]

LITERATURE: unpublished

When this sheet was with Annamaria Edelstein, London, Chiappini di Sorio confirmed the attribution to Schiavone. This attribution has thus far not been discussed in the literature on the Dalmatian master.

When two strongly individual artists work in close proximity, their competitive instincts usually ignite a certain friction and, on occasion, generate mutual interest and admiration as well. The present sketch seems to document such an encounter, although positive results are harder to define. When, in 1558–59, Paolo Veronese was concluding his work in the nave of S. Sebastiano, Venice, he delegated much—if not all—of the *Twelve Apostles* cycle, which occupied the three triangular pendentives above the monks' choir's supporting wall, to his younger brother Benedetto, who had assisted him in the decoration of the church since 1556.

Only eight of these mural paintings survive, but the formats of all twelve are recorded on a sheet of twelve studies (no. 316, Devonshire Collection, Chatsworth). Since the Chatsworth version differs in detail, as well as in entire figures, from the finished paintings, it must be preparatory to them, and although its quality is quite good it betrays the more haltingly illustrational handling of Benedetto. Two other sheets (no. 7548 S, Gabinetto Disegni e Stampe degli Uffizi, Florence; formerly on the London art market) reproduce in random juxtaposition all twelve of the figures in the Chatsworth drawing. Also clearly imitative of Paolo's chiaroscuro drawing mode, they are inferior in their grasp of form and must have been for shop reference, although Benedetto might also be their author. At lower center on the Chatsworth sheet and at the left of center on the Uffizi derivation one finds St. Andrew with his cross in the same format as the finished painting, but with many significant differences. The most notable of these is the saint's left hand, which rests atop the cross's arm in the drawings, but against its side in the mural.

The Katalan sketch of St. Andrew follows the format of Benedetto's drawing and must, therefore, be based on it, rather than on the painting. Its handling is not, however, reflective of any member of the Caliari family shop. Instead, it shows all the characteristics of the mature drawings of Andrea Schiavone. Although he retains the Caliari chiaroscuro medium, Schiavone allows the pen to dominate here with a wiry, nervous, scratchy pattern that skitters over the sheet in a style close to that of his compositional study (no. 1580, Albertina, Vienna) for the *barco* of S. Maria del Carmine, Venice, or the sketch for *Christ at the Pool of Bethesda* (Kurt Einhorn, Düsseldorf). The former may be dated to just after 1551 and the latter to about 1551–55.

Schiavone was commissioned to paint the *terra verde* frescoes in the Grimani chapel around 1553, and the adjacent monochrome frescoes and the altarpiece, *Christ on the Road to Emmaus*, for the Pellegrini chapel shortly after 1557. Paolo Veronese began work in the S. Sebastiano sacristy in 1555, continued in the church proper the following year, and would gradually take over almost all of the church's decoration over the following decade. Thus, between 1553 and 1557, Schiavone was at work on two of the six lateral chapels in S. Sebastiano and might well have anticipated a continuing share in the church's embellishment had not Paolo's sparkling new classical style thrown the Dalmatian master's murkier paintings into eclipse. He was thus squeezed out of any further work at S. Sebastiano.

Despite what we assume to be his disappointment with this loss in the highly competitive Venetian artistic scene, Schiavone reacted with characteristic enterprise. Always an acquisitive observer

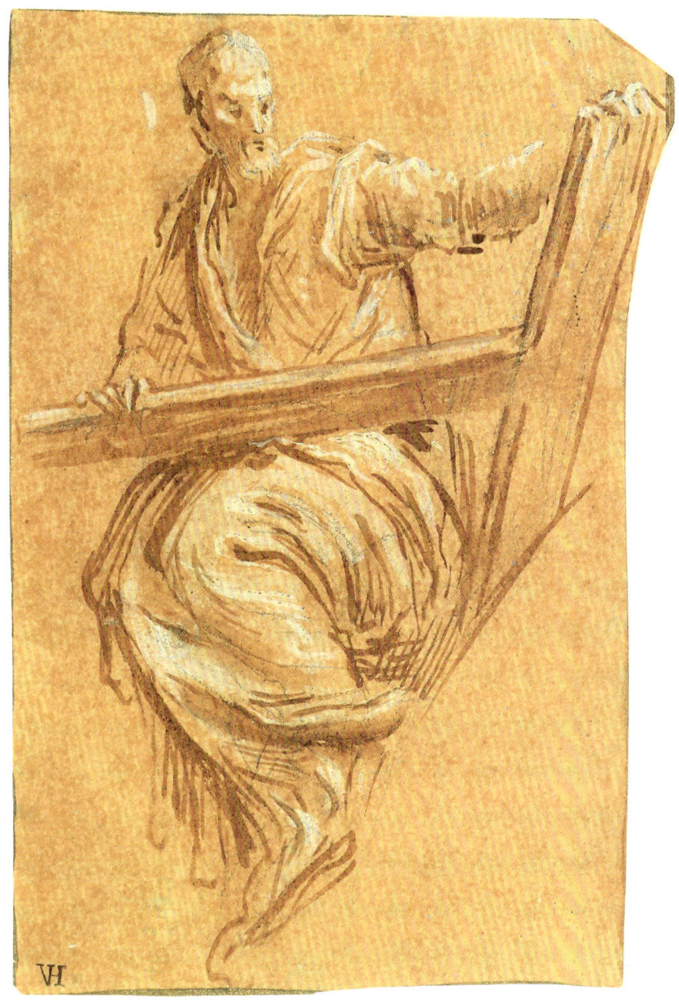

of others' work, he seems to have decided to learn from the experience and sat down to copy Benedetto's St. Andrew drawing, either the original or, more probably, the Uffizi copy. Although he was once again omnivorous in his taste, Schiavone remains unmistakably himself in the highly keyed refinement of this little sketch, which must date to about 1559. He would not again respond so openly to Veronese's influence.

WRR

Francesco de' Rossi, called Francesco Salviati
Florence, 1510–Rome, 1563

10 *Design for a Round Platter, with the Chariot of Neptune and Dolphins* (ca. 1550)

Pen and brown ink, with brown wash, over traces of black chalk, heightened with white; circumferences traced with a compass (mark of fixed point in the center); corners cut; laid down

277 x 275 mm (10 7/8 x 10 3/4 in)

Provenance: unidentified collection (L. 474); private collection, Milan; [Christie's, London, 19 July 1993, lot 14]

Literature: Bertelà 1980, 199 n. 479; Mortari 1992, 234–35, no. 374

Exhibitions: *Il Primato del Disegno*, Palazzo Strozzi, Florence, 1980

This drawing has been connected by Mortari, following Bertelà, to studies by Francesco Salviati for similar compositions: *Design for a Platter with Neptune in the Center*, at Windsor (inv. 2082)[1]; and *Design for a Platter with the Fall of Phaeton*, formerly in the Ellesmere collection.[2] This platter may have been intended as part of a service decorated with the signs of the zodiac, this one representing Scorpio. The date of circa 1550 proposed by Michael Hirst for the Ellesmere drawing,[3] and accepted by Mortari, would hold also for the present drawing. Other designs for round platters of this type are to be found in the Victoria and Albert Museum, London, with *The Fall of Phaeton*[4]; and in the Pushkin Museum, Moscow, with *The Triumph of Galatea* (inv. 10900),[5] but these do not have the quality of drawings by the artist's own hand. Indeed, the Victoria and Albert Museum drawing was earlier given to Benvenuto Cellini.[6]

Mariette, who owned the Ellesmere drawing, thought it to be by Giulio Romano.[7] The purpose of these designs is uncertain (Mariette believed them to be intended for execution in ceramic). At least one known example of a ceramic platter inspired by a design of Salviati's exists, with *The Visitation* as its subject, in the Roman church of S. Francesco a Ripa, "but the plate seems more to be a fake"[8] and shows an entirely different sort of decoration. The drawings in question would appear to be intended for execution by a goldsmith. It should be noted that Salviati's earliest artistic activity took place in the shop of a Florentine goldsmith named Diaceto, where he diligently trained himself to draw, along with his young companions in the studio.[9]

The greatest influences on Salviati as a decorative artist were Giulio Romano, Cellini, and Michelangelo, whose drawing, *The Fall of Phaeton*, is particularly relevant in this instance. To these names should be added those of Polidoro da Caravaggio and Perino del Vaga, to whom a number of very fine decorative projects by Salviati have on occasion been attributed, among them the *Helmet* in the Louvre (inv. 6126).[10]

An important group of drawings for decorative objects by Salviati has survived. Among the better known of these drawings are studies in the Uffizi Gallery for the *Farnese Casket* (Capodimonte Museum, Naples). Other sheets continue to appear on the art market.[11] Several projects by Salviati are known through numerous copies, including an important group at the Victoria and Albert Museum.[12] Another interesting group of decorative drawings given to Salviati was to be found in the Einar Perman collection, Stockholm.[13] Thirteen of these served as models for the Victoria and Albert Museum drawings.[14] These drawings, some of which still appear on the market (Emmanuel Moatti, Paris), are not original drawings by Salviati, even if the inventive quality is often remarkable, as in the case of *Design for an Octagonal Platter, with Ceres on a Chariot in the Center*.[15] Salviati, who detaches the detail from the decorated form and therefore breaks a rigid adherence to tradition, greatly contributed to the development of ornamental art in the sixteenth century. The red chalk study, *A Reclining Male Nude*, at the Getty Museum (inv. 86.GB.574),[16] in its impeccable modeling, is evocative of the enamel-like figures painted by Zucchi but it also brings to mind the smooth and polished surface of metal. It may well be a detailed study for a type

1. Popham and Wilde (1949; cat. no. 893, fig. 170); Mortari (1992; 282, cat. no. 582, fig. 170).

2. Sotheby's, London, 5 December 1972, lot 87; 9 April 1981, lot 71; Mortari (1992; 225, cat. no. 320).

3. See the sale catalogue of 9 April 1981, above.

4. Ward-Jackson (1979, cat. no. 286); Mortari (1992; 228, cat. no. 335).

5. Maiskaia (1986, cat. no. 14); Mortari (1992; 239, cat. no. 396).

6. Wooburn sale, Christie's, London, 5 June 1860, lot 250.

7. Sale catalogue, Paris, 1775, no. 597: "Un Bassin de forme ronde...." "C'etoit autrefois l'usage chez les Grands d'étaler sur leurs buffets de ces faïences ornées de peintures, qui se fabriquoient dans le Duché d'Urbin, et qui souvent étoient exécutées sur les Dessins des meilleurs maîtres: ce dessin, dont la touche est spirituelle, est exécutée au bistre" [It was the custom in great families of the past to display on "buffets" the ceramic pieces which were manufactured in the duchy of Urbino, and which were based on drawings by the best artists; this drawing with its spiritual touch, is executed in brown wash].

8. Wilson (1987; 177, cat. no. 275).

9. Vasari (1963–64, 5:509–10).

10. Monbeig Goguel (1970, pl. XX).

11. Design for a Chalice, *from the Mariette collection; Colnaghi, London, June 1982, lot 43.*

12. Ward-Jackson (1979; 284–307, with bibliography); Mortari (1992, 227–30).

13. Boerner, Düsseldorf, October 1970, lots 57 and 58, figs. 20 and 21.

14. Hayward (1962, 157–64); Hayward (1965, 114–49).

15. Kaufman Collection (1969, cat. no. 91).

16. Goldner and Hendrix (1992, cat. no. 43)

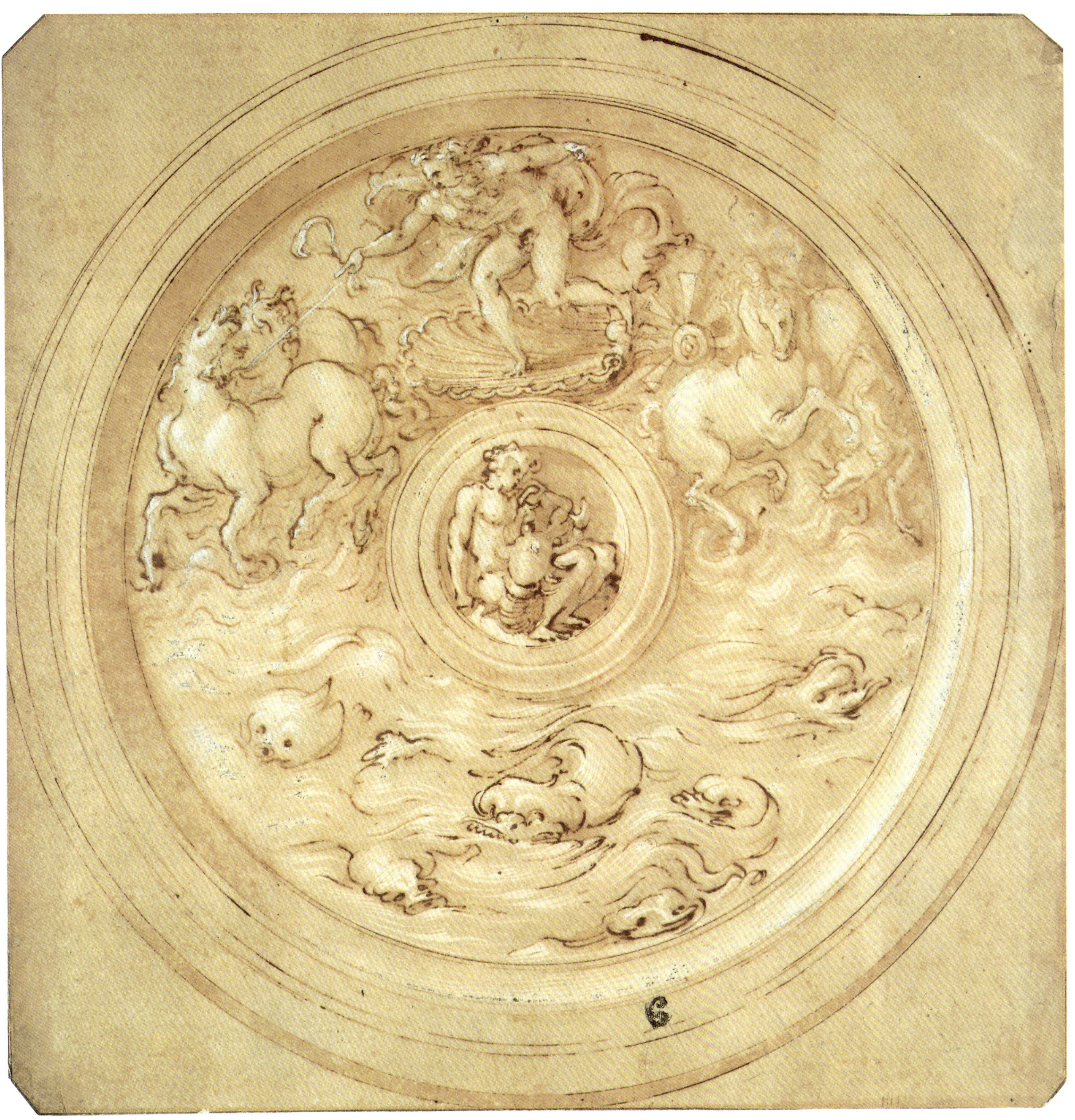

of figure in a similar position found in a design in the now-dispersed Kaufman collection. These ornamental inventions could be used several times in the execution of the object. This gives sheets such as the present one, in which the artist gives free rein to the fluid style of his *cappriccio*, and whose originality is unquestionable, an even greater value.

CMG

Giorgio Vasari

Arezzo, 1511–Florence, 1574

11 *Bacchanal* (1559–60)

Pen and brown ink, finished with black chalk; numerous brown stains; cut at bottom; laid down; inscribed in pen and brown ink, then crossed out, *Jules Romain*; inscribed in pencil, *Francesco Primaticio*

282 x 285 mm (11 1/8 x 11 1/4 in)

Provenance: private collection, Paris; Hôtel Drouot, Paris, 31 March 1993, lot 67; [Hôtel Drouot, Paris, 27 May 1994, lot 36]

Literature: Davis 1979, 215–16; Davis 1981, 127, under cat. no. 24f; Markova 1992, 237–41 and fig. 2

Although this drawing was presumed lost until it reappeared on the Parisian market in 1993, its photograph in the Bernard Berenson photographic collection at Villa I Tatti near Florence had been noted by Charles Davis (1979 and 1981). In his view, this study was related to the project for a fresco on the Bacchanal theme at the Villa Giulia in Rome, which Vasari had intended to paint in 1553, before his departure the same year to decorate the ceiling of the loggia in the *nymphaeum*. Its iconographic content precisely matches the mythological scene described in an *invenzione* that the renowned humanist Annibale Caro, Vasari's good friend, wrote specifically for the pope's villa, "per la Vigna di papa Giulio l'anno 1550": "Bacco ubriaco con la sua compagnia di baccanti huomini e donne, satiri, con Sileno, Priapo coronati di ellera, di papini et di fichi, con otri e tazzoni di vino, chi si leva et si sporga con alcuni tirsi coperti d'ellera la punta et tutti insieme faccino strepito e fallino" [Drunken Bacchus with his company of men and women bacchantes, satyrs, with Silenus and Priapus, all crowned with ivy, sprays of plants, and figs, and with goatskins and goblets full of wine, which are being raised and tilted, and with some *thyrsi*, their tips intertwined with ivy, and all of them together are making an uproar and falling about].[1]

In fact, Vasari also treated the same subject in an oil painting whose composition was known through a highly elaborated drawing of exceptional quality at the Louvre (inv. 2157),[2] and a similar engraving by Fernando Gregori (Bibliothèque Nationale, Paris). Included in a volume that reproduced the paintings of the Gerini collection in Florence, the engraving had long constituted the sole trace of Vasari's work.[3] Drawing upon the visual evidence of the Louvre study and the engraving, Vittoria Markova was able to locate the painting at the Radiscev Fine Arts Museum, Saratov.[4] With its vertical composition still set in the original frame, the *Bacchanal* of the Russian museum, on loan from The Hermitage, had lost its initial attribution. The *Bacchanal* was the pendant piece of the beautiful *Toilette of Venus* (inv. 2777, Staatsgalerie, Stuttgart).[5] During the eighteenth century, the two paintings were brought together once again in the Gerini collection, one of the most important in Florence at that time. We do not know who commissioned the works nor the year they were executed despite the mass of documents handed down by Vasari (autobiography, correspondence, *zibaldone*, and ledger). The style suggests that these paintings date from his mature period, circa 1559 or 1560.

This drawing, which was only recently acquired by Jak Katalan, is unquestionably related to the Gerini painting, and not to the projected fresco for the Villa Giulia. It can be seen as a version that was worked out in great detail, then put aside. The medium—essentially pen and ink with finishing touches in very finely sharpened black chalk that throws some lighted forms into relief—and the fluid, sinuous style comprise the same technique he used in the conclusive Louvre study mentioned above. The lower part of the drawing, which was cut, must have also included the rest of the powerful, recumbent form of Silenus drinking, no doubt little different from the figure in the definitive version. There is another study for the *Bacchanal* in pen and ink alone, without any addition of black chalk, which corresponds to a decisive step in the final process of its elaboration (inv. 620 F, Uffizi).[6] In this sketch, the underlying composition, later used in the accomplished Louvre drawing and the Saratov painting, had already been established; even then, the artist had in mind the effect of an antique bas-relief that he wanted to create. However, the style is much freer, and more appealing in the completed project.

1. *Davis (1981, 126–27).*

2. *Monbeig Goguel (1972, cat. no. 222).*

3. *Monbeig Goguel, ibid.; Markova (1992, fig. 7).*

4. *Markova (1992; 238, fig. 1).*

5. *Ewald (1981; 74–75, fig. 308); Corti (1989; 103, cat. no. 80).*

6. *Davis (1981; cat. no. 24a, fig. 146).*

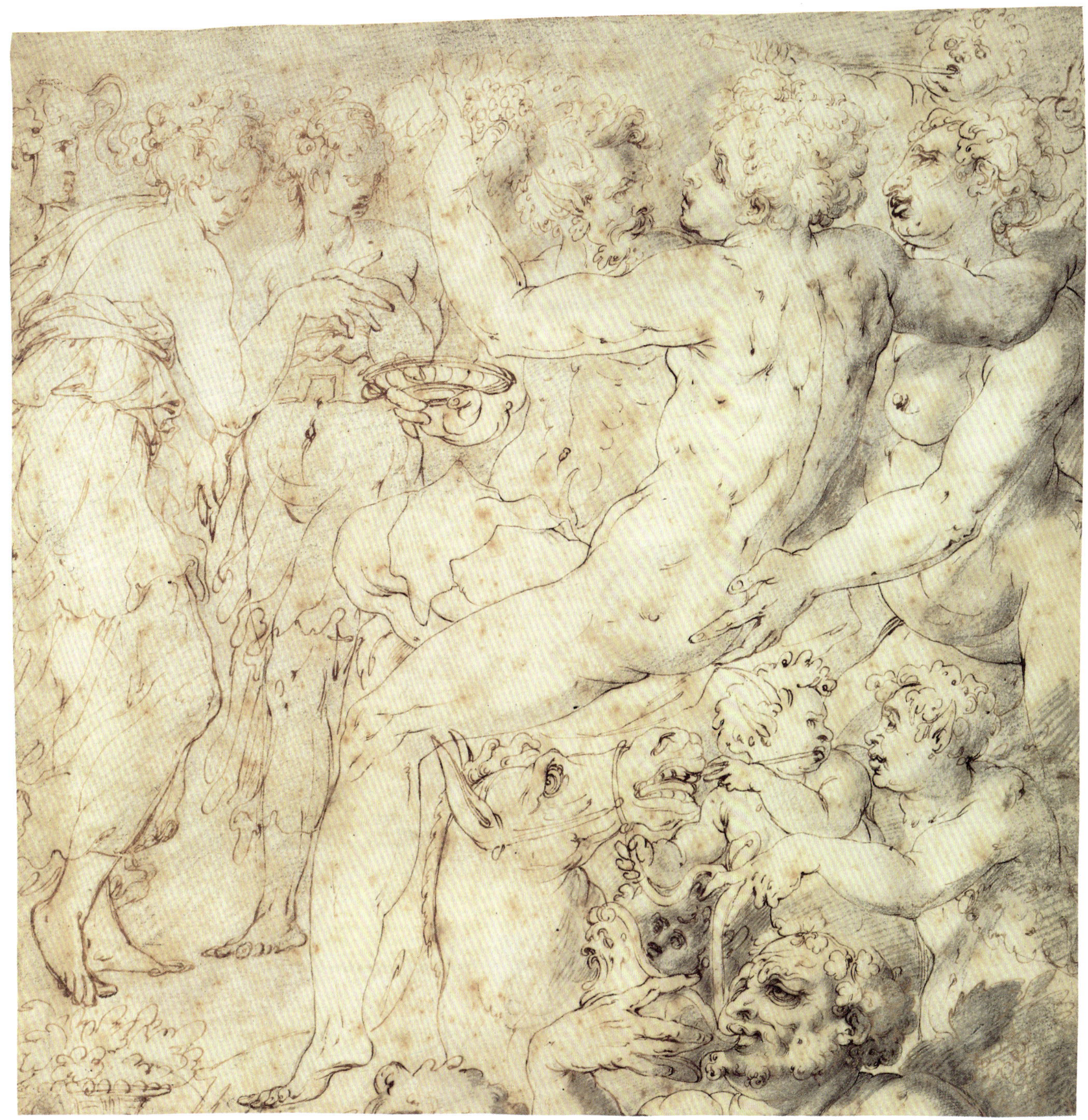

7. *For the most recent appraisal of these drawings, see Sisi (1992, cat. nos. 2.8 and 2.9).*

8. *On this question, see Monbeig Goguel (1990, 121–30).*

The perfect mastery of long unbroken lines gives the highly finished drawings of the Louvre and the Katalan collections a most distinctive appearance. They seem to have been inspired by a graphic ideal that Antonio Pollaiuolo had attained one century earlier in his well-known studies, *Adam and Eve* (inv. 95 F and 97 F, Uffizi).[7] Above and beyond Pollaiuolo's model, this type of drawing goes back to the ancient Etruscan tradition of outlined figures on painted vases or lightly engraved on round metal mirrors. Like Battista Franco or Cristofano Gherardi, Vasari excels at the use of pen and ink, representing forms with well-balanced continuous strokes, without resorting to washes. For these draftsmen, this style of drawing relates to subjects or motifs taken from antiquity,[8] though it is less a matter of archeological truth than the artistic gift for creating an aesthetic atmosphere, in particular by the capture and crystallization of the contour.

CMG

Lelio Orsi

Novellara, 1511–Novellara, 1587

12 *Fall of Men and Horses* (ca. 1565)

Pen and brown ink and wash over black chalk with traces of red chalk, heightened with white; collector's indistinct dry stamp

197 x 265 mm (7 3/4 x 10 1/2 in)

Provenance: unidentified collector; Los Angeles, private collection; [Sotheby's, London, 1 July 1991, lot 37, as Bolognese School, sixteenth century]

Literature: unpublished

When it appeared for sale at Sotheby's in London, this drawing was interpreted as the *Death of the Children of Niobe*, though it is impossible to affirm with certainty its true subject matter. The vertiginous scene does seem to illustrate the myth of a sidereal battle of extraordinary violence. Horses and horsemen, the latter entirely nude or scarcely draped, have been hurled into the void. The tuft of plants in the foreground on the left and the sketchy indications of land forms betoken the terrestrial reality where the final outcome of the catastrophe takes place. In the upper part of the image, parallel lines seem to indicate the border for a decorative frame.

Visually, the drawing belongs to a tradition of battle scenes inspired by ancient bas-reliefs and disseminated by engravings such as the one attributed to the Master B with the Dice, which purportedly reproduces an invention by Giulio Romano.[1] Nonetheless, the dazzling mastery of spatial effects does not recall compositions after bas-reliefs, but rather the whirling celestial turmoil of Primaticcio's paintings for the Royal Château at Fontainebleau. Recently, Vittoria Romani drew my attention to the role played by Primaticcio in the development of illusionist painting in Northern Italy, which can be explained not only by the dissemination of engravings after his work at Fontainebleau, but also by his regular trips to the region.

This drawing is part of the world of Pellegrino Tibaldi and Giovanni Francesco Bezzi (Il Nosadella). The attribution of the drawing could be nudged in this direction, and the name of Lelio Orsi compellingly imposes itself in view of the unmatched expressive verve and marvelous ease that characterize the art of the master of Novellara. The doubts expressed by Vittoria Romani, in conversation about this attribution, do not in any way concern the surprisingly free and faultless quality of the draftsmanship. Worthy of note is the kinship between the motif of the horseman on the right, freeing himself from the enveloping drapery, and the figure, *Night*, represented by Guido Reni in his project for the Palazzo Zani in Bologna, which was formerly included among the works of none other than Lelio Orsi (inv. 6681, Louvre, Paris).[2] Orsi painted a similar figure, though turned in the opposite direction, in the *Deluge* (detached fresco, ca. 1565, Galleria Nazionale, Parma), similarly influenced by Pellegrino Tibaldi.[3]

Battle scenes with horses and chariot races seem to have aroused the unflagging interest of Lelio Orsi, whether he used a pen alone, with much denser strokes, as in the drawing acquired by the Louvre (inv. RF 43385) after the exhibition in Reggio Emilia in 1987,[4] or whether he employed a technique close to that of Tibaldi, as is the case here. Orsi's catalogued drawings are often much more laden with white highlights and dark washes, for example the series of studies for friezes depicting *Allegories of the Seasons* at the Louvre (inv. 3640, 10379, 10380, 10381).[5] Despite the tendency of many previous art historians to the contrary, one must be extremely wary of the alterations undergone by these as well as the drawings from the Everard Jabach collection, which disfigured the artist's true graphic quality. In my opinion, the disparity between the Katalan drawing and the drawings just mentioned has to do with their different states: the former has retained its original clearness unspoiled, in sharp contrast to a sheet such as *Apollo's Chariot*, which was heavily retouched by a seventeenth-century hand.[6]

In the final analysis, intact original drawings by Orsi are quite rare, especially among his decorative projects. One must always return to the touchstone of Orsi's studies, that is, those that display the

1. Masseri (1993; cat. no. 51, ill. p. 60).

2. Cordellier (1987; 81–82, fig. 17).

3. Reproduced in Clerici Bagozzi, Pirondini, and Frisoni (1987; 140, cat. no. 123).

4. Clerici Bagozzi, Pirondini, and Frisoni (1987, cat. no. 131).

5. Romani (1984, 28 n. 20 and figs. 11–14); Clerici Bagozzi, Pirondini, and Frisoni (1987, cat. nos. 10–13).

6. Paris, private collection; see Clerici Bagozzi, Pirondini, and Frisoni (1987, cat. no. 15).

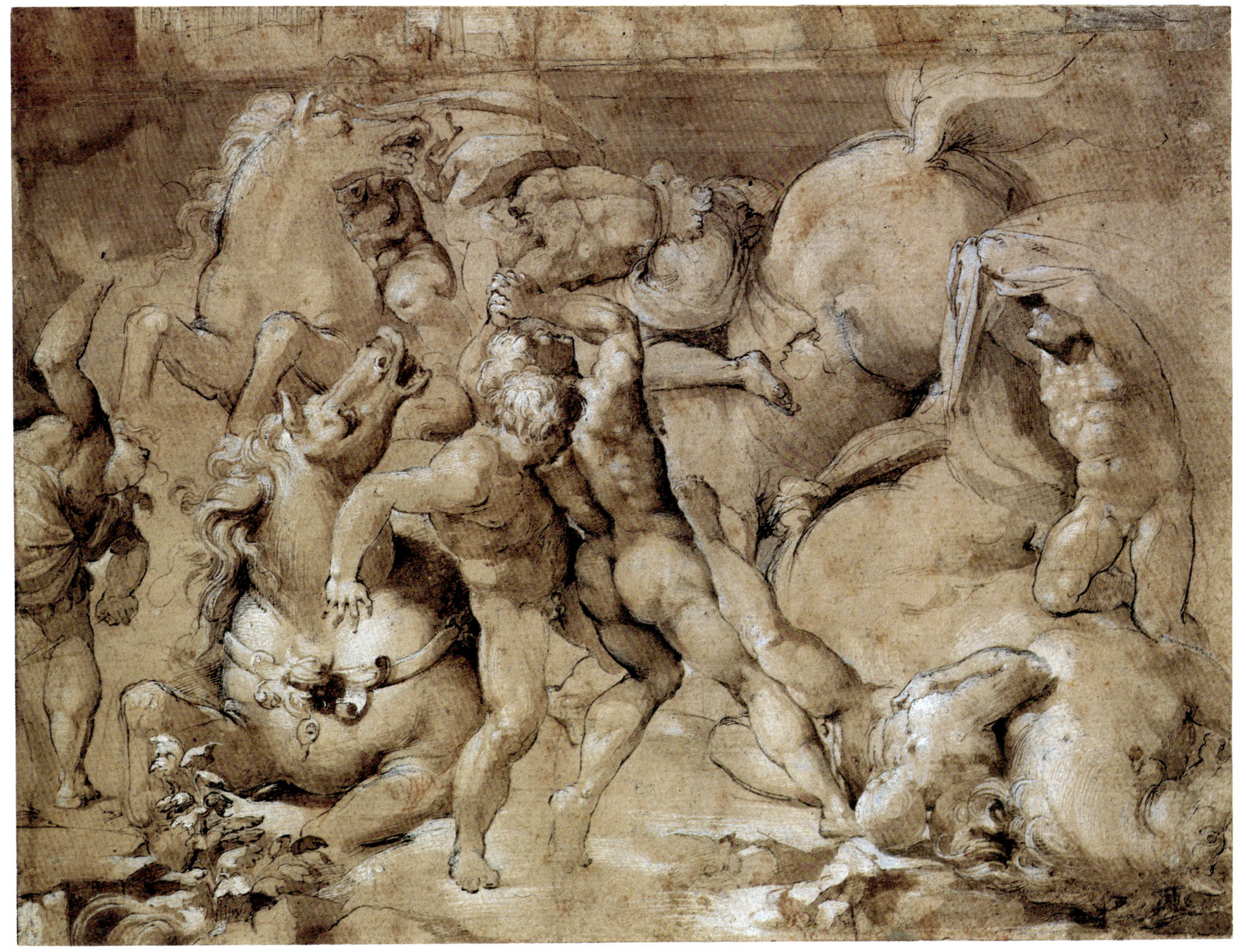

7. Clerici Bagozzi, Pirondini, and Frisoni (1987, cat. no. 59).

qualities one finds in *Frieze with a Putto in a Cartouche* (inv. 1643 E, Uffizi Gallery).[7] The highly illusionistic character of the present work suggests that it was made circa 1565, but the dating of Orsi's drawings, like other aspects of his work, remains an extremely complex question.

CMG

PROSPERO FONTANA

Bologna, 1512–Bologna, 1597

13 *Two Music-Making Angels* (ca. 1579)

Pen and brown ink and wash, laid down

112 x 90 mm (4 3/8 x 3 1/2 in)

PROVENANCE: seventeenth- or early-eighteenth-century English collector, (L. 2908, misidentified in Sotheby's 1994 catalogue as Nicholas Laniere); Victor Bloch ([?], according to inscription on mount); [Sotheby's, London, 18 April 1994, lot 2, as attributed to Ludovico Carracci]

LITERATURE: unpublished

The sheet, once attributed to Ludovico Carracci, demonstrates upon closer reading that it is still part of late-mannerist culture, particularly in the composition of the figures of the two plastically defined angels. The intriguing idea that the drawing might be by the Bolognese painter, Prospero Fontana, whose graphic work has been the object of many studies,[1] is justified by the stylistic comparison of the sheet with *Time and Fate* in the Uffizi Gallery, Florence (inv. 109066F).[2] This securely attributed drawing by Fontana is related to the oval stucco field at the center of the ceiling in a ground-floor room of the Villa Giulia, Rome, for which there is another preparatory study at Windsor Castle.[3] A reading of the stylistic characteristics of the Katalan drawing reveals the lessons learned from Giorgio Vasari, one of the principal reference points in the formation of the Bolognese painter. The drawing might be associated with the decoration of the crossing of the church of S. Pietro, Bologna, which depicts *God Blessing, with Music-Making Angels,* which was Fontana's last important public commission, dated 1579.[4]

MDG

1. *Gere (1965, 199–206); Davidson (1969, 404–9); Pillsbury (1976, 127–46).*

2. *Petrioli Tofani (1985; 29 n. 45, fig. 40); Di Giampaolo (1989b, 188 n. 89).*

3. *Popham and Wilde (1949; 353–54, no. 1066, pl. 85, inv. 5990); Gere (1965; 200 n. 9, fig. 43).*

4. *Fortunati Pietrantonio (1986; 1:348, reproduced on 409).*

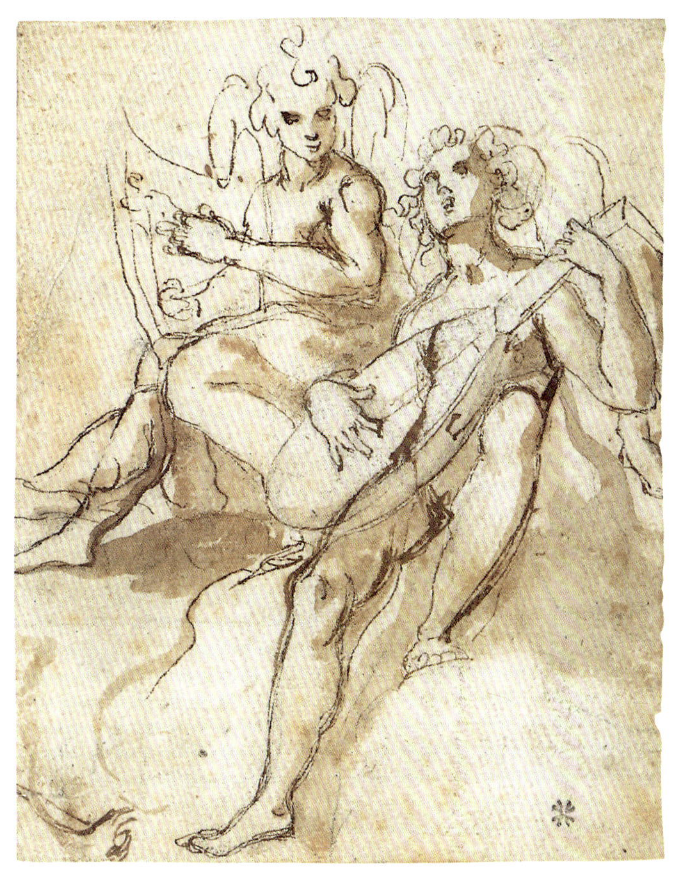

Taddeo Zuccaro

Sant' Angelo in Vado, 1529–Rome, 1566

14 ### *The Triumph of Bacchus* (ca. 1563)

Pen and brown ink with brown wash over black chalk; inscribed on back of mount in Jonathan Richardson, Sr.'s hand, *Federigo Zuccaro in Caprarola vicino a Roma J.R.*

157 x 421 mm (6 3/8 x 16 5/8 in)

Provenance: Jonathan Richardson, Sr. (L. 2184); Charles Rogers (L. 624); Sir Thomas Lawrence (L. 2445); Samuel Woodburn; Christie's, London, 4 June 1860, part of lot 1074; Sir Thomas Phillipps; T. Fitzroy Fenwick; Dr. A. S. W. Rosenbach, New York; Philip and A. S. W. Rosenbach Foundation, Philadelphia; British Rail Pension Fund; [Sotheby's, New York, 11 January 1990, lot 24]

Literature: Richardson the Younger 1722, 291; Gere 1969, 109, 203, cat. no. 217, pl. 138; Gere 1970, 127, cat. no. 3; Griswold and Wolk-Simon 1994, 68–69, cat. no. 75

Exhibitions: *Sixteenth-Century Italian Drawings in New York Collections*, Metropolitan Museum of Art, New York, 1994, cat. no. 75

Although the details and sources of inspiration for this drawing may be interpreted in different ways, the reliability of the elder Richardson's inscription should be trusted with the important correction that the drawing is an excellent example of Taddeo Zuccaro's draftsmanship and not Federico's. While Federico inherited the Farnese Villa project and its preparatory drawings after Taddeo's death, he noted that the paintings in the Camera dell'Autunno were entirely by Taddeo's hand.[1]

It has been noted by Gere and Wolk-Simon that the initial inspiration for this drawing lies in antique models and a design by Perino del Vaga for a carved crystal made for the collection of Taddeo's patron, Alessandro Farnese.[2]

Between the drawing and painting stages, the *Triumph of Bacchus*'s composition was considerably simplified. Several of the retinue, most notably Silenus on his donkey, were omitted, as were a number of background elements. The chariot of Bacchus is centered in the painting, and the entire composition is rendered in an oval format rather than a rectangular one. This was certainly done to increase the legibility of the composition when seen from the floor of the small room.

JM

1. Vasari (1906; 7:109 n. 1).

2. Gere (1969, 203); Griswold and Wolk-Simon (1994, 83–84). The crystal and its preparatory drawing in the Louvre are illustrated in Armani (1986, 196–97).

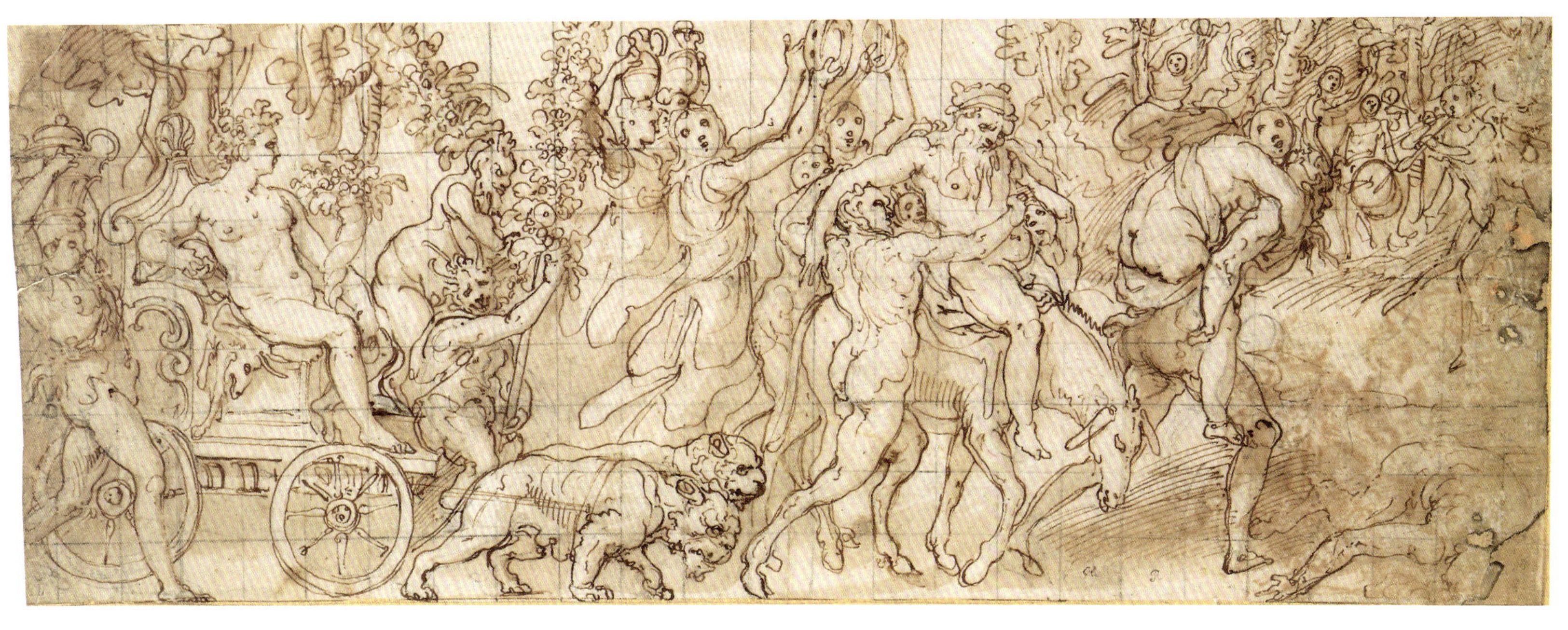

Niccolò Circignani, called Il Pomarancio

Pomarance, ca. 1517/24–Città della Pieve, after 1597

15 *The Two Marys and St. John at the Foot of the Cross* (1594–96)

Black chalk, pen and brown ink, and brown wash, laid down, with an inscription on the backing, *Forse del Roncalli*

192 x 208 mm (7 1/4 x 8 1/8 in)

Provenance: The Edward James Foundation; [Christie's, London, 18 April 1989, lot 64, as attributed to Central Italian School ca. 1580]

Literature: unpublished

The attribution of this sheet to Niccolò Circignani, called Il Pomarancio, which was previously attributed to "Central Italian School circa 1580,"[1] is supported by a comparison with several drawings securely attributed to the master, whose work has been carefully studied only recently.[2] We refer in particular to a sheet in the British Museum, London (inv. 1945-7-13-233),[3] which is related to the vault decoration of the Chapel of St. Helen in Sta. Croce in Gerusalemme, Rome, completed in 1593. Similar stylistic elements, derived from the art of the Zuccari, which are present also in Il Pomarancio's pictorial work, were executed, according to Baglione (1642), with "buona prattica...e diligenza e studio," and are noticeable in the group of drawings at Christ Church Picture Gallery, Oxford.[4] The Christ Church group is connected with the frescoes of the Palazzo della Corgna in Castiglione del Lago, which show episodes from the life of Ascanio della Corgna, patron of the work, who engaged the artist during the last decade of the century.

MDG

1. *See cat.*, Old Master Drawings, *Christie's, London, 18 April 1989, lot 64; with an inscription on the verso,* Forse del Roncalli *[Possibly by Roncalli].*

2. *Sapori (1982, 27–61 and n. 393); Turcic' (1983, 271–74); Gere and Pouncey (1983; 1:54–56, 2:pls. 59–63).*

3. *Gere and Pouncey (1983; 1:55, 2:pls. 61, 63).*

4. *Byam Shaw (1976, 1:77–78 and nn. 166-177; all previously catalogued under the name Bernardo Castello).*

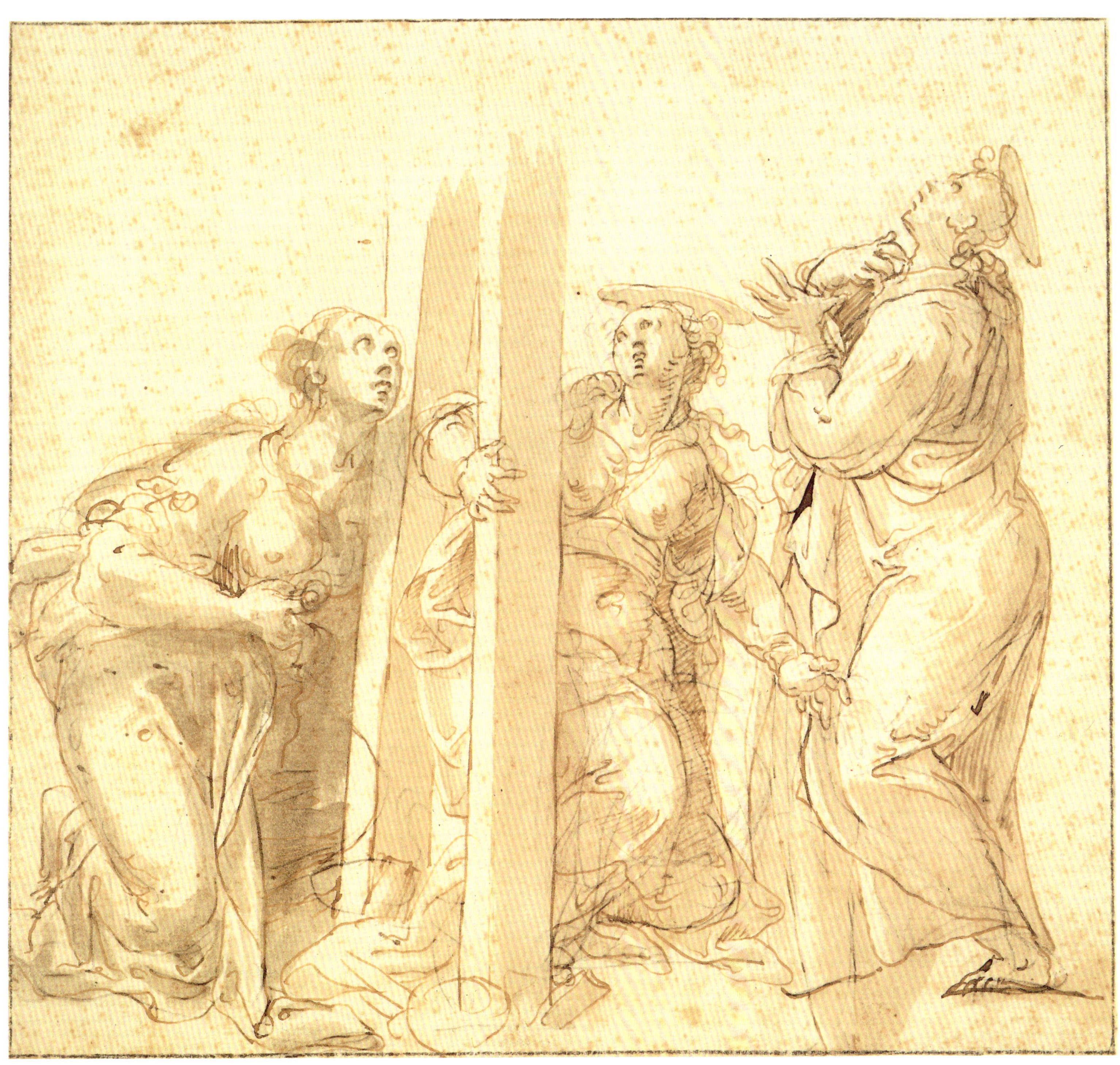

Federico Barocci

Urbino, ca. 1535–Urbino, 1612

16 *Head of a Man Looking Down* (1580–83)

Black and colored chalks on blue paper

201 x 197 mm (7 7/8 x 7 3/4 in)

Provenance: said to be from an album of drawings put together G. Piancastelli (1845–1926); [Sotheby's, New York, 14 January 1992, lot 40]

Literature: unpublished

This drawing is a typical study by Federico Barocci, an excellent draftsman, whose drawings have survived in large numbers, which allows us to follow the steps of his graphic development in detail. Dozens of drawings for the altarpiece, the *Martyrdom of S. Vitale*, for example, are known, for which the Katalan drawing is most likely a study, the features of the bearded face being quite similar to those of soldiers in the finished painting. The altarpiece, commissioned for S. Vitale in Ravenna in 1580 and completed in 1583, is now in the Brera, Milan.

Sotheby's sales catalogue suggests that the drawing is preparatory for the *Martyrdom* and that it depicts the soldier wearing a helmet and holding a staff, witnessing the martyrdom from the left middle ground. The hatching, however, would suggest a more vertical position of the head, if not a slight tilt toward the right. Jak Katalan has observed the strong similarity of the study with the soldier whose head appears at the knee of the turbaned ruler at right. There remain, however, doubts about the identification, since the eyebrows do not correspond between study and painting, nor does the line over the forehead describe unquestionably the line of the helmet, which should be expected in a study in so advanced a state of preparation.

PD

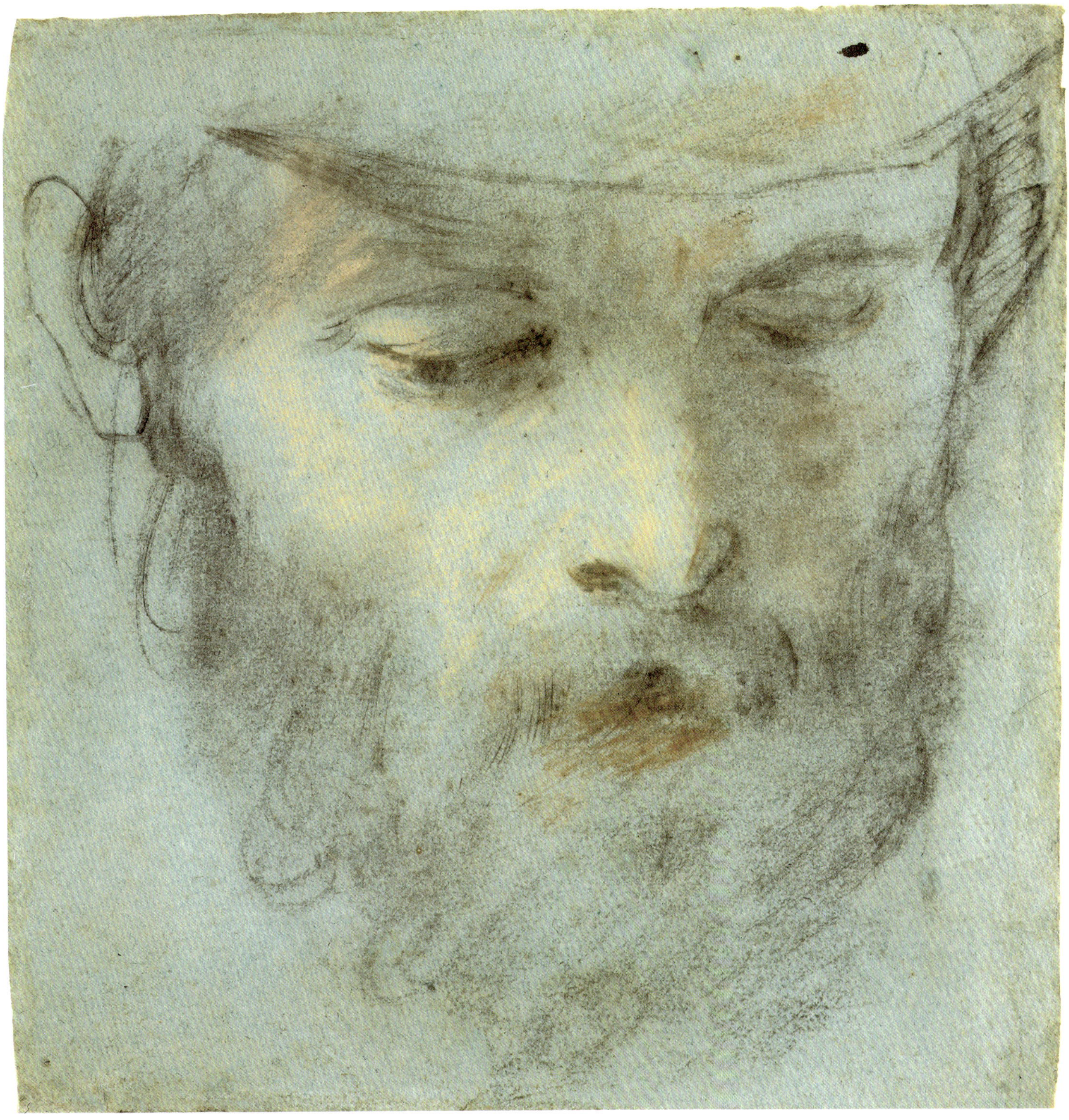

Giovanni Battista Naldini

Florence, 1537–Florence, 1591

17 Recto: *Hercules and the Nemean Lion* Verso: *Hercules and the Cretan Bull* (ca. 1565)

Pen and brown ink over black chalk

195 x 319 mm (7 5/8 x 12 1/2 in)

Provenance: Hôtel Drouot, Paris, 11 March 1985, lot 120; [John Morton Morris, London, 1986]

Literature: Griswold and Wolk-Simon 1994, cat. no. 32

Exhibitions: *Sixteenth-Century Italian Drawings in New York Collections*, Metropolitan Museum of Art, New York, 1994, cat. no. 32

The mythological subject of this drawing is exceptional in the graphic *oeuvre* of Naldini, which is rich in religious themes, battle scenes, figure studies, copies after the antique, and even a few allegories and landscapes. He demonstrates, moreover, an impressive mastery of movement in this depiction of violent combat between the hero, nude and unarmed, and the animal forces against which he opposes the virile mass of his body. The references to antique models are unmistakable. The style of this double-sided sheet recalls both the expressive studies of Pontormo, who was Naldini's teacher, and the work of Florentine artists of the later seventeenth century, such as Baldassarre Franceschini, all of which have a baroque exuberance. Like Naldini, Franceschini begins by laying down his forms quickly with a few seemingly disorderly lines of red chalk, which he then reinforces with a pen heavily loaded with ink. The way in which the theme of heroic combat has been interpreted by Naldini looks less like that of his Florentine contemporaries than the way his subject was explored by the young Annibale Carracci in the Palazzo Fava in 1584.

This drawing was probably made in the Florentine context of the court of Cosimo I de' Medici, with whom the theme of the Labors of Hercules was associated as a metaphor for the benefits brought by a prince to his subjects. It was used, for example, for the decoration of *apparati*. Six statues representing the Labors of Hercules, now preserved in the Palazzo Vecchio, were made around 1562 by Vincenzo de' Rossi for Cosimo I. A room in the Suite of the Elements (*Quartiere degli Elementi*) in the Palazzo Vecchio is dedicated to this ancient hero.[1] The two episodes represented in Naldini's drawing appear there. According to the documents, this room was decorated by Vasari, assisted by Marco da Faenza, in 1556–57, a time when Naldini, apprenticed to Pontormo, was no longer part of Vasari's team of artists. Thus, the sketches on Naldini's sheet, which William Griswold correctly interpreted as studies for a ceiling (see exh. cat. cited above), cannot be associated with this room. It is not impossible, on the other hand, that Naldini's drawing was used in the preparation of tapestry cartoons, prepared by Giovanni Stradanus, for a set illustrating the life of Hercules, recorded in documents of the Florentine weaving workshops in 1565.[2] The scene, *Hercules Killing the Centaurs*, is still in place in the *Quartiere degli Elementi* .[3]

From the time Naldini returned to Florence from a study trip to Rome in 1560, he was protected by Monsignore Vincenzo Borghini, a key figure at the court of Cosimo I, and by Giorgio Vasari. The main monographic study on Naldini is Paola Barocchi's article, which fully explores the role of his collaboration with Stradanus.[4] Several of Naldini's studies for Florentine commissions in the mid-1560s, for example for the *Pietà* in S. Simone and *The Way to Calvary* in the Badia, are comparable to the present drawing, which is one of the most beautiful by this artist.

CMG

1. Allegri and Cecchi (1980, 97–101).

2. Allegri and Cecchi (1980, 100).

3. Ibid.

4. Barocchi (1965, 3–47, cat. no. 31).

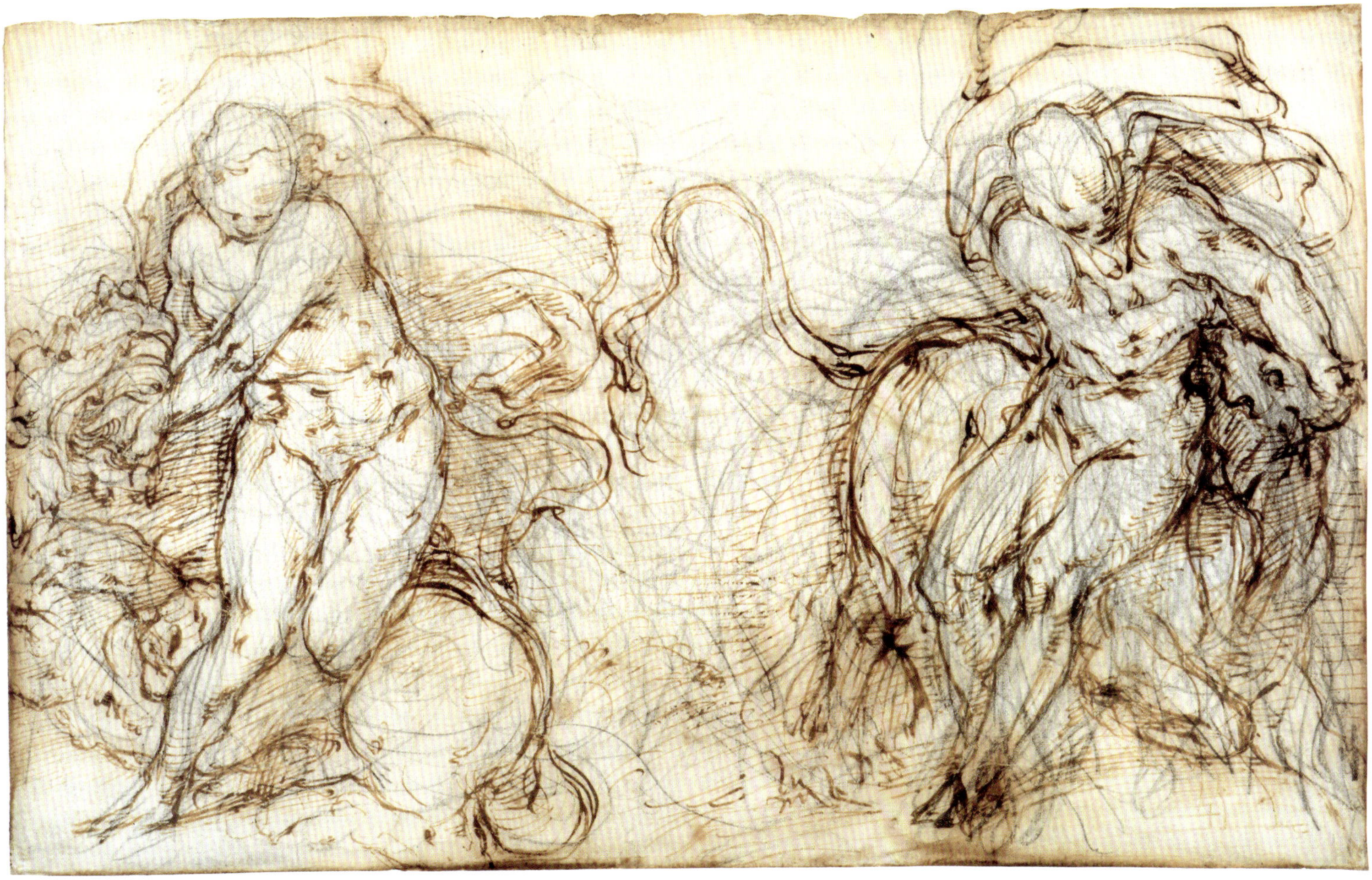

Recto

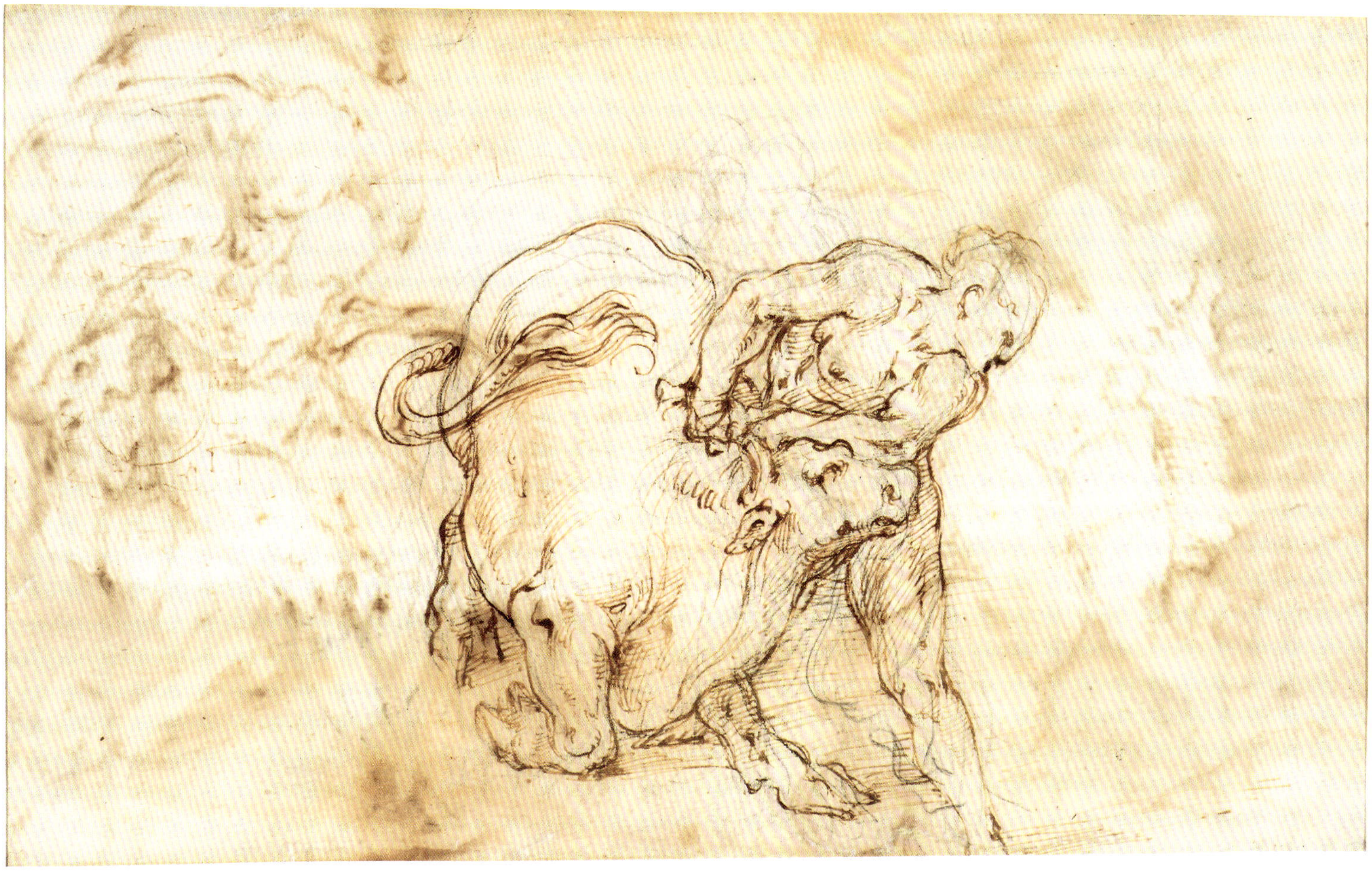

Verso

Andrea Michieli, called Vicentino

Vicenza (?), ca. 1542–Venice, 1617

18 Recto: *Crucifixion* Verso: *Battle of Spoleto* (1575–76)

Red chalk (recto and verso) on ivory paper; inscribed in pen on the recto, *15*

287 x 203 mm (11 1/4 x 8 in)

Provenance: probably once in the collections of Padre Resta and Lord Somers; [Christie's, London, 10 December 1991, lot 129]

Literature: unpublished

This impressive sheet can probably be identified as C III in the inventory of drawings assembled by the *marchand amateur*, Padre Resta, for Lord John Somers in London. It was then ascribed to Tintoretto. When it appeared at auction (Christie's, London, 10 December 1991, lot 129) an attribution to Andrea Vicentino was proposed at the suggestion of Terance Mullaly, but it has not otherwise been discussed in the literature.

Little is known about the early years of Andrea Michieli's career, either as a painter or as a draftsman. He was born in Vicenza, probably in 1542, and it has been proposed that he received his earliest training in the studio of Giovanni Battista Maganza the Elder (cf. cat. no. 20). This apprenticeship would reasonably fall between about 1555 and 1560, but no works datable to earlier than the last decade of the century are reliably attributed to him. His definitive transfer to Venice doubtless fell shortly before his first inscription in the Fraglia dei Pittori there in 1583. Thus, his beginnings between about 1560 and 1583 remain uncertain, but lacking any firm evidence for his activity in Vicenza, his awareness of—if not full participation in—the Venetian artistic scene may have come in the 1570s. However, no drawings have been securely dated to these years.

The ambitious compositional study for a *Crucifixion* on the recto does not relate directly to any known painting by Andrea Vicentino, but a few details reflect passages of Tintoretto's *Crucifixion* (Scuola di S. Rocco, Venice) of 1565, while Vicentino's *Crucifixion* in turn influenced later treatments such as those of Passignano, whose vertical version (S. Marziale, Venice) can probably be dated to 1586, like its signed and dated pendant, *Resurrection* by Aliense; or Leonardo Corona's horizontal treatment (S. Fantin, Venice), done toward the end of the century for the Scuola del Sacramento. Since Tintoretto was commissioned to decorate the choir of S. Marziale with these subjects in 1551, murals that were lost at an early date, it remains a question as to whether all of these, including the present drawing, might not reflect this unknown *Crucifixion* by Tintoretto.

The surprising sketch on the verso has not heretofore been identified as after Titian's great *Battle of Spoleto*, the mural painted for the Sala del Maggior Consiglio of the Palazzo Ducale in 1538 after a quarter century of procrastination on the part of Titian. The mural was an immediate sensation and suddenly changed the direction of Venetian painting. Before it was destroyed by fire in 1577 the mural had attracted not only the attention of Venetian artists, but also engravers such as Giulio Fontana from Verona, who reproduced it in 1569. Perhaps the best record of its appearance is a painting (Uffizi, Florence) that may be pertinent to this discussion. The Katalan drawing is clearly after the right half of the original mural and not after either Fontana's engraving, or another reproductive print (Albertina, Vienna) that is more faithful to Titian's original. The drawing is responsive to pictorial effects, such as the reflection on the shields of the brigade of soldiers at upper center, the torrents of rain at top, and the details of costume such as the slashed jacket of the general's page at lower right. That a few spatial relationships—for example, the banner on the bridge, which appears slightly further to the left in the drawing—are not like that of any other copy, confirms the freehand character of the sketch that, had a print been its model, would have conformed to that norm. In short, this is a drawing done before the great fire of 1577 destroyed the mural.

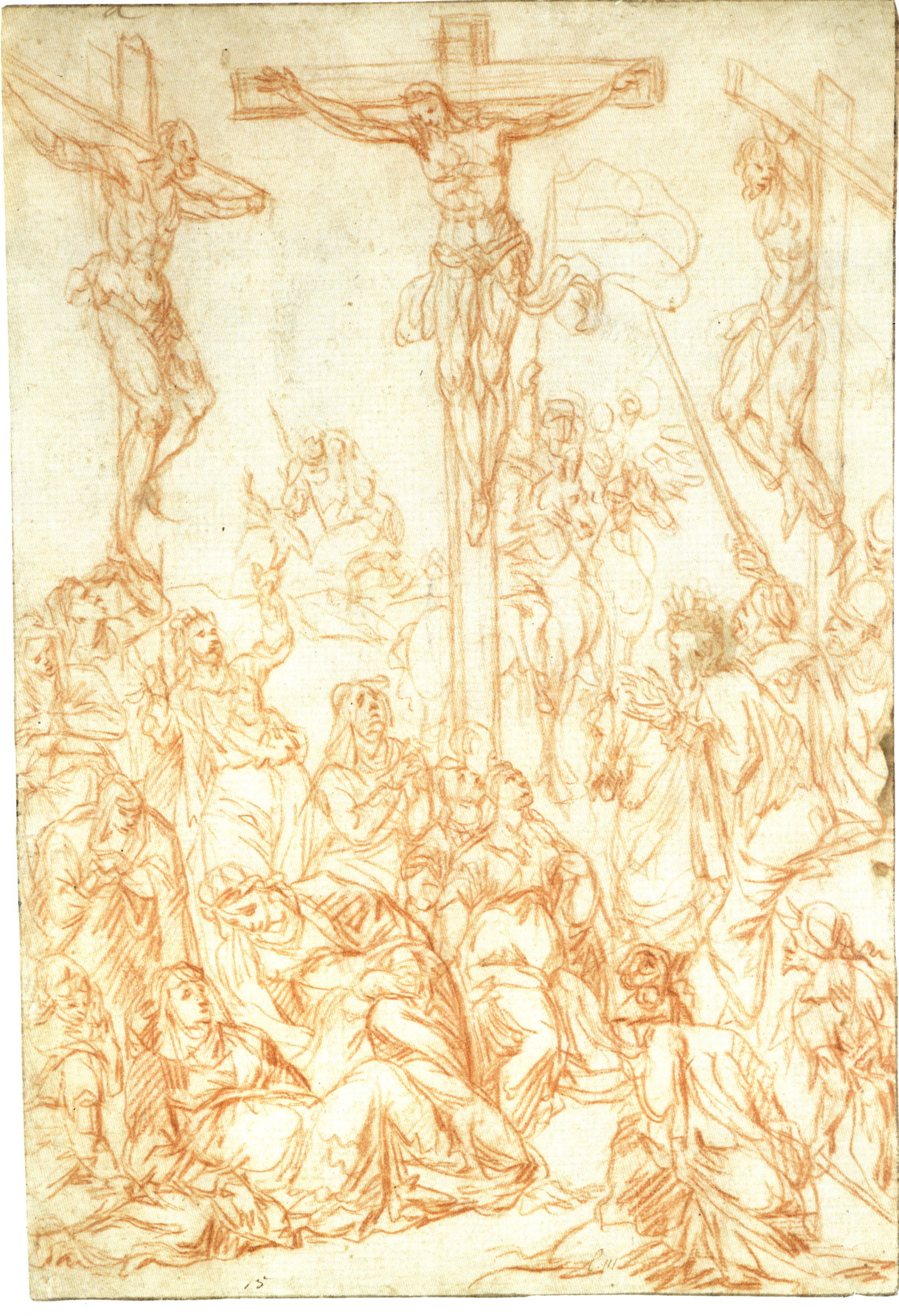

Recto

1. Tietze and Tietze-Conrat (1944; 180, cat. no. 747).

Still another sheet helps to clarify the role of the Katalan sketch. A page formerly in the Paul Oppè collection, London, contains on its recto studies made from two murals in the Sala del Maggior Consiglio. At top is Tintoretto's *Excommunication of Frederick Barbarossa* and below, rotated ninety degrees, Veronese's *Barbarossa Receives the Antipope Octavian*. Both were burned along with Titian's *Battle* in 1577. On the verso of the Oppè sheet one finds six sketches after Veronese's ceiling in the Sala del Collegio, a work documented as in-progress between 1575 and January 1577. Thus, the Oppè drawing may be dated with some precision between 1575 and the end of 1576.

Although the Oppè drawing has been ascribed to El Greco,[1] it is clearly by the same hand as the Katalan drawing. They share a splintered, rapidly approximate handling of the sharpened chalk, a caricatured shorthand of accented facial features, a nervous exaggeration of gestures, and the same reddish-orange chalk. This medium was seldom adopted by native Venetian draftsman, but in Vicenza it still found adherents. Federico Zuccaro had introduced it into Venice around 1562–63 specifically as an appropriate medium, with black and white chalk added, for copying other artists' paintings. Before it was trimmed at top and bottom, the Oppè drawing was about the same size as the Katalan sheet; they were probably once pages from the same sketchbook of the type in which a young beginner recorded his impressions of pictures in the Palazzo Ducale and elsewhere.

The attribution of all these drawn copies to Andrea Vicentino presents the obvious difficulty of our almost complete ignorance of his early work. The chalk drawings of his presumed teacher, Giovanni Battista Maganza, remain a mystery, but Maganza's pen-and-wash studies project a similar agitated impulse to staccato line. Circumstantial but striking parallels between this sheet and early black chalk drawings by Alessandro Maganza (cf. cat. 20), who was also a pupil of Giovanni Battista, suggest a common matrix. Among Andrea's later black chalk figure studies, *Seated Male* (no. Dyce 239, Victoria and Albert Museum, London) is more assured and contained in contour, but it shares many graphic mannerisms with both the recto and verso of the Katalan sheet.

We would, albeit with a reserve based on a lack of comparative material, suggest that the young Andrea Vicentino visited Venice in 1575–76 and there copied the famous paintings in the Palazzo Ducale as part of his education. From this sketchbook we are able to identify the Oppè and Katalan sheets. It is not to be ruled out that the *Crucifixion* on the recto of the latter is also based on an as-yet-unidentified work by another master. From his drawing after Titian's *Battle of Spoleto* Andrea progressed to the large painted copy of that mural now in the Uffizi, and somewhat later consulted his drawing for motifs used in the *Children of Niobe* (Castle Gallery, Prague), in which several motifs from Titian's composition are closer in detail to those in the present drawing.

WRR

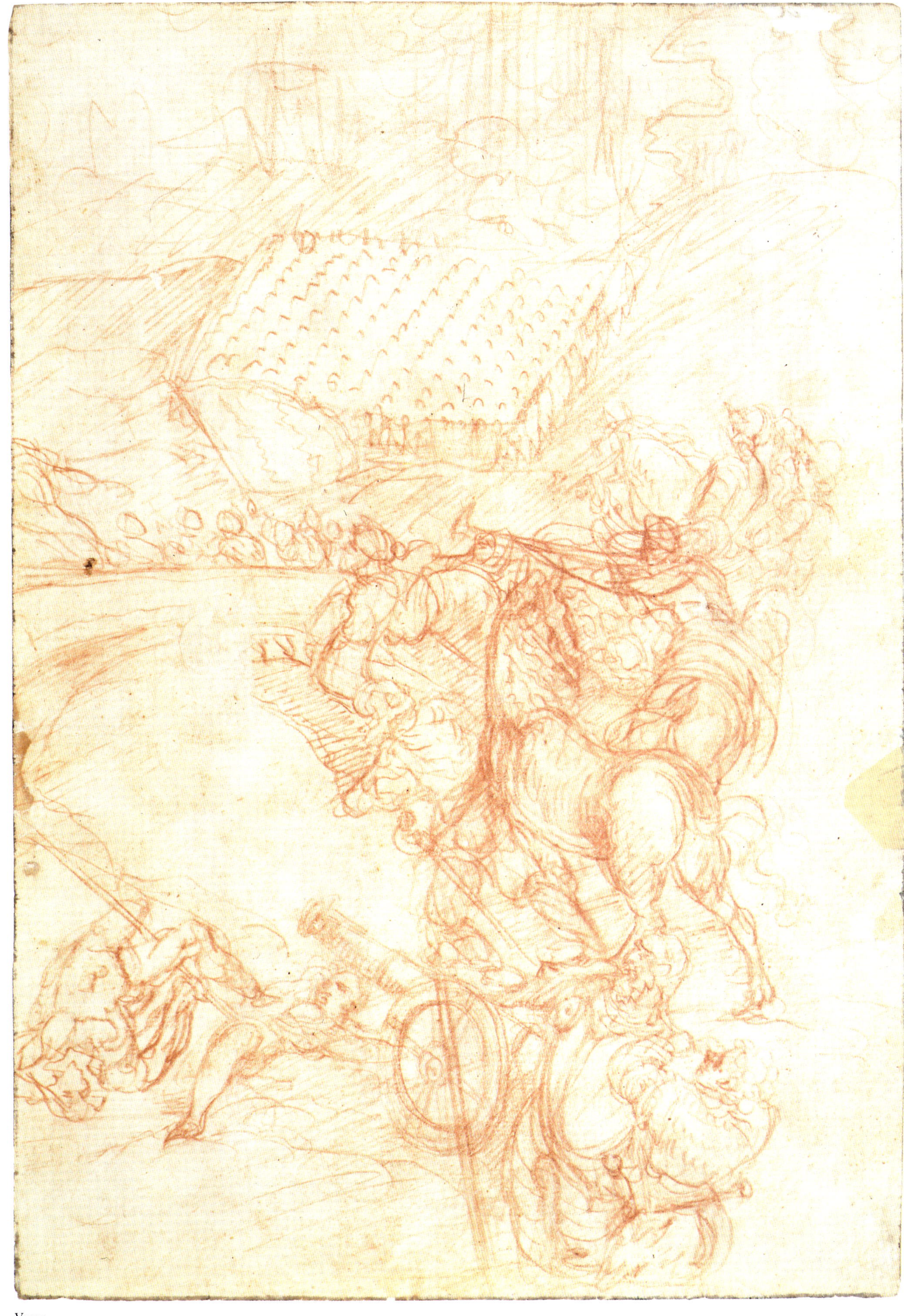

Verso

Jacopo Negretti, called Palma il Giovane
Venice, 1548–Venice, 1628

19 ### Recto and verso: *Studies for a Flaying of Marsyas* (ca. 1580)

Pen and brown ink with bistre wash over light black chalk on ivory paper; inscribed in pen in a late-sixteenth-century hand, *Molto Mag. o sig. Compari oss;* and in pencil in a late-eighteenth-century hand, *Palma Vecchio*

198 x 284 mm (6 6/8 x 10 3/16 in)

Provenance: Stephen Schwarz collection, New York; [Sotheby's, New York, 16 January 1986, lot 56]

Literature: Tietze and Tietze-Conrat 1944, 216, cat. no. 1054

The inscription of Palma's uncle's name reflects a confusion occasionally encountered among collectors in the nineteenth century, but it is doubtless a misinterpretation of a traditional ascription to Jacopo Palma il Giovane. The Tietzes confirmed this attribution with a date of 1580–90+ (cited above). At its most recent sale (New York, Sotheby's, 16 January 1986, lot 56) this was repeated. Stefania Mason Rinaldi has generously reviewed my ideas about it and has confirmed Palma's authorship.

Jacopo returned from his central Italian travels by 1570. By 1578 his reputation was such that he was invited to share, along with Tintoretto and Veronese, the painting of the three major fields of the ceiling of the burned Sala del Maggior Consiglio in the Palazzo Ducale. Leaving aside juvenalia drawn in Rome prior to his return, Palma at once demonstrated his extraordinary capacity to synthesize the various currents of draftsmanship that coexisted in Venice in the 1570s. From Titian he learned how to use black and white chalk; from Tintoretto, a ductile and expressive black chalk line; and from Veronese, the lightning-fast use of pen and tensile line. It is primarily this elegant, linear fluidity of Veronese that is Palma's inspiration in the Katalan drawing, a mode that would remain constant until after 1600, when age and repetition vitiated its spontaneity.

This series of spirited sketches of Apollo skinning the satyr Marsyas, who had lost his musical challenge to the deity of classical harmony, includes Apollo in the act of flaying the bound Marsyas and several sketches of an observer to the right who seems to be another satyr. In both idea and detail, Palma reflects Titian's great, late *Flaying of Marsyas* (Archiepiscopal Palace, Kromeriz), a work that must have remained in Venice after Titian's death in 1576, since we know at least one contemporary copy (art market, Venice) by a painter from the circle of Palma. The primary variation of this format is found on the recto, where Apollo with his laurel wreath is studied thrice at left and more fully in the ensemble at right, in which he directs the flaying rather than executing it himself.

Palma began his exploration of the theme on the verso with a prominent Marsyas hung head down from a tree as the skinner flays his upper thigh. The artist then briefly considered Marsyas upright, further to the right, turning the paper ninety degrees clockwise to repeat his second idea with an elaborating pictorial wash. Finally, the artist concluded at the lower corner, where Marsyas returns to his first position with a pair of flanking flayers and the freshly added figure of the spectator Apollo with his lyre. Pleased with this last solution, Palma then turned the sheet over to create a conflation of his first and fourth ideas from the verso in the light sketch at top center, then dropped to lower right for the most complete study, one in which the second executioner is replaced by the standing Apollo, who imperiously directs the grisly operation. Almost as an afterthought, the artist's hand moved left to clarify Marsyas's pose and explore three variations for Apollo, now seen from his left side.

This fresh, flexible exploration of visual ideas is not a direct preparation for any known painting by Palma. His only surviving canvas of this theme (Herzog Anton Ulrich Museum, Brunswick) resembles the composition of the primary figures in the drawing, most particularly the most finished version at lower right of the recto. The personages represented in the painting do not, however, correspond with those in this study. Midas, who plays a major role in the Brunswick painting, is not present in this drawing. Since the attendant in the upper sketch on the recto, who might have been Midas but for his satyr's

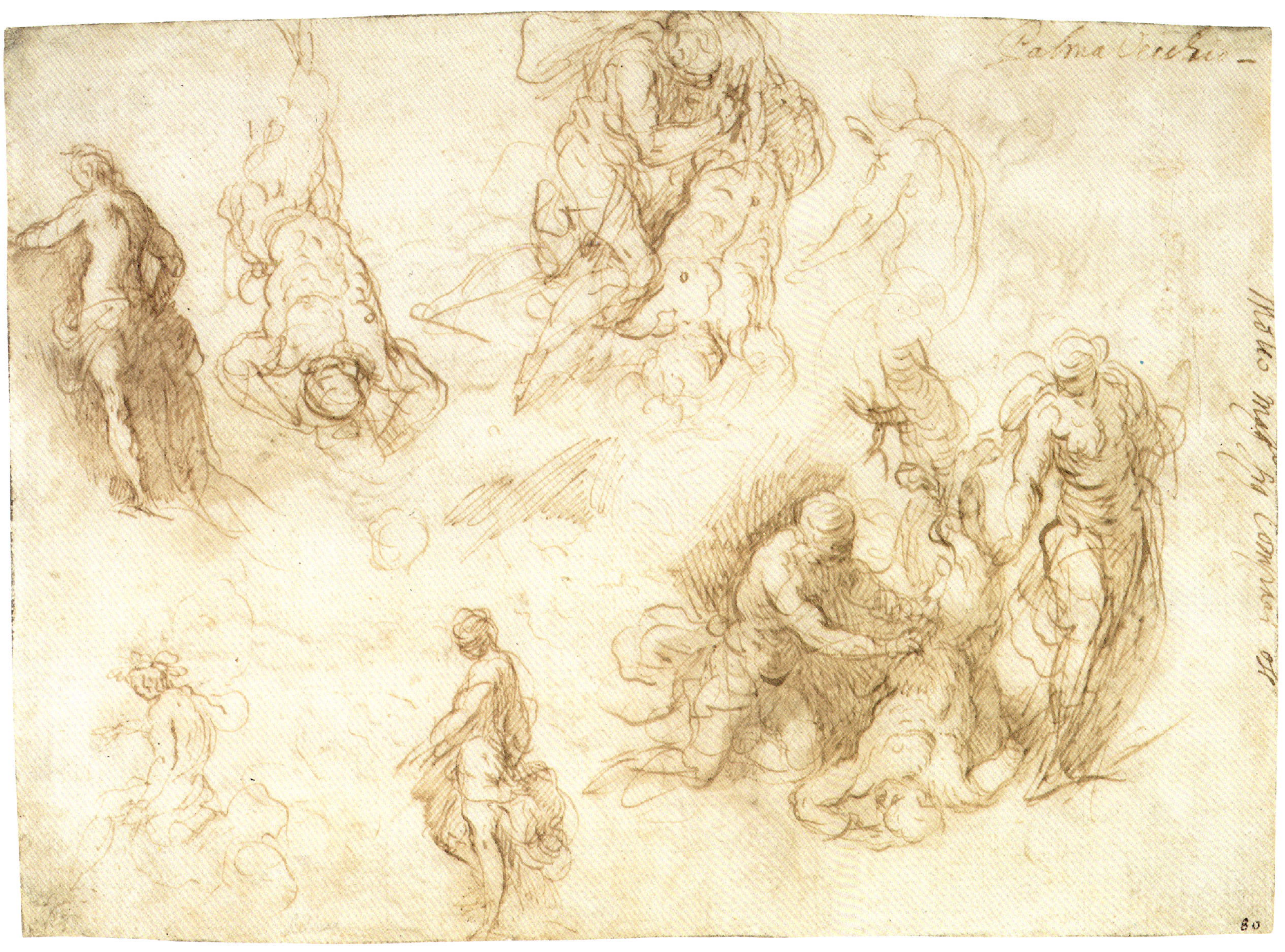

Recto

1. *Mason Rinaldi (1984; 77, cat. no. 37).*

anatomy, would be used in reverse for the figure of Marsyas in the Brunswick pendant painting, *Contest Between Apollo and Marsyas*, it is clear that Palma probably remembered his earlier Marsyas composition in this drawing, when he conceived the Brunswick paintings. Mason Rinaldi has convincingly dated the Brunswick pendants to 1610–15.[1]

The style of this sheet fits best with Palma's works of around 1580. The first, looser studies on the verso have the same improvisational freshness found in the nude studies (formerly Pietro Scarpa, Venice) done in 1578 for *Venice Crowned by Victory* (Sala del Maggior Consiglio, Palazzo Ducale, Venice), one of Palma's first great public commissions after his return to the Serenissima. The more finished studies for Apollo on the recto resemble the sketches (Museum of Art, Ann Arbor) that were preparations for the *Assumption of the Virgin* (Pinacoteca Querini Stampalia, Venice) of mid-1582. Although this spirited pen work would persist in sketches such as that (no. 3497, Staatliche Graphisches Sammlung, Munich) which Palma did in preparation for the façade frescoes commissioned by Alessandro Vittoria in 1592, they are already more diaphanous in touch and lack the firm control evident a decade earlier. We would, therefore, suggest that this fine sheet be dated very close to 1580.

WRR

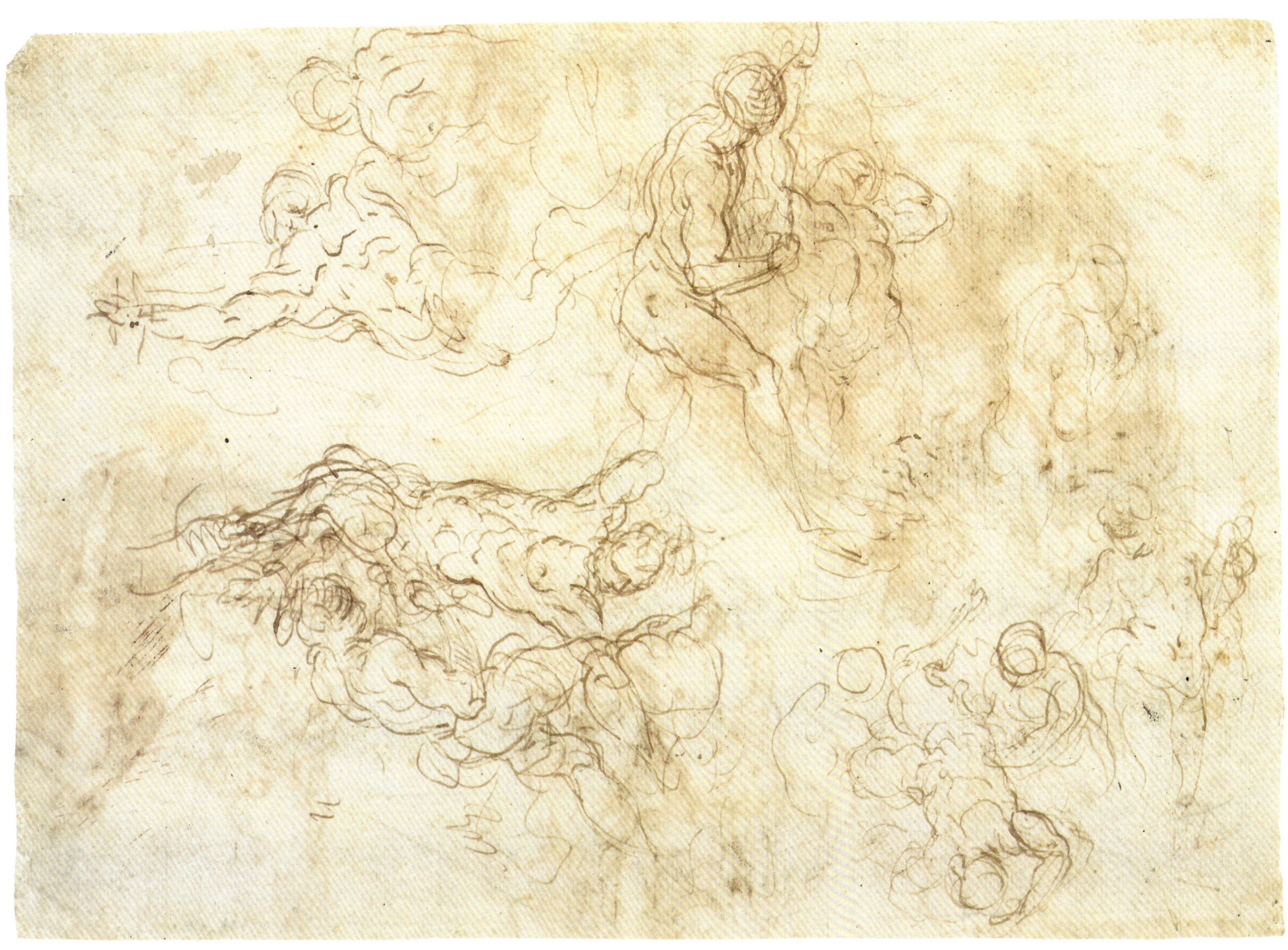

Verso

Alessandro Maganza

Vicenza, 1556–Vicenza, after 1630

20 *Design for an Allegorical Ceiling* (1590–1600)

Pen and brown ink over light black chalk on ivory paper

352 x 271 mm (13 7/8 x 10 5/8 in)

Provenance: Philip Leroux collection, London; Lodewijk Houthakker collection, Amsterdam; [Hazlitt, Gooden and Fox, 1992]

Literature: Fenyö 1958, 62; Scholz 1959, cat. no. 32; Kollewijn 1985, 31, cat. no. 32; Fuhring 1989, cat. no 298

The catalogue of the exhibition of architectural drawings from the Houthakker collection wrongly traces this sheet to the Scholz collection in New York. That sketch[1] is another study by Alessandro Maganza, but is different in medium and dimensions from the present sheet. Kollewijn published the present spirited sketch under Maganza's name, described it as a study for a ceiling in which the artist omitted the architectural environment since that would be left to an *enquadratura* specialist or a stucco sculptor.[2]

The drawing's subject seems to be an allegory of the patron who commissioned it. In the flat, central, rectangular field one might identify the flying figure of Virtue or Harmony seated on the winged figure of Vice holding serpents and a lyre. She is surrounded by a cloud bank on which seven planetary deities recline. Clockwise from the top they are: Jupiter, Mars, Saturn, Mercury, Luna, Venus, and Sol. Here, Maganza was obviously inspired by the vault of Veronese's Sala dell'Olimpo in the Villa Barbaro, Maser, even to the details of pose in certain figures.

The four episodes that fill the curved surfaces where the ceiling joins the walls are less clear. At the top a male figure embodying Peace sets fire to a stack of armor, while a female, possibly Abundance, proffers a vase. Along the right side a victorious youth in a chariot is greeted by two women, one holding a crown and a vase, while the other at right proffers a laurel wreath and a caduceus. Below, a female figure surrounded by animals, probably Circe, offers a circlet to a recoiling male, who would be Ulysses. At right a seated, bearded figure gestures to three males who appear to offer instruments of science and architecture. The general meaning of the ensemble appears to be a celebration of celestial harmony that presides over the virtues of a noble gentleman, doubtless the Vicentine patron who commissioned the frescoes to embellish his family palace. Early sources do not, however, describe a secular ceiling by Maganza that might fit this program, and no such ceiling appears to survive today.[3]

Alessandro Maganza is the most striking example of an unusual syndrome that characterized much of the painting done in Vicenza in the late Renaissance. Doggedly academic in a hybrid pictorial style, he would be entirely forgotten today were it not for his brilliant drawings. His early training as a draftsman was with his father, Giambattista il Vecchio, whose drawings depend on the example of Paolo Veronese, with whom the elder Maganza collaborated on the costumes for the opening production of *Oedipus* at the Teatro Olimpico in 1584. Alessandro continued to be inspired by Paolo's fluent handling of pen and ink, producing a sizable surviving drawing *oeuvre* that is spontaneous, expressive, and capable of continual—seemingly effortless—invention, a quality almost entirely absent from his paintings.

The clear response to Veronese's drawings that is so evident in this fresh and vital sketch suggests that it be dated rather early in Alessandro's career, that is, during the ninth decade of the century, before the tenebrist wash experiments that dominate his handling of the medium after 1600. Its exact place in his *oeuvre* must await the publication of Mason Rinaldi's authoritative study of Maganza's drawings in relation to documented paintings.

WRR

1. Fuhring (1989; 262–63, cat. no. 298); Scholz (1959, cat. no. 32).

2. Kollewijn (1985; 31, cat. no. 32).

3. Fenyö (1958, 62).

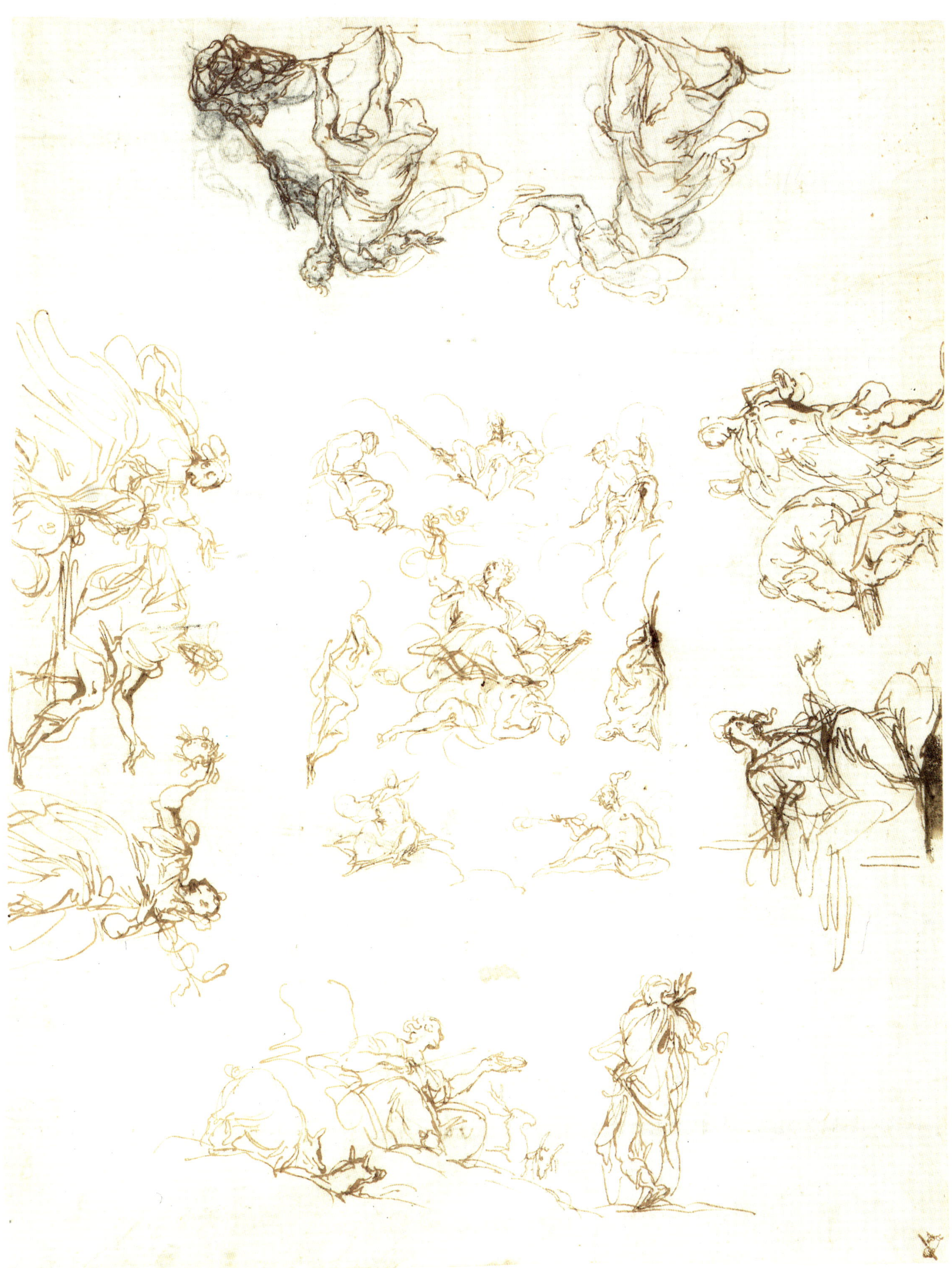

DOMENICO ROBUSTI, called TINTORETTO

Venice, 1560–Venice, 1635

21 *Study for 'Christ Washing the Feet of the Apostles'* (1590–95)

Oil paint on blue paper; inscribed on the verso, *Nz/A.V.*; on the back of the mount *,42* and *Tintoretto*

261 x 221 mm (10 1/4 x 8 5/8 in)

PROVENANCE: H. Fleischauer collection (L. 1306b); perhaps Lady Diana Duff Cooper collection, London; [Christie's, London, 8 April 1986, lot 19]

LITERATURE: unpublished

This strong study bears a traditional attribution to Jacopo Tintoretto, recently revised (Christie's, London, 8 April 1986, lot 19) to that of his son Domenico, a view confirmed in written communications by David Rosand and Paola Rossi.

The drawing's subject is Christ washing the feet of the Apostles, in which the kneeling, aureoled Christ at left turns to receive a bucket of water from an attendant, while an Apostle, studied here from a nude model according to the familiar Robusti shop practice, strips in preparation at right. Other servants heat water at the fireplace in the background. The intersection of forms at left suggests that the sheet has been severely cut and that the full composition followed the standard Tintoretto format as a horizontal with Christ near the center. Its composition would have resembled the painting of this subject (National Gallery, London), which Jacopo Tintoretto painted around 1566 for S. Trovaso, Venice, but the style and handling of the drawing are clearly incompatible with such a date. Much later, around 1592, the Robusti shop returned to this subject in a discursive mural (S. Moisè, Venice), the preparation of which Domenico and other assistants participated in. Again, however, none of the figures in this late version is sufficiently close to those in the drawing to suggest a direct connection between them.

Domenico Robusti was born in 1560, and would have received his paternal training between 1574 and 1578. Taking his inspiration from Jacopo's rare but dynamic compositional drawings in mixed media, such as the sketch (1579, no. 1031, Capodimonte, Naples) for the *Battle of the Taro* (Alte Pinakothek, Munich), Domenico quickly made the oil sketch on blue or brown prepared paper. This was his preferred medium for *concetto* drawings, compositional ideas that he frequently revised in multiple repetitions in his search for just the right formal solution. This highly original approach to the preparatory sketch is best seen in the more-than-a-hundred oil sketches (nos. 1907-7-17-1 to 1907-7-17-90, British Museum, London; and elsewhere) that all seem to date from his mature years around the end of the century and into the early seicento.

The Katalan sheet, in contrast with those fluent studies, is brusque, abrupt, and startlingly willing to abandon *grazia* for an energetic realism that is in many passages abrasively ugly. Its impetuous vulgarity is that of an impatient youth who thrashes about in an unfocused effort to free himself from the routine discipline of the family shop. Indeed, its figural motifs and the slashing use of highlighting resemble passages in paintings such as the *Last Supper* (S. Giorgio Maggiore, Venice), a mural of 1592–94, a painting in which his participation was more extensive than is usually thought. Domenico's independent paintings, such as the *Baptism of Christ* (Museo del Prado, Madrid; formerly Sandborn collection, London), or the *Martyrdom of St. Stephen* (S. Giorgio Maggiore, Venice) of 1593–95, have the same abrupt chiaroscuro and acrobatic poses found in the Katalan drawing. An intermediate stage in Domenico's working procedure may be found in the phantasmagorical *Battle* (Museum of the Rhode Island School of Design, Providence), a rapid preliminary chiaroscuro sketch in oil on canvas. All of these related pictures may be dated to the years 1594–96, and are more elegantly ordered than the Katalan drawing. Domenico's compositional study for *Martyrdom of St. Stephen* (no. L. 12, Christ Church College Museum, Oxford) shares an impatient energy with the present sheet. All of these associations suggest that we may date this drawing to the years 1590–95.

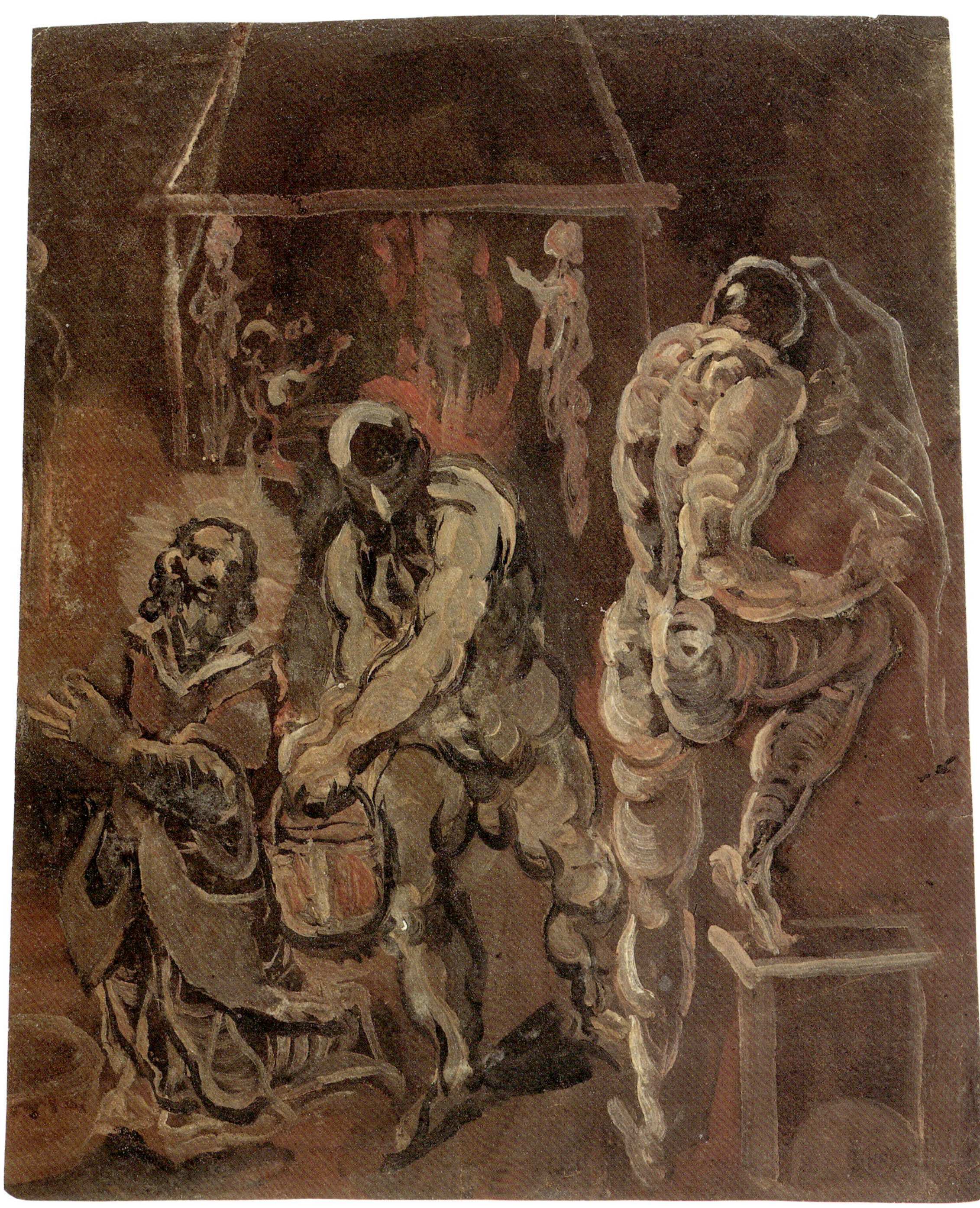

The relation between Robusti father and son is analogous to that of Giambattista and Domenico Tiepolo a century and a half later; the primary device used by Domenico to escape the abstract ideality of the paternal example was an energetic and cynical embrace of the harshly realistic aspect of his subjects. This homely directness takes on an expressionistic intensity in Domenico's drawings, a powerful originality that had but limited appeal to a still-younger generation in search of classical order. In our own century, its cruel energy seems once again deeply communicative.

WRR

LEANDRO DAL PONTE, called BASSANO
Bassano, 1557–Venice, 1622

22

Recto: *Woman Milking a Goat* Verso: *A Nursing Child on its Mother's Lap* (ca. 1595)

Black chalk, heightened with white chalk (recto and verso) on slightly faded gray-blue paper

199 x 189 mm (7 7/8 x 6 7/16 in)

PROVENANCE: Stephen Schwarz collection, New York; [Sotheby's, New York, 16 January 1986, lot 67, as Jacopo Bassano]

LITERATURE: Fröhlich-Bum 1931–32, 121–28; Tietze and Tietze-Conrat 1944, 52, cat. no. A 175; Arslan 1960, 358

This informal but evocative sketch was attributed by Lili Fröhlich-Bum to Jacopo Bassano on the basis of a supposed relationship to the *Annunciation to the Shepherds* (Accademia di S. Luca, Rome).[1] Tietze and Tietze-Conrat thought it was not even Venetian, an opinion apparently accepted by Arslan, who listed it with the distant Dal Ponte shop or wrongly attributed works.[2] More recently, it was sold as by Jacopo (Sotheby's, New York, 16 January 1986, lot 67).

Patently Bassanesque, this motif of the group may be traced to an invention by Jacopo, not the Roman *Annunciation to the Shepherds* that is a replica by Francesco Dal Ponte, but rather to the first version (National Gallery of Art, Washington) that was painted around 1559 by Francesco's father.[3] There, however, the animal is a cow, and it is not until the 1570s that the stock figure of a kneeling woman is combined with a goat. Even then, the goat's frequent appearances are quite distinct in pose and detail from the recto of the Katalan drawing. Perhaps the direct model may be found in *Spring* (Galleria Borghese, Rome), a variant of Jacopo's original set of *Seasons* painted by Francesco around 1577 and frequently replicated by several members of the Dal Ponte shop. Despite these multiple points of reference to paintings produced by several members of the Bassano shop, the motif on the recto of this sheet does not correspond exactly with any known picture.

The very rough sketch on the verso, only recently revealed during restoration, is severely cut at left and is so summary in execution as to defy identification. Nonetheless, a few details can be figured out. The fragmentary form at left appears to depict a seated woman, her dress tied at the shoulder but lowered to expose her left breast to a small child, who leans forward to nurse. The prototype for this may be found in the woman and child at center foreground in *Jacob's Journey* (Royal Collections, Hampton Court) of ca. 1563, but it does not reappear in this drawn format in any known subsequent painting. If one rotates the sheet thirty degrees clockwise, the recumbent child, the woman, and significant details closely resemble the figures at lower left in the *Miracle of the Loaves and the Fishes* (formerly in the refectory at Montecassino; destroyed 1943). This large mural had been commissioned from Francesco but was not even started at the time of his suicide in November 1592. Leandro assumed responsibility for the mural, painted the *modello* (formerly in the Earl of Spencer collection, Althorp House)—in which the nursing woman appears in reverse at right center—and finished the mural in 1594. We would, therefore, tentatively associate the verso with this project and date it to 1593–94.

Most of Leandro's studies for the Montecassino painting (Gabinetto Disegni e Stampe degli Uffizi, Florence; Departement des Arts Graphiques, Louvre, Paris; etc.) of the coeval *Meeting of Pope Alexander III and Doge Ziani* (Consiglio dei Dieci, Palazzo Ducale, Venice), another project inherited from Francesco, as well as preparatory sketches (Departement des Arts Graphiques, Louvre, Paris; Carnegie Institute, Pittsburgh; Ratjen Foundation, Vaduz) for the *Martyrdom of St. Lucy* (S. Giorgio Maggiore, Venice), Leandro drew in 1594. They display an abrupt, energetic, rather scratchy handling of the medium consonant with both recto and verso of the Katalan study. We would, therefore, confirm its attribution to Leandro, loosely associate it with pictures of the mid-1590s, and date it to these years.

WRR

1. Fröhlich-Bum (1931–32, 121–28).

2. Tietze and Tietze-Conrat (1944; 52, cat. no. A 175).

3. Arslan (1960, 358).

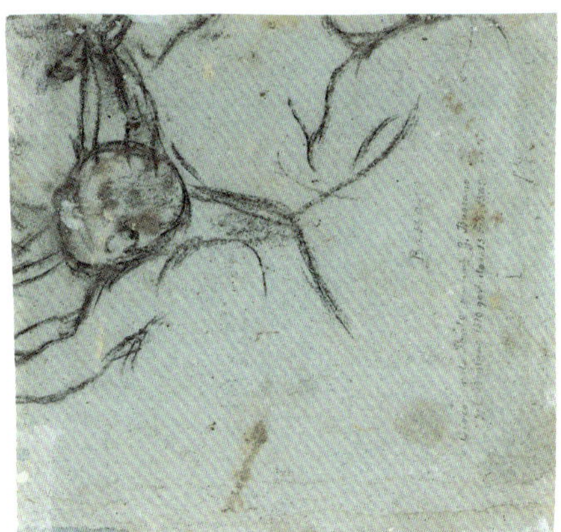
Verso

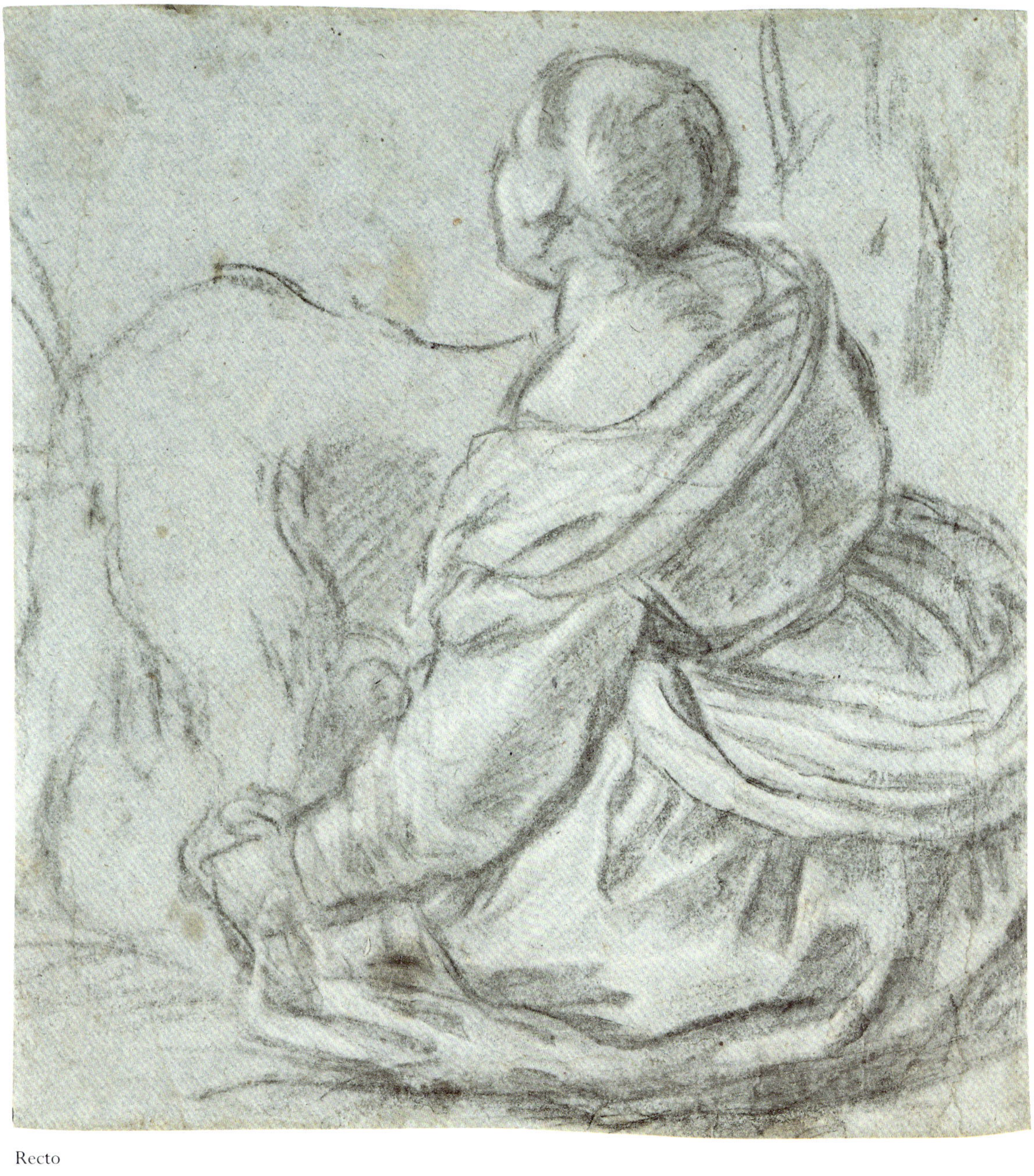

Recto

Camillo Procaccini
Bologna, ca. 1555–Milan, 1629

23 *St. Benedict and St. Scholastica at Table* (1610–20)

Red chalk, squared in red chalk

182 x 170 mm (7 1/8 x 6 5/8 in)

Provenance: Giuseppe Vallardi (L. 1223); Carlo Prayer (L. 2044); Juan and Felix Bernasconi; Christie's, London, 6 July 1987, lot 73; [Marcello Aldega and Margot Gordon, 1991]

Literature: Aldega and Gordon, 1988, cat. no. 8

As Philip Pouncey was the first to recognize, the drawing represents St. Benedict, the founder of western monasticism, and his sister St. Scholastica, the abbess of a convent in Piombarcola, at their yearly meeting at Montecassino.

The work is typical of Camillo's finished chalk drawings. Close comparisons may be made between *St. Benedict and St. Scholastica at Table* and sheets such as the *Flying Angels*, preparatory for the Milanese Duomo sacristy ceiling of 1611 (F235 inf. n. 982, Ambrosiana, Milan; and 662, Accademia, Venice)[1]; or the *Adoration of the Shepherds* (C 731-3/5395-5, Castello Sforzesco, Milan) for the painting in S. Vittore al Corpo, Milan of 1615–16[2]; or the *Shepherds* (3816, Windsor Castle), a study for the *Adoration of the Shepherds* (Brera, Milan) of about the same date.[3] Also relevant are two studies for the laterals in the Pisani Chapel in S. Nicolò dei Tolentini, Venice of around 1618 (23716, Berlin-Dahlem and Maser Collection, Chicago).[4] This wide dating, covering most of the second decade of the seventeenth century, is indicative of the steady character of Camillo's art. Despite the fact that the drawing is squared for transfer, the picture has not yet come to light. Precise dating would only be possible if the finished work, with relevant documents, were to be found.

NWN

1. Neilson (1979; 23–24 n. 27; 146, fig. 193; 168, fig. 195).

2. Neilson (1979; 46 n. 61; 153, fig. 206).

3. Neilson (1979; 26–27 n. 33; 171, fig. 213). See also Neilson (1989, 353 n. 249) for further discussion of the date of the altarpiece.

4. Neilson (1979; 70–71 n. 101; 127, fig. 253; 130, fig. 260).

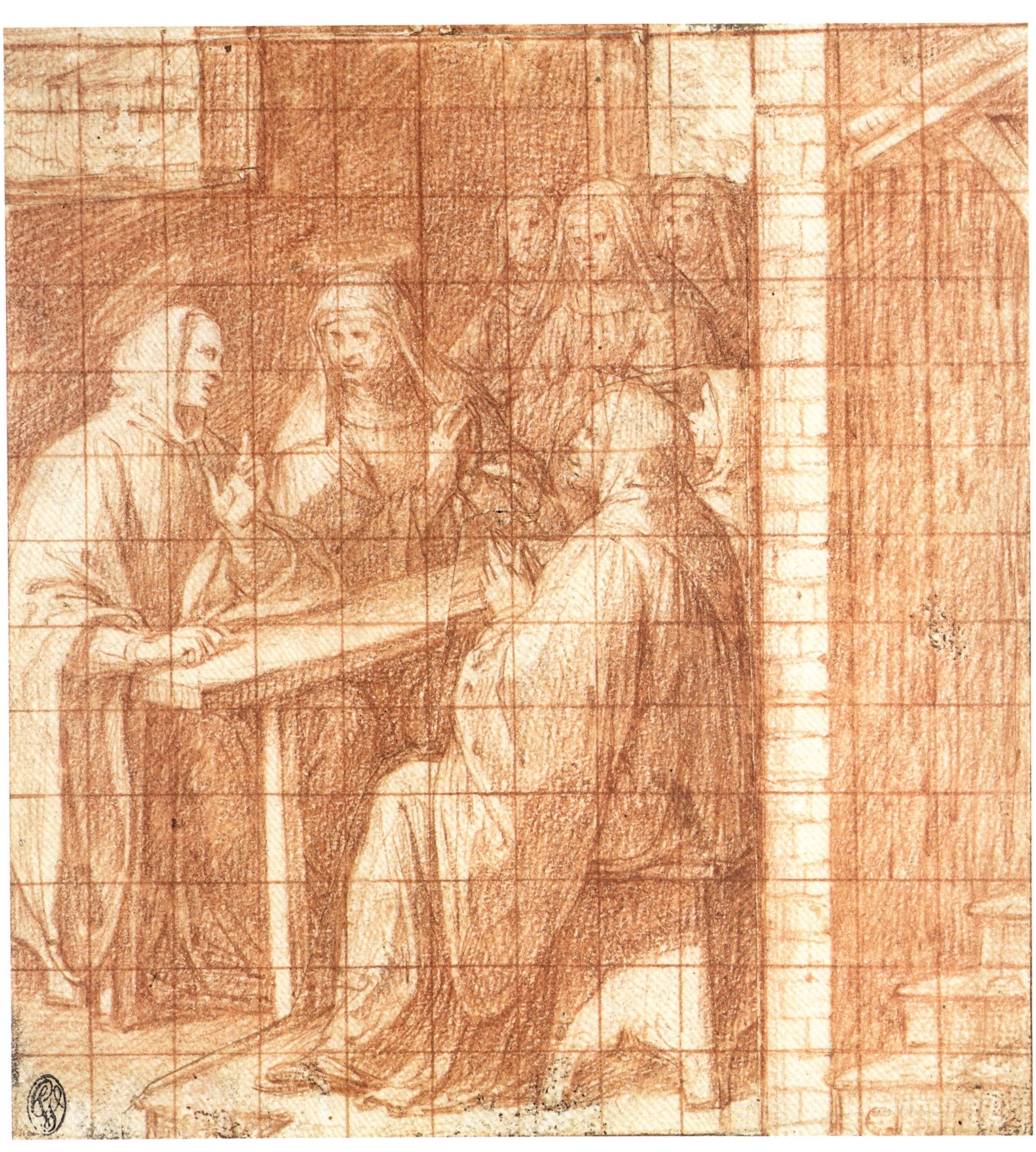

Bartolomeo Cesi

Bologna, 1556–Bologna, 1629

24 *Study for a Standing Figure* (ca. 1584)

Red and white chalk on blue paper

283 x 195 mm (11 1/8 x 7 5/8 in)

Provenance: Alessandro Maggiori (with the attribution, "Il Cesi fece"; L. 3005b); Breschi (L. 2079b); Argentieri (L. 4866); [Aldega and Gordon, New York, 1992]

Literature: Aldega and Gordon 1988, cat. no. 13

The fresco cycle on the walls and ceiling of the church of Sta. Maria dei Bulgari in Bologna, depicting *Scenes from the Life of the Virgin* was destroyed in World War II. The cycle represented an important stage in Cesi's artistic career, as Graziani acutely observed in his fine monographic study of the artist, which appeared in 1939.[1] It was considered by Francesco Arcangeli to be "il più bel ciclo pittorico bolognese della pittura di Controriforma..." [the most beautiful Bolognese pictorial cycle of the Counter Reformation].[2] We know from a document that, by 1584, work on the decorative complex had progressed to the point that Cesi could supervise in person a project for the Certosa di Maggiano, near Siena.[3] There are numerous drawings related to the frescoes, a group of which were known to Graziani.[4] They were later studied by Johnston and Forlani Tempesti and in more recent studies.[5] The drawings allow us to characterize the working methods of the master through an understanding of the techniques he employed. The *modello* in the Uffizi Gallery, Florence (inv. 7269F; pen, ink, and brown wash) for *The Coronation of the Virgin*, originally at the center of the ceiling in Sta. Maria dei Bulgari,[6] should be added to the series of drawings related to *The Death of the Virgin*.[7] The Katalan sheet is related to the figure at left in the fresco, *Charity and Truth* (see the reproduction in Fortunati Pietrantonio [1986, 820]); it should be placed close in time to the execution of the painting, unlike the well-known sheet in the Uffizi Gallery (inv. 781E), which is correctly considered to represent an early idea for the central part of the fresco.

MDG

1. *Graziani (1939, 54–95).*

2. *Arcangeli (1959, 54).*

3. *Bagnoli (1978, 36).*

4. *Graziani (1939, 94–95).*

5. *Johnston (1973, 32–35); Forlani Tempesti (1977, 2:486–98). Di Giampaolo (1988; 92–94, 161–71); Di Giampaolo (1989b, 286); Zacchi (1991, 111–25 and n. 743).*

6. *Di Giampaolo (1990, 30–31).*

7. *Di Giampaolo (1988, 162).*

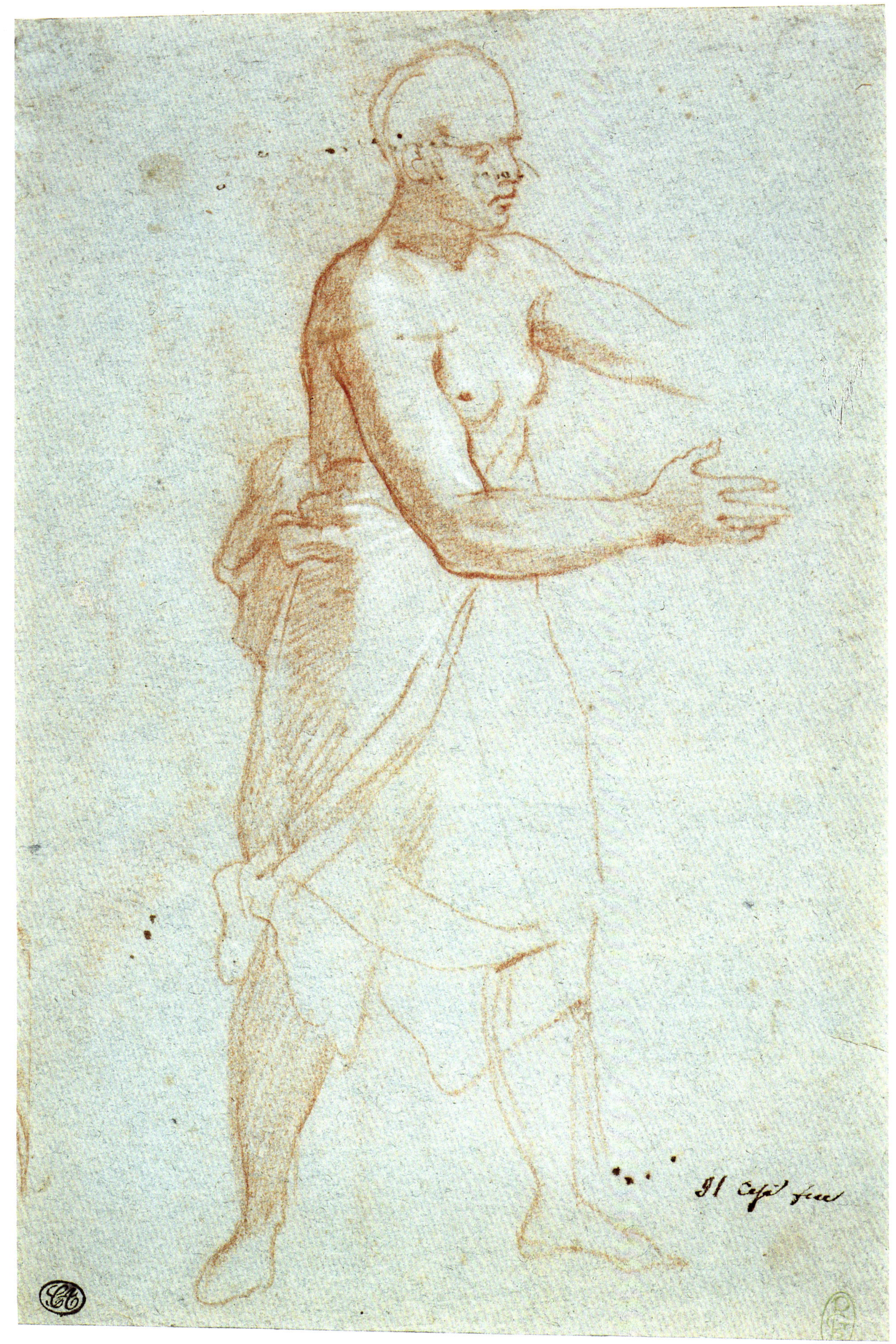

BERNARDINO POCCETTI

Florence, 1548–Florence, 1612

25 *Portrait of a Young Man in Period Costume, Hand Resting on a Staff* (ca. 1600)

Black chalk; torn lower left corner reinserted and completed before addition of stamp; laid down

225 x 160 mm (8 7/8 x 5 1/2 in)

PROVENANCE: Thomas Dimsdale (according to nineteenth-century inscription on old mount); unidentified collector, blue ink stamp; [Hôtel Drouot, Paris, 15 May 1992, lot 31, attributed to Bartolomeo Cesi]

LITERATURE: unpublished

Following the Florentine tradition as it had been practiced since the beginning of the sixteenth century, Bernardino Poccetti, a consummate painter of figures, would make separate studies for each one before transferring them to his frescoes.[1] These frescoes took up the better part of his career, and Poccetti was indeed the foremost specialist of religious narratives in cloisters and church interiors in Florence and all of Tuscany during the years immediately before and after 1600. The natural poise of the figures who populate these compositions, and the quality of their depiction, both lively and simple, refined but without affectation, add up to a Florentine version of realism, which at the time affected all the Italian schools of painting, whether they were the Carracci in Bologna or the nascent influence of Caravaggio in Rome (1598–99, Chapel of St. Matthew, S. Luigi de' Francesi). One could also compare—the better to distinguish between them—the drawing shown here with *Head of a Young Boy*, attributed to an anonymous member of the Brescian school circa 1600, that recently came onto the art market.[2] Some of Poccetti's drawings were formerly classified among the works of the Bolognese school, for example, *A Young Man Lying on a Bench, Sleeping* (inv. 7351, Louvre, Paris). Motifs such as *A Man Drinking*, made famous by Annibale Carracci's rendering of the subject in 1581 (Cleveland), were also treated by Poccetti,[3] though the latter, like the Florentines in general, had a different feeling for the individualization of his subjects. The strong features of the young man in the present drawing, the elongated line of the eyes and the full lips, call to mind an Asian model. The stylization of the face is underlined by the elegance of the costume, particularly the headdress crowned by a plume and a jewel. There is no figure corresponding to this young man in any of Poccetti's known paintings.

In about 1600, in the Franciscan cycle of lunettes in the cloister of the Church of Ognissanti, Jacopo Ligozzi also took to painting elegant young gentlemen. This is how he portrayed St. Francis sharing his cloak with the beggar and kissing the leper,[4] whereas in the lunette, *Preaching to the Sultan*, there is a young man with a staff—as in Poccetti's drawing—who is standing in the foreground, though seen from behind.[5] Significantly, Poccetti's figure is slightly foreshortened. Perhaps the drawing originally represented a full-length figure to be placed in the foreground of a painting such as the lunette of the *Appearance of the Virgin to the Seven Saintly Founders of the Servite Order* in Pistoia, dated 1602.[6]

CMG

1. *Hamilton (1980, 7–22).*

2. *London, Richard Philip, reproduced in* Burlington Magazine *135, no. 1080 (March 1993): p. x.*

3. *Voss and Planiscig (n.d., pl. 37).*

4. *Conigliello et al. (1989, 42–43).*

5. *Ibid., 64–65.*

6. *Falletti et al. (1992, fig. 78).*

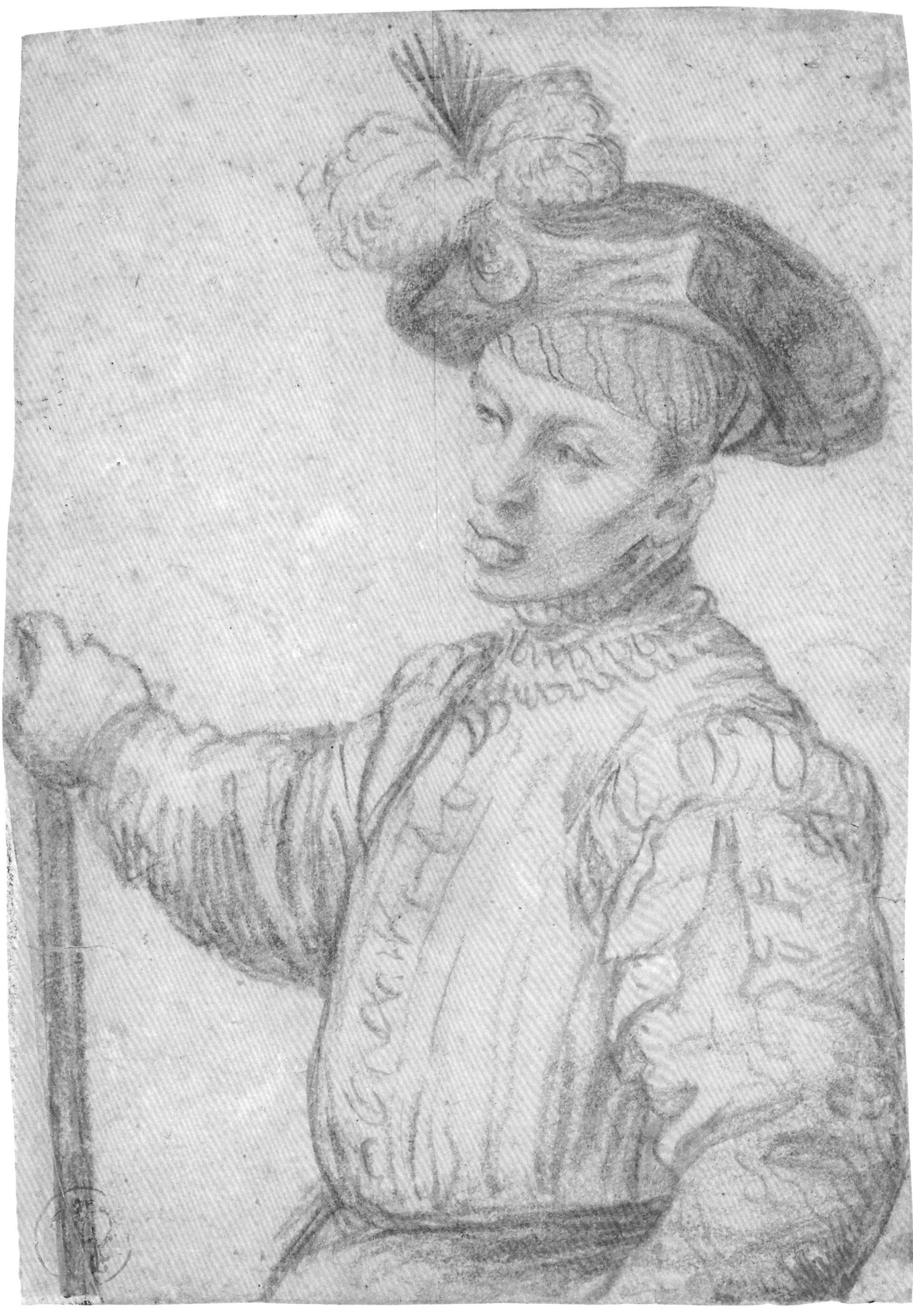

ANDREA BOSCOLI

Florence, ca. 1560–Florence, 1607

26 ### *A Horse Seen from Behind*

Red and black chalk; inscribed in pen and brown ink in upper right corner, *M.4.*

226 x 136 mm (8 7/8 x 5 3/8 in)

PROVENANCE: E. Bouverie (L. 325); Sotheby's, London, 5 December 1977, lot 65; Jacques Petit Hory, Paris; private collection, Los Angeles; [Katrin Bellinger, Munich, 1991]

LITERATURE: Bellinger 1991, cat. no. 20; Griswold and Wolk-Simon 1994, cat. no. 40

EXHIBITIONS: *Sixteenth-Century Italian Drawings in New York Collections*, Metropolitan Museum of Art, New York, 1994, cat. no. 40

This drawing by Andrea Boscoli belongs to a group that includes a large number of studies drawn from live models and done in red chalk, frequently combined with black chalk, as is the case here. The bulk of these studies consists of full-length figures, often nudes, and anatomical details such as the unpublished drawing, *Hands* (private collection, Paris), or *A Head Seen from Behind*.[1] Animal studies are rare.[2] Boscoli enrolled at the Accademia del Disegno in Florence in 1584. In contrast to the work of contemporary Florentine draftsmen such as Jacopo da Empoli, the drawings by Boscoli that concern us here are characterized by the choice of unusual points of view and the recurrent rendering of volumes by facets and planes, revealing wide, empty spaces. The subtlety of this technique allows the artist to push forms to the point of abstraction. Boscoli's prodigious skill gives the "natural," so dear to the hearts of the Florentines, a tense, anticonformist slant. When he copies Michelangelo, he sometimes manages to set off a motif in such a nonacademic manner that the figures take on a decidedly bizarre quality; for example, in the unpublished copy of a motif from the lower left side of the *Last Judgment* in the Sistine Chapel (inv. 783, Louvre, Paris). The style of his drawings, which are innumerable, is in most instances easily recognizable. In 1959, Anna Forlani had already counted more than three hundred, and since then numerous other sheets have come to light. Filippo Baldinucci's comment might expand our insight into the nature of Boscoli's virtuosity as a draftsman: "Disegno si bene, che i suoi disegni, senza mancare di una franchezza, e bravura di tocco straordinario, no paion fatti al naturale, ma copiati a tutto suo agio da altri disegni. Hanno in sé una certa vaghezza cagionata da alcune risentite macchie, e attitudine con disinvoltura, e scioglimento di parti, che dà altrui nell'occhio assai, questo pero cagiona in loro il difetto di potersi dire alquanto ammanierati" [He drew so well that his drawings, despite their straightforwardness and an extraordinary mastery of touch, do not seem to be done from life, but copied at leisure from other drawings. They possess a certain beauty engendered by various heartfelt blotches, postures of great freedom and nonchalance, and careful selection of parts, which strike the eye of all and sundry, but the deficiency resulting from all this is that they can be said to be somewhat mannered].[3]

Drawings of horses had a privileged status among Florentine draftsmen such as Naldini, Stradanus, Empoli, and Giovanni Bologna, but the object of these studies varied widely. There is a great difference between Stradanus's almost emblematic studies of horses designed for engravings of the most handsome specimens in Don Juan of Austria's royal stables[4] and Boscoli's drawing shown here. It is possible that the artist did not make use of a live model, but rather a sculpture, a wax model, or a bronze statuette in this work.[5]

CMG

1. *Gaud collection sale; Sotheby's, Monaco, 20 June 1987, lot 23.*

2. Camel *(inv. 860 Orn, Uffizi); Forlani (1959, cat. no. 30), cited with complementary references by Griswold and Wolk-Simon (1994).*

3. *Baldinucci (1846, 2:76–77).*

4. *See the sheet presented by E. Moatti in New York, sale cat., Jack Kilgore and Co., Inc., May 1994, cat. no. 5.*

5. *Griswold and Wolk-Simon (1994).*

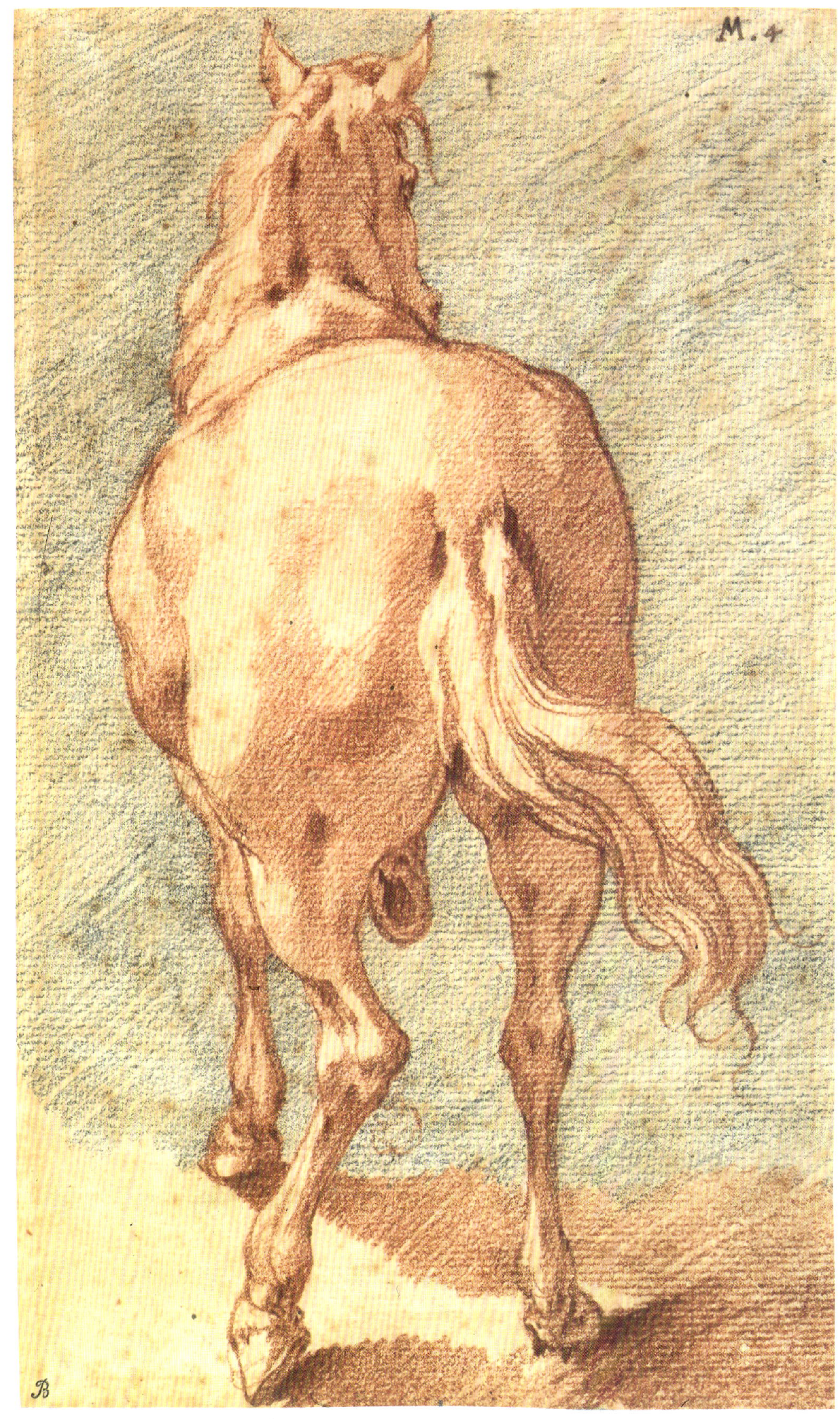
M. 4

Ludovico Cardi, called Il Cigoli

Cigoli, near S. Miniato, 1559–Rome, 1613

27 Recto: *Studies of Tityus* Verso: *Assorted Figure Studies* (ca. 1613)

Pen and brown ink with wash over red chalk (recto); pen and brown ink and black chalk (verso)

132 x 195 mm (5 3/16 x 7 5/8 in)

Provenance: [Sotheby's, London, 13 April 1992, lot 211, as Neapolitan School]

Literature: unpublished

Ludovico Cardi, who is better known by his nickname taken from the village near S. Miniato where he was born, might be considered the Annibale Carracci of Florence. Almost exact contemporaries, both artists participated in the stylistic revolution in the last quarter of the sixteenth century that challenged the artificial sophistication of late *maniera* with an art more closely based on the direct study of nature. Cigoli was, however, a more conservative artist than any of the Carracci, and his Florentine roots manifest themselves in his tighter surface finish and in the inspiration from the works of Florentine predecessors such as Andrea del Sarto, although he was also deeply affected by the work of Federico Barocci. His drawings and paintings show a special interest in dramatic light effects, which also separates them from those of his Florentine predecessors and contemporaries.

Jak Katalan spotted this characteristic example of Ludovico Cigoli's draftsmanship in a sale catalogue, where it was labeled "Neapolitan School". It is an intriguing sheet that displays Cigoli's drawing technique at its most varied and experimental. On the recto, five sketches experiment with designs for a picture of Tityus having his liver pecked at eternally by a vulture, a subject not known to have been painted by Cigoli. Three sketches on the left explore the formal relationship between the man and the bird, a fourth sketch shows a barely indicated figure, but a fifth one above it has been worked up with wash, provided with a setting, and even squared for transfer. Many such sheets of sketches that explore a variety of possible poses for key pairs or groups of figures in a proposed painting by Cigoli are known, though none that demonstrate the creative process from tentative idea to final resolution with the diagrammatic clarity of this particular example.[1] An especially apt comparison is the verso of a sheet in the Louvre with assorted sketches for a painting of Narcissus reclining by a pool and contemplating his reflection.[2] The most finished sketch is elaborated in a full-page study on the recto of the sheet. Viatte dated the drawing late in Cigoli's career and noted that this mythological subject is not known to have been painted by him. Indeed, mythological themes are rare throughout his career; his production consisted mainly of religious subjects, and then of portraits.

While the attribution of this double-sided sheet to Ludovico Cigoli is secure, only tentative connections can be made between any of the sketches and known commissions. The dominant figure on the verso is a seated male figure facing right and pointing with his right arm, drawn with bold, expressive, angular, and broken pen strokes. Cigoli made similarly expressive pen drawings in his last years in Rome. An especially close parallel is offered by a study in the Uffizi connected with his fresco of *Tobias and the Archangel* in the Villa Arrigoni (Muti) in Frascati, where the hands also look like mittens.[3] A composition study for Cigoli's painting, *Christ's Appearance to St. Peter* of 1607, also in the Uffizi, uses the same bold, zigzag contours for the principal figures seen in the Katalan drawing.[4] The slight pen sketch of a reclining male nude seen from the back on the lower left of the verso looks like the twin of a dead youth in the foreground of a drawing in the Uffizi for a scene of St. Felicity witnessing the martyrdom of her children.[5]

All the stylistic parallels for both recto and verso indicate that the Katalan drawing was made relatively late in Cigoli's career. The artist may have begun to explore mythological themes while depicting the story of Psyche in 1611–13 for the Casino of Cardinal Scipione Borghese, who employed Guido Reni, Agostino Tassi, Orazio Gentileschi, Giovanni Baglione, and others to decorate his summer residence on the Quirinale before abandoning it in 1616 to focus his energies on the Villa

1. *Chappell et al. (1979; cat. no. 75, verso).*

2. *Viatte (1981–82, cat. no. 23).*

3. *Chappell et al. (1979; cat. no. 89, verso).*

4. *Chappell et al.(1979, cat. no. 93).*

5. *Chappell (1992, cat. no. 66a). The altarpiece was commissioned in 1606, but was not completed until 1610.*

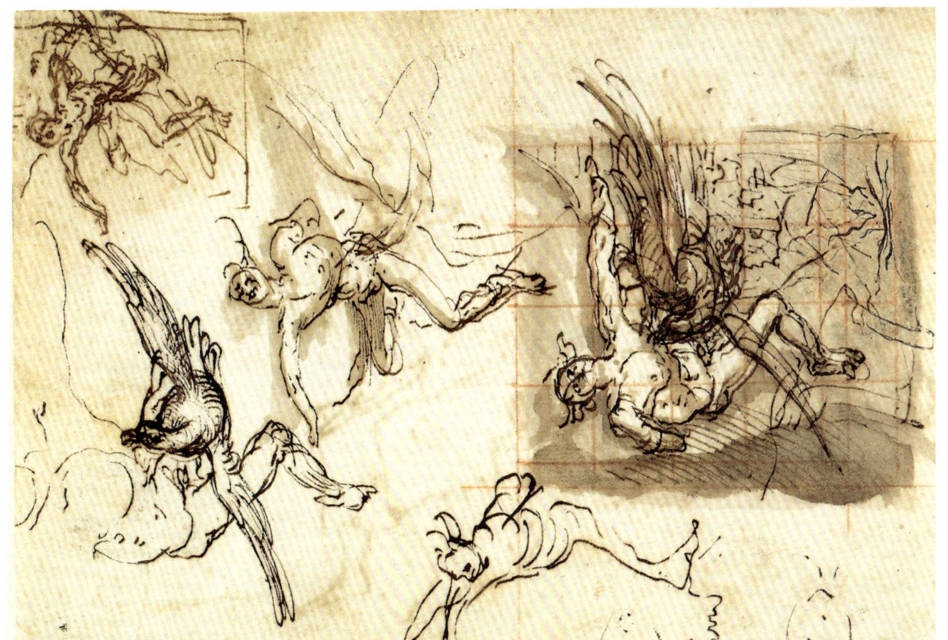

Recto

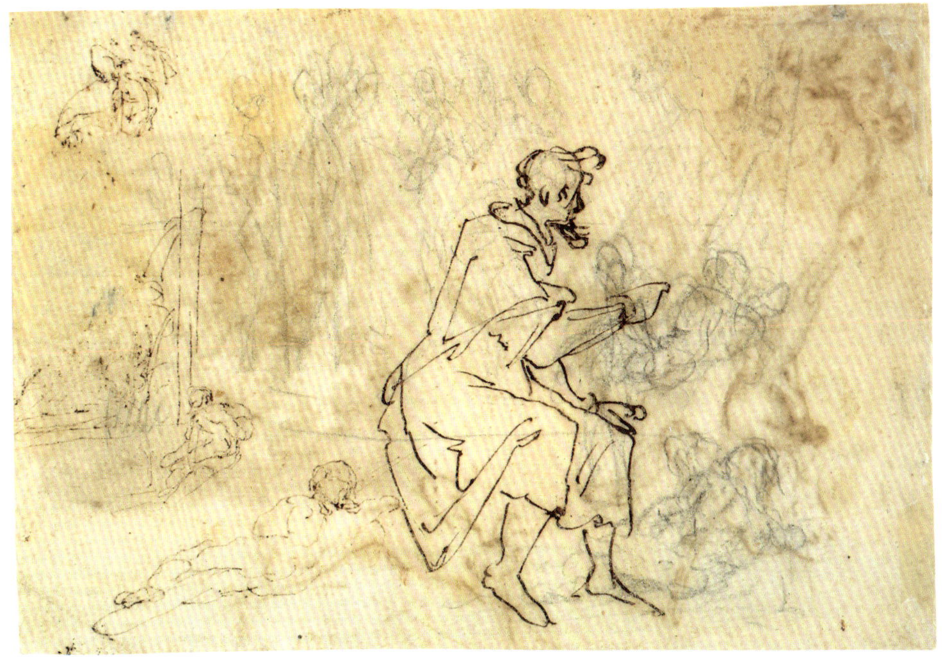

Verso

Borghese.[6] Perhaps Cigoli hoped to receive further commissions from the cardinal, or maybe the stories of Narcissus and Tityus were also contemplated for a different iconographical program than that which was finally chosen. As pointed out, the reclining male figure might be a rejected proposal for one of the grisaille satyrs and nymphs who recline on the arches of the lunette-shaped fields, or for the cloud-borne man in the lower left of the ceiling scene of *Psyche before Jupiter*.[7] Finally, the seated man can best be connected with a late commission designed by Cigoli but carried out by his then-young assistant, Sigismondo Coccapani, the scene of St. Antoninus giving alms to a poor man taken from two false beggars in the cloister of S. Marco, Florence, painted in the year of Cigoli's death.[8] None of Cigoli's other seated male figures facing left come as close as this witness of the miracle does to the depicted age, costume, and gesture seen in Katalan's sketch. Cigoli was only fifty-four when he died. The drawing may thus be among the last that he made before that premature event.

ASH

6. For the most recent summary account of Cigoli's fresco cycle, detached when the Casino was destroyed in the nineteenth century and now kept in the Museo di Roma, see Faranda (1986, 99–102 and cat. no. 84).

7. Letter from Jak Katalan to Anne Sutherland Harris. Also see Faranda (1986, 99 and pl. XLVIII). The figure is in the reverse direction, but is one of the rare back view nudes in Cigoli's oeuvre, *so the connection is worth consideration.*

8. See Viatte (1981–82; 44, cat. no. 25), which illustrates the scene and a composition study by Cigoli for the fresco.

Francesco Vanni

Siena, 1563–Siena, 1610

28 *St. Blaise and St. Catherine of Alexandria Receiving the Crown and Palm of Martyrdom* (1595–1605)

Black and white chalk, squared in red chalk; borderlines in pen and black ink; laid down; inscribed at lower left in pen and ink, *23;* the mount at lower right inscribed in pen and ink, *29*

204 x 160 mm (7 31/32 x 6 9/32 in)

Provenance: Gasparo Mola; Padre Sebastiano Resta (L. Sup. 2992a); Edward Clive, first earl of Powis; by descent; the earl of Plymouth; Christie's, London, 1 July 1986, Lot 118; [Nissman, Abromson & Co., 1989]

Literature: Andrews 1969, cat. no. 88; Nissman, Abromson & Co. 1989, cat. no. 14; Griswold and Wolk-Simon 1994, cat. no. 101

Exhibitions: *Italian 16th-Century Drawings from British Private Collections*, Scottish Arts Council, Edinburgh, 1969, cat. no. 88; *Sixteenth-Century Italian Drawings in New York Collections*, Metropolitan Museum of Art, New York, 1994, cat. no. 101

Both saints are depicted kneeling, with the attributes of their martyrdom: St. Blaise is in bishop's attire, with the iron wool comb with which he was martyred, and a palm; St. Catherine, crowned, is shown with a fragment of the wheel with which she was tortured before being beheaded, and a palm. An angel hovering above them approaches with the crown and palm of martyrdom.[1]

The attribution of this typical drawing was first suggested by Peter Anselm Riedl, who dated it to between 1595 and 1605, but was unable to connect it with an extant work by the master.[2] In his view it could have been made in preparation for a church banner.

PD

1. Andrews (1969, cat. no. 88).

2. Nissman, Abromson & Co. (1989, cat. no. 14).

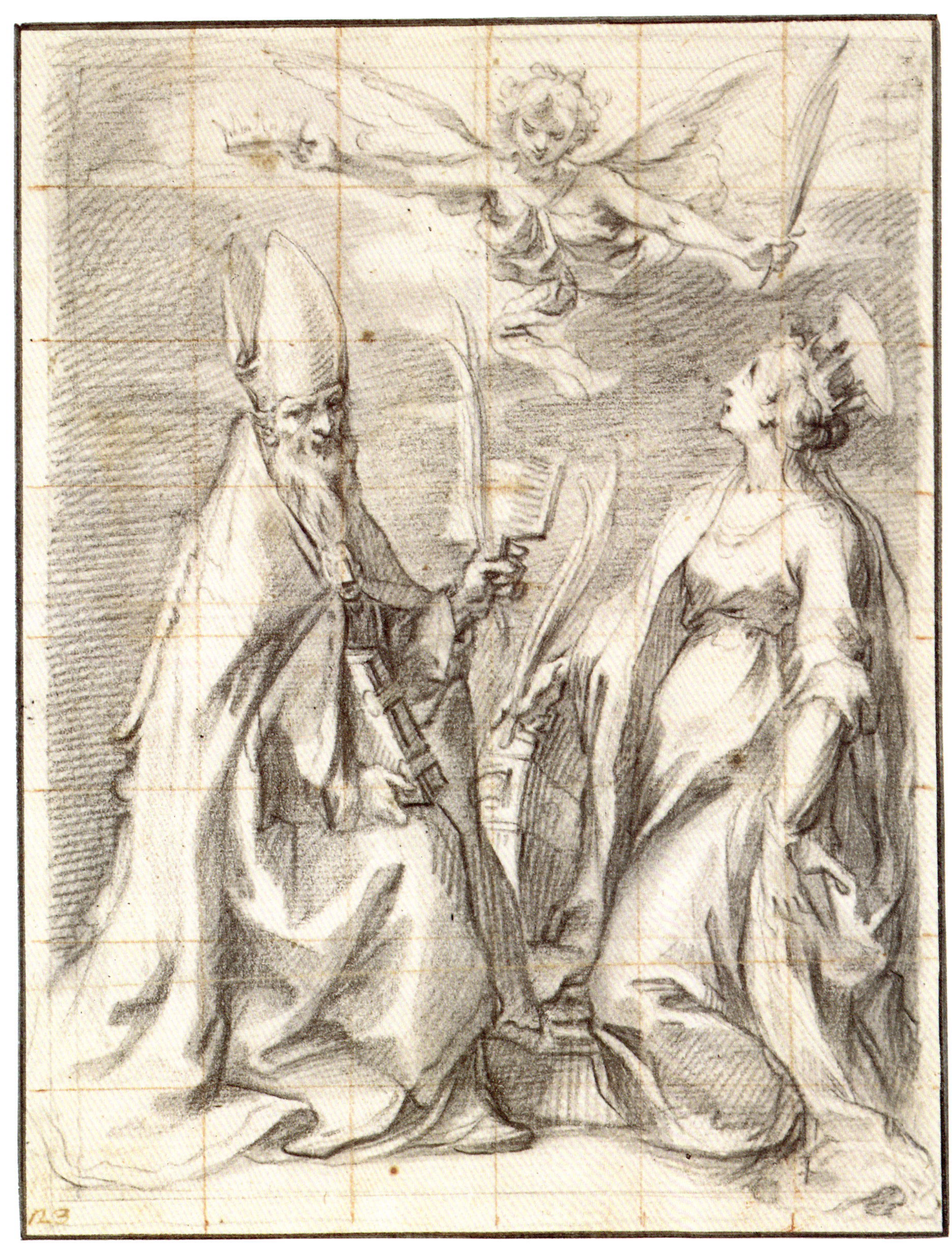

Giovanni Alberti

Borgo S. Sepolcro, 1558–Rome, 1601

29 *Nude Man Supporting the Aldobrandini Coat of Arms* (ca. 1596)

Black and red chalk on cream paper

135 x 198 mm (5 3/8 x 7 3/4 in)

Provenance: Hans Calmann; Sotheby's, London, 7 December 1976, part of lot 31; Marcello Aldega, Rome; [Christie's, London, 20 April 1993, lot 24]

Literature: Aldega, 1980, cat. no. 26

This drawing is one of a sizable group preserved in both public and private collections connected with decorative commissions that Giovanni and his brother Cherubino (1553–1615) carried out in the Vatican for Pope Clement VIII Aldobrandini.[1] Of these, the decoration of the Sala Clementina (1596–1600) especially impressed the biographer, Giovanni Baglione, who called it "one of the most beautiful works of this type carried out in our time," and claimed that Giovanni Alberti had no rival when it came to painting illusionistic perspectives ("ebbe genio a far mirabili prospettive"), and further that his figures on the vault were far better than those by his brother.[2] The strong foreshortening of the muscular male figure in this drawing, which portrays a hand of which only knuckles and a little finger are visible, and which creates the chest and the complex interlace of bone and muscle of the steeply angled back with little more than one inflected contour line, would seem perfect proof of the particular artistic genius of Giovanni Alberti. Yet scholars who have studied the brothers' work have been unable to separate their hands definitively, and their drawings are sometimes attributed to both. Those, however, that emphasize foreshortening and give the figures more sculptural mass, as with this example, are generally assigned to Giovanni, an attribution preferred for this sheet.

This figure is connected with a male nude on the center of the west side of the vault of the Sala Clementina. He reclines on a broken pediment to the left of Clemency, who is seated in the middle of the pediment, armor beneath her feet and an olive branch in her right hand.[3] He holds up the crenellated bar of the Aldobrandini arms, thus making clear the connection between the virtue of clemency and Pope Clement VIII. There are other studies for this commission in the Metropolitan Museum of Art, New York and the Ashmolean Museum, Oxford, in addition to those in Rome already cited.[4]

The Alberti brothers were born in Borgo San Sepolcro, a town with long-standing political and artistic connections with Florence. Their father, Alberto, an architect and wood carver, had established a second studio in Rome by 1566, and had had occasional commissions from Duke Cosimo I de' Medici in Florence. Thus the Alberti sons had opportunities to study both Florentine and Roman *maniera* painting and drawing before arriving in Rome, where they were settled from ca. 1580. Alberto and Cherubino bought a cartoon by Giulio Romano in 1571, and Cherubino made an engraving after Federico Zuccaro's *Coronation of the Virgin* in SS. Trinità dei Monti in 1572. Both Cherubino and Giovanni also made drawings after Michelangelo and Taddeo Zuccaro.[5] Their drawings are not so smoothly articulated and elegantly contoured as those of the Zuccari, but some debt to their drawing style is evident. If less polished, the Albertis' best drawings convey energy and movement in a way quite exceptional for mannerist drawings. The exhibited sheet captures all these qualities with unusual economy and precision.

ASH

1. Abromson (1978; 531 f., esp. 533 f.); Hermann-Fiore (1983, cat. nos. 20–33).

2. Baglione (1642, 70). The fresco above the cornice level is given to Giovanni by Baglione, but Hermann-Fiore attributes preparatory studies for the vault to both brothers, who probably collaborated on this vast project.

3. Hermann Fiore (1980; 39f., fig. 17). I am grateful to Morton Abromson for helping me to make the right identification.

4. Parker (1956, cat. no. 70 and pl. 24); Bean (1982, cat. nos. 2–3).

5. Hermann-Fiore (1983, cat. nos. 20–33). The chronology on 27–34 is especially helpful. For drawings after other artists, see cat. nos. 3–12, 148–151, and 155–157.

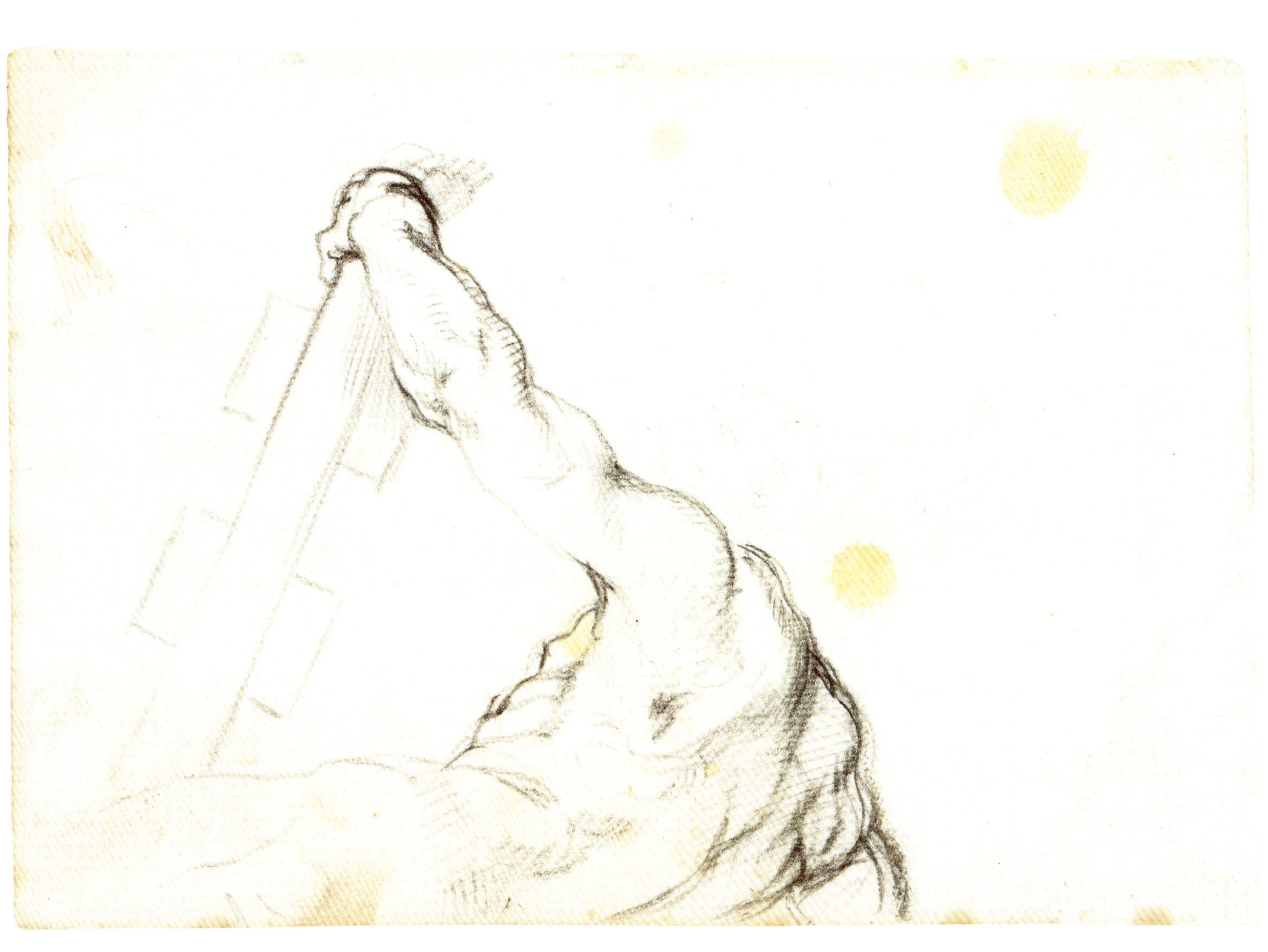

Ludovico Carracci

Bologna, 1555–Bologna, 1619

30 a, b *Two Drawings After Pellegrino Tibaldi's Ceiling Fresco in the Sala di Ulisse, Palazzo Poggi, Bologna* (ca. 1580)

Pen and brown ink with brown wash

175 x 268 mm (6 7/8 x 10 1/2 in) each

PROVENANCE: Pierre-Jean Mariette (L. 1852); Count J. P. van Suchtelen (L. 2332); Hôtel Drouot, Paris, 7 June 1989; [London, Kate Ganz, 1991]

LITERATURE: Bohn 1992a, 400–402; Feigenbaum 1992, figs. 5 and 6; Bohn 1993, 230–31 and figs. 1 and 2

Ludovico Carracci was one of the key painters of the early Italian baroque period who, with his cousins Annibale and Agostino Carracci, founded an art academy in Bologna that trained several major Italian painters of the next generation. A brilliant and innovative iconographer, whose paintings are notable for their dramatic lighting and versatile emotional expressiveness, Ludovico was also a prolific draftsman who produced some four hundred surviving drawings.

The calligraphic pen style of these two sheets, with its curlicues and flourishes, is not typical of the artist's mature drawings but recalls the draftsmanship of Ludovico's mannerist predecessors. Thus these may be Ludovico's earliest extant pen drawings, datable to around 1580.

The drawings reproduce two of the *ignudi* and part of the framework of Pellegrino Tibaldi's famous ceiling fresco in the Palazzo Poggi, Bologna. The Carraccis' seventeenth-century Bolognese biographer, Count Carlo Cesare Malvasia, noted that Ludovico esteemed Tibaldi, Nicolò dell'Abbate, and Francesco Primaticcio more than any of his compatriots and taught his students to draw from their works in the Palazzo Poggi and elsewhere.[1] The Katalan drawings are two of only three known drawings by Ludovico after these artists, although many more such drawings must once have existed, by Malvasia's account.[2]

Pierre-Jean Mariette, who once owned these two sheets and placed them together on a single mount, explained their inception based on another passage in Malvasia's biography. The latter had noted that before designing the Farnese Gallery (in 1597–1600), Annibale had drawings made in Bologna after Tibaldi's frescoes.[3] Mariette believed that these drawings were made by Ludovico and sent to Annibale in Rome, but the style of the two sheets suggests a date much earlier than the late 1590s.[4]

BB

1. Malvasia ([1678] 1841, 1:332–33).

2. The third drawing, which was discovered by Sylvie Béguin and is known to this writer only from a photograph, is in the Musée des Arts Decoratifs, Paris. It copies another ceiling by Tibaldi in the Palazzo Poggi (discussed and illustrated in Feigenbaum [1992, 306 and fig. 7], without inventory number or further information).

3. "Ed Annibale (come altrove si disse) stando in Roma, prima di fare lo scomparto della Galleria Farnese, fece disegnarsi in Bologna, e mandarsi quello del Tibaldi, suddetto nella saletta abbasso del palagio de' detti Poggi, disegnandone uno su quella similitudine...." (Malvasia [1678] 1841, 1:333)

4. Mariette's opinion was recorded in an inscription on the mount: "Haec ornamenta quae Peregr. Tibaldi in quodam conclavi aedium Card. Poggii Bononiae depinxit, ab Ann Carraccio sese ad opus Farnesian-accingente, rogatus delin & per litteras Romae mittebat." See Bohn (1992a, 402). Feigenbaum (1992, 306) evidently accepts the dating in the late 1590s implied by the story.

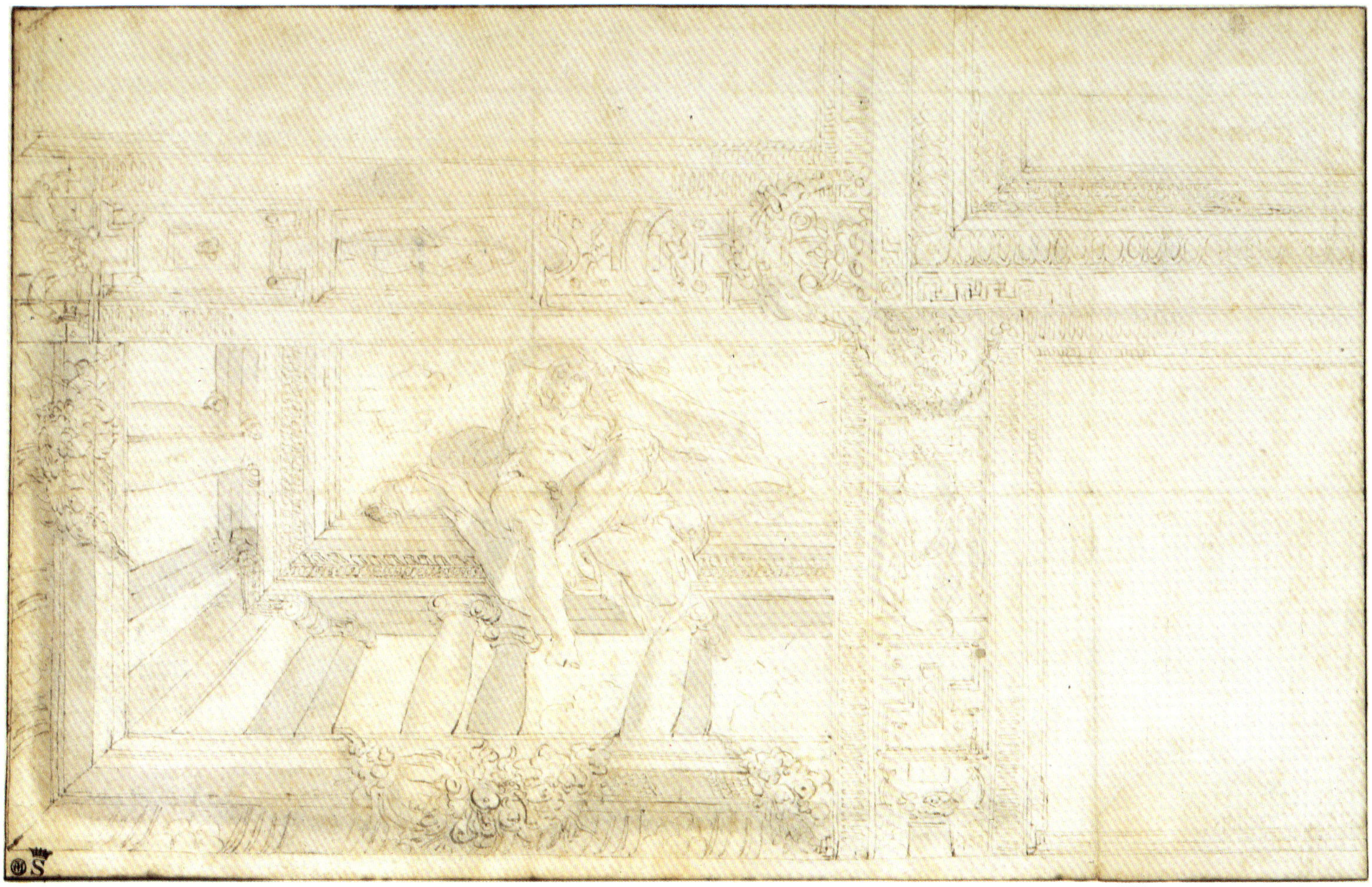

30 a

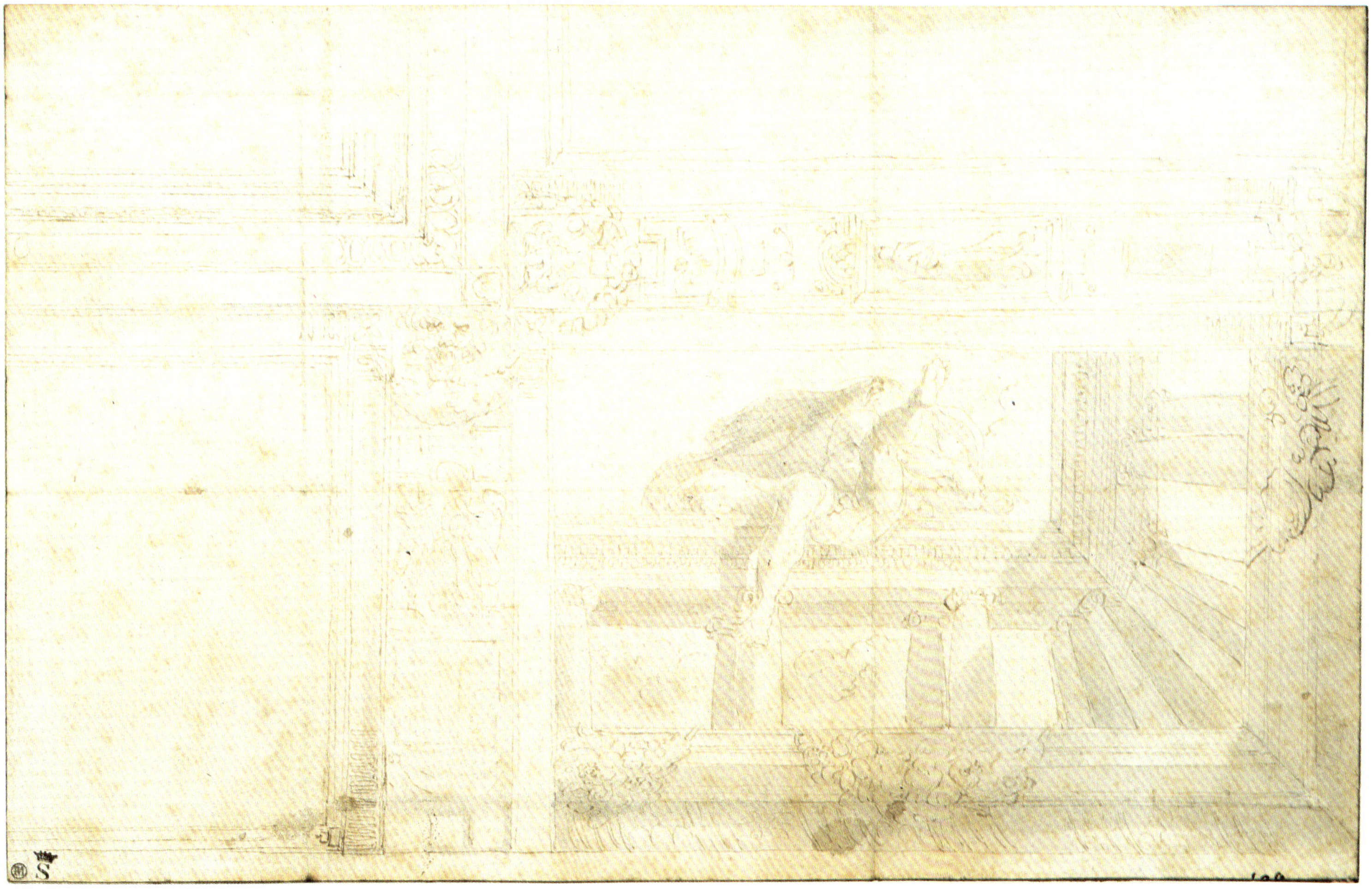

30 b

Ludovico Carracci

Bologna, 1555–Bologna, 1619

31 *The Head of a Young Man Looking Down to the Left* (1584–85)

Oil on paper, laid on card

290 x 213 mm (11 7/16 x 8 3/8 in)

Provenance: private collection, England; [Christie's, London, 19 April 1988, lot 50]

Literature: unpublished

The comparison between the *Head of a Young Man* with that of the youth in the Pinacoteca Capitolina, Rome (inv. 159),[1] previously attributed to Annibale Carracci, and more convincingly to Ludovico around 1582–83, as proposed by Francesco Arcangeli and, with some doubts, by Denis Mahon,[2] brings up once again the problem of portraits by Ludovico, whose production in this genre was quite slight in comparison with that of Annibale and Agostino Carracci.

In the Pinacoteca Capitolina *Head*, the expression of the face and the composition based on diagonal lines make one think, in fact, of the early style of Ludovico; the two "portraits" are similar in the way the artist handles the strokes, showing a freshness and immediacy that, I would hazard to say, anticipates impressionist painting. Both Stephen Pepper and Denis Mahon (in conversation) date this *bozzetto* to around 1584–85. What is more, Pepper suggests that the painting presents stylistic affinities with the figure bending to administer strokes of the whip in the famous *Flagellation* in Douai (Musée de la Chartreuse),[3] with the soldier to the right who cracks the whip, and its related drawing in Chatsworth (inv. 410, Devonshire Collection), also recently brought to the attention of scholars.[4]

MDG

1. Feigenbaum (1993; 6 n. 3, with bibliography).

2. Arcangeli (1956, 106 n. 2); Mahon (1957, 196).

3. Arcangeli (1970, 204 n. 56); Feigenbaum (1993; 15–16 n. 7, with bibliography).

4. Rosenberg (1965, n. 69); Benati (1991; 17, with bibliography).

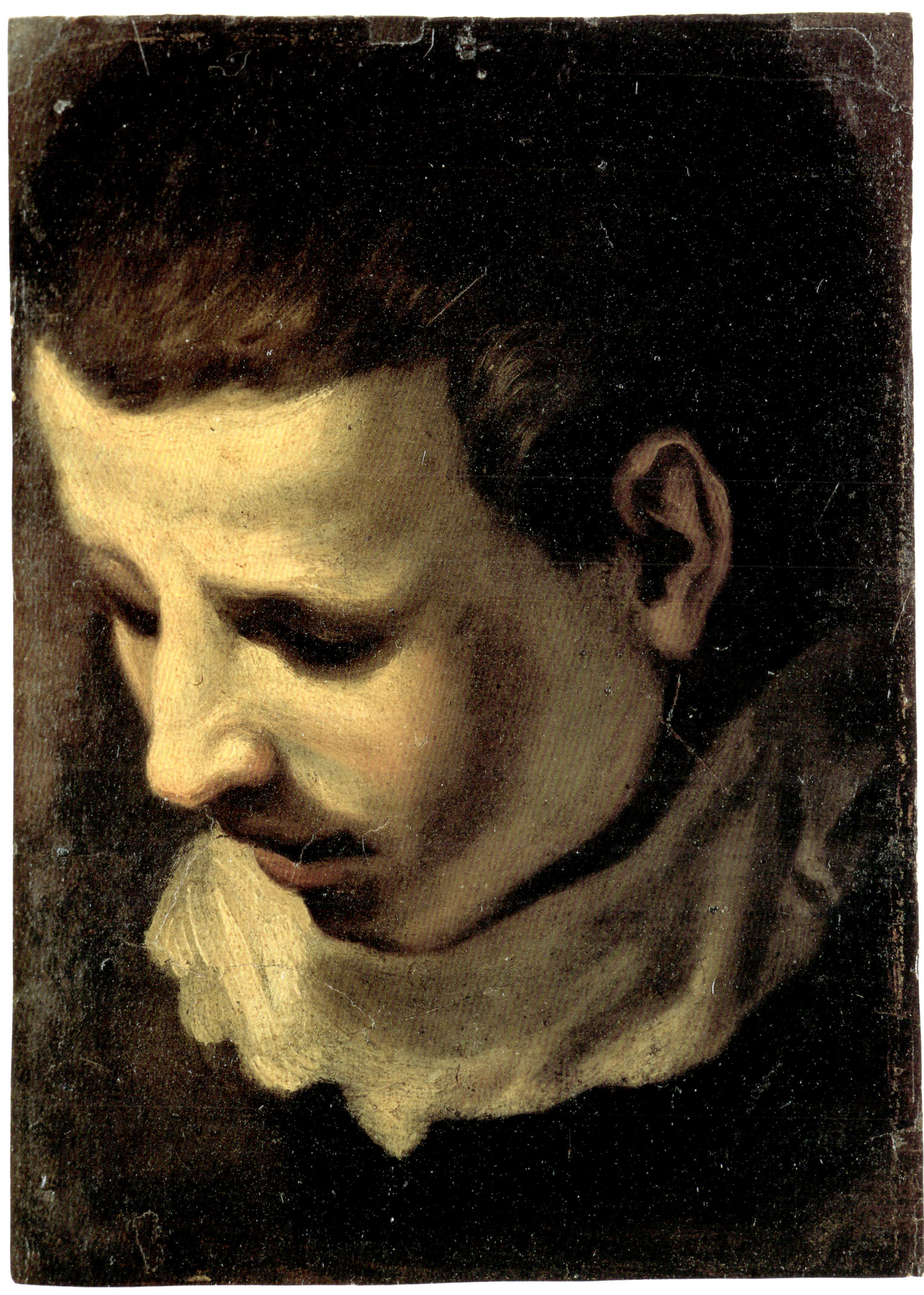

Agostino Carracci

Bologna, 1557–Parma, 1602

32 Recto: *Study for the Engraving of St. Jerome* Verso: *Study of Angels in the Clouds* (ca. 1600)

Black chalk, pen, and brown ink (recto and verso); inscribed 5, in brown ink, followed by *Ag. Caracci* in black chalk, on the verso

127 x 117 mm (5 x 4 5/8 in)

Provenance: Baron Landau Finaly (L. 1334c), no. 417; [Richard Day Ltd., London, 1987, as Bolognese School]

Literature: Bohn 1994, under cat. no. 219

1. See Bohn (1992b, 125–28) for several examples of this confusion.

2. On these six other drawings, see Bohn (1994, under cat. no. 219). Four of these drawings were previously published by DeGrazia Bohlin (1979) and DeGrazia (1984, both under cat. no. 213); two other drawings published by DeGrazia Bohlin are not accepted by this writer as autograph works.

3. Frankfurt, Städelsches Kunstinstitut, inv. 5656, recto and verso in pen and brown ink; 173 x 271 mm; first ascribed to Agostino by Pepper (1971, 44).

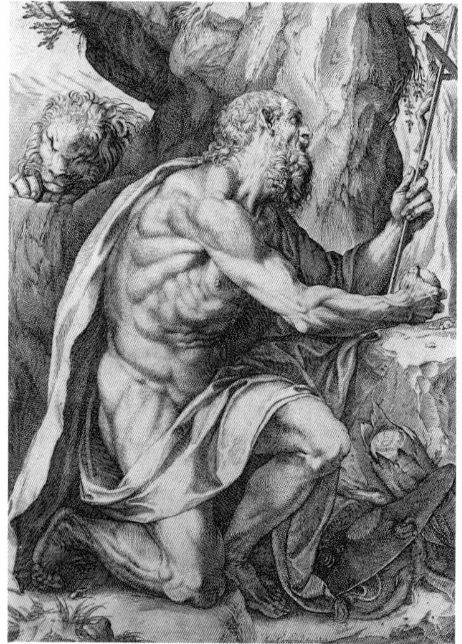

Fig. 4: Agostino Carracci, *St. Jerome*, Metropolitan Museum of Art, New York

The only full-time printmaker of the three Carracci, Agostino produced over two hundred engravings in the course of his twenty-seven-year career. Although he was also a prolific draftsman, Agostino's drawings have been less studied than those of Annibale and Ludovico and have been frequently confused with sheets by both Annibale and Ludovico.[1]

No such problems are posed by this drawing, since the recto is an autograph preparatory study for one of Agostino's most famous engravings, *St. Jerome*, (Fig. 4) which the artist left unfinished upon his death in Parma in 1602. Malvasia's account that the print was completed at Ludovico's request by Francesco Brizio (ca. 1574–1623) has been accepted by most scholars.

This drawing is probably the earliest extant study for the print, for which six other autograph preparatory drawings are known.[2] The Katalan sheet rapidly sketches a first solution for the saint's kneeling pose; the positions of the arms, legs, and draperies have yet to be finalized. An angel holds up the crucifix that is the subject of St. Jerome's devotion. In the next study for the print, in Frankfurt, the crucifix is supported only by the rock; in the final version, the saint himself holds the crucifix in his left hand.[3] The vigorous pen style of the Katalan drawing, with its reliance on rapid parallel slashes for interior modeling, is very similar to the Frankfurt sheet.

Although the verso is not connected to any known work, it was probably a preparatory study for a heraldic engraving, in light of the crown held aloft by the five angels. Agostino designed and engraved seven known heraldic prints during the 1590s, and this sketch was probably made for a project of this nature.

BB

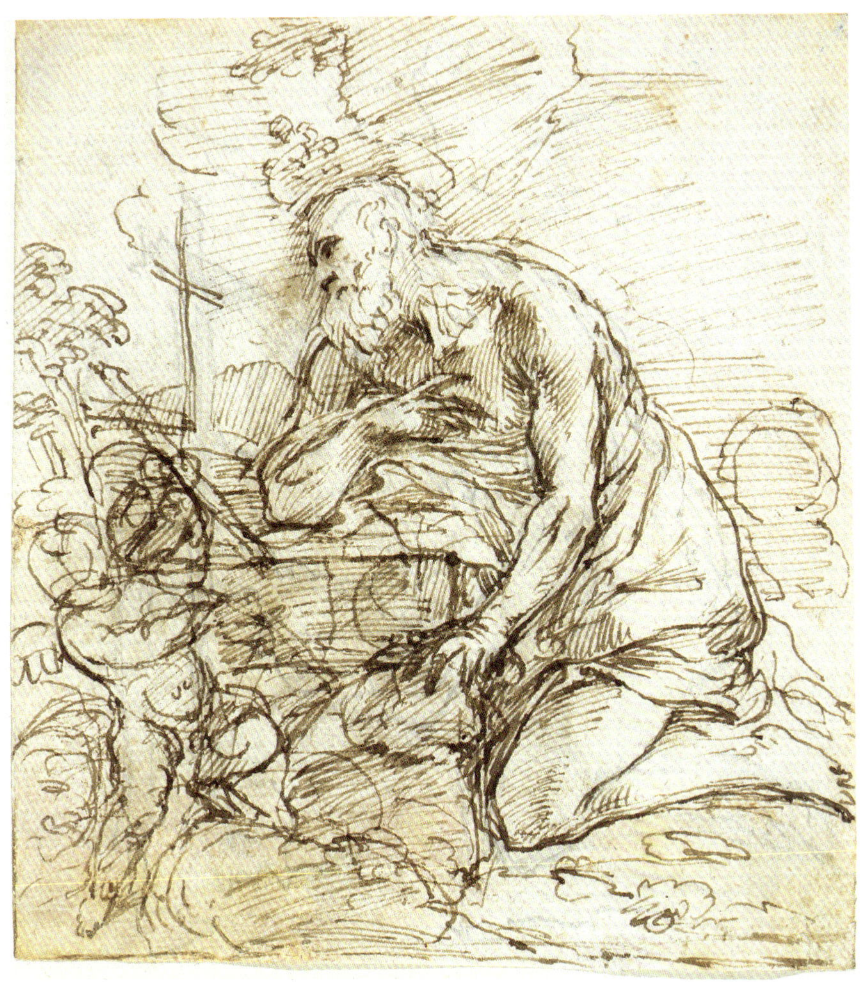

Recto

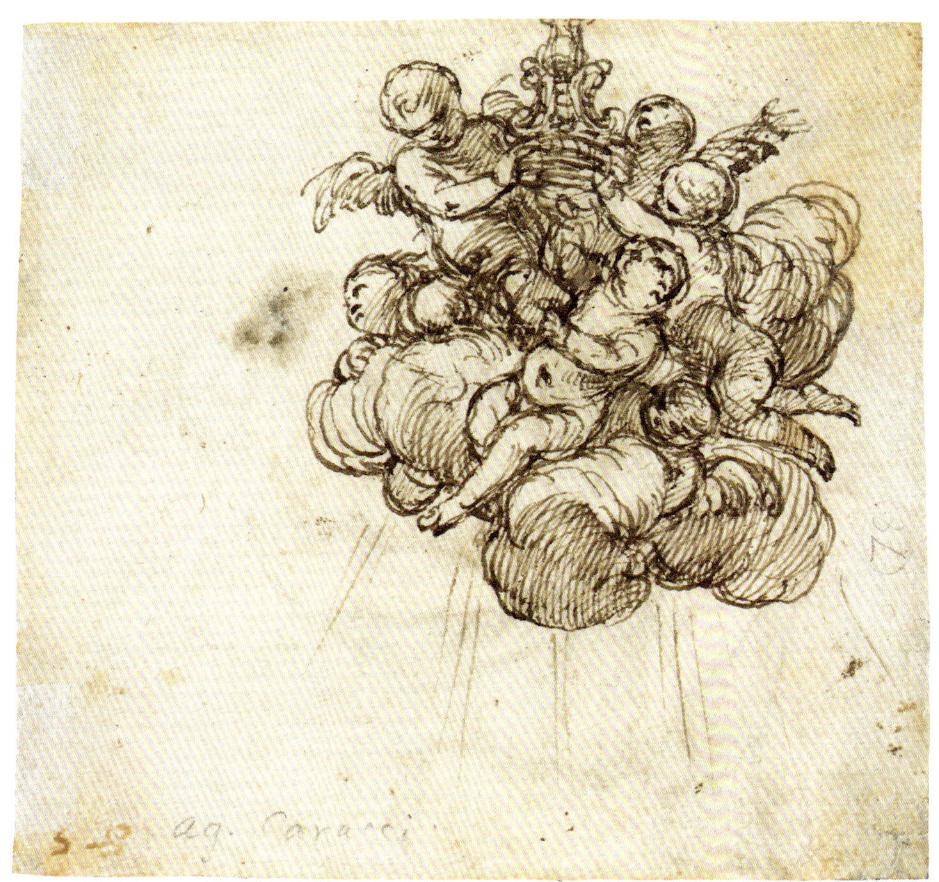

Verso

Annibale Carracci

Bologna, 1560–Rome, 1609

33 *Three-Quarter-Length Study of a Male Nude, his Back Turned, Holding a Staff (?) in his Left Hand* (ca. 1590)

Red chalk, the tip of the top right corner made up

290 x 227 mm (11 3/8 x 8 7/8 in)

PROVENANCE: Padre Resta; Lord Somers, no. 61n. (L. 2981); Jonathan Richardson, Sr. (L. 2184), his mount with attribution, *Annibale*, and shelfmarks, *Z.17./DD.21./Zh 42. EE. 14. X.43.*, and inscription, *Annibale Carracci con questo forte Contorno dava fortezza alle Figure. / P. Resta*; Sir Joshua Reynolds (L. 2364); Sir Samuel Woodforde, Bt., who is thought to have been given the drawing by Sir Joshua; Frank Woodforde, his nephew, by whom presented 12 September 1875 to John C. Eccleston, D.D., Rector of St. John's Church, Clifton, Staten Island, New York, by whom extensively inscribed on the backing; Christie's, New York, 12 January 1988, lot 22; [Christie's, New York, 11 January 1989, lot 37A, as attributed to circle of Annibale Carracci]

LITERATURE: unpublished

The figure, seen from behind, with its head of rebellious curls turned to the right, was drawn by the painter in an improvised movement: the act of catching hold of a support with the left hand. The body, struck by natural light from the right, is modeled in a uniform chiaroscuro that emphasizes its plasticity and creates the effect of immediacy; it conforms to the inscription on the back of the mount in the hand of Jonathan Richardson, Sr., attributed to Padre Sebastiano Resta, which reads, "Annibale Carracci con questo forte Contorno dava fortezza alle Figure." Drawings that fulfill the same function, both intellectually and in their relation to a project, are: *Half-Length Figure of a Young Rower* in the Accademia, Venice[1]; *Study for a St. Sebastian* in the Galleria Estense, Modena[2]; *Reclining Male Nude*, formerly in the Squire collection, London,[3] which can be associated with the well-known sheet in the Louvre, Paris (inv. 7321), depicting a youth in the act of taking off his shirt, directly related to the figure performing the same action in the lower left of the altarpiece in S. Gregorio, Bologna, dated 1585[4]; the two studies for *Youth Seen from the Front* in the British Museum, London (invs. 1903-6-29-2; 1943-10-9-36); and, finally, the series of nudes in the Uffizi Gallery, Florence (invs. 1540F, 12374F, 12417F, 17092F, and 3656S; previously attributed to Guercino) in which the human figure, studied from a live model, appears in all its spontaneity in the various movements of daily life.

MDG

1. *Moschini (1931, 77); Di Giampaolo (1993; 54 n. 33, reproduced).*

2. *Di Giampaolo (1989a, 200).*

3. *Cf. Edinburgh Festival Society (1972; 10 n. 22, reproduced on 55).*

4. *Posner (1971; 2:pls. 21a, 21d).*

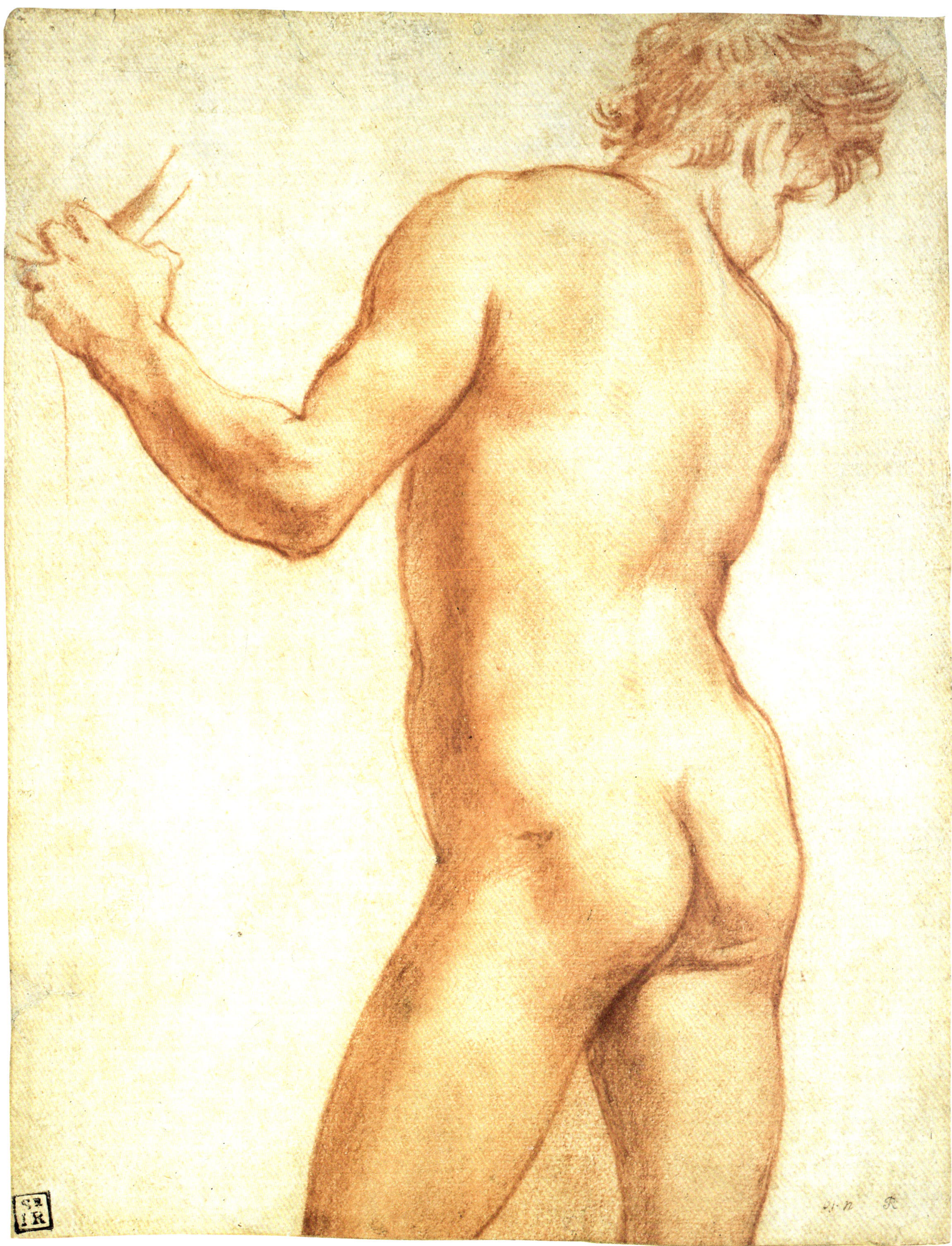

Annibale Carracci

Bologna, 1560–Rome, 1609

34 *Landscape with Men Playing a Ball Game* (1598–99)

Pen and brown ink on buff paper

100 x 268 mm (4 x 10 1/2 in)

Provenance: W. Mayor (L. 2799); Colnaghi, 1949; [Christie's, New York, 10 January, 1990, lot 44, as attributed to Domenichino]

Literature: unpublished

Landscape painting and drawing were diversions for Agostino and Annibale Carracci.[1] Not until the seventeenth century did any Italian painters specialize in this genre, and while Annibale's rare landscapes, drawn and painted, were enormously influential, he always considered himself a history painter and would be surprised to learn how esteemed his landscape production has become. His lunette painted in 1603–4 for a chapel in the Palazzo Aldobrandini in Rome, depicting the Flight into Egypt, is reproduced in every essay on the ideal landscape style and in most surveys of seventeenth-century art. Its calm expanse of water framed by trees and bordered by low slopes of land, with a castle at the summit and vistas to the left and right, is both a convincing portrait of the Roman *campagna*, with its fortified hill towns, and a perfectly orchestrated presentation of deep space that draws us back slowly to enjoy its pleasant prospects. The spectator can trace the journey of the Holy Family alighting from the boat in the foreground, and imagine their slow crossing from the far shore with the grazing sheep on the nearby slopes.

The evolution of such a perfectly designed, large-scale landscape composition implies a long process of artistic maturation, yet Annibale painted relatively few independent landscapes, and the attribution to him of most of them has been challenged at some time. His landscape composition drawings, none of which can be connected definitively with an accepted painting as a preparatory study, allowed him to plan these expansive views on a practical scale.[2] Their hallmark is an exceptional sure-footedness when placing succeeding planes of space defined by the bank of a river, the brow of a sloping hillside, or a clump of trees. The confidence and speed with which they are drawn is all the more impressive for being executed, in most cases, in ink without any chalk underdrawing. Analysis of these spatial transitions in the work of his imitators always reveals weaknesses in the delineation of spatial recession, as well as in either a mechanical imitation of his graphic technique or graphic mannerisms never found in his drawings. The recent literature is full of drawings by P. P. Bonzi, Francesco Brizio, and similar hands optimistically associated with the most highly regarded of the Carracci.[3] Even separating the landscape studies of Annibale from those by his brother Agostino is not easy, and the problem of copies is acute.[4]

Proving that a Carracci-like landscape drawing is by Annibale, therefore, is no simple matter. In the case of the drawing exhibited here, however, close stylistic parallels with two universally accepted drawings by Annibale, one of which is connected with a painting also universally accepted as his work, makes the task relatively straightforward. The first drawing is the study in Frankfurt connected with the *Bacchus and Silenus* (National Gallery, London), dated to about 1599 by Posner.[5] Although the figures are much larger in the Frankfurt drawing (Fig. 5), the foreground is similarly sketched, with a few long lines and small circles indicating stones or pebbles. A distant mountain on the horizon, drawn with one vivid contour line and some horizontal parallel hatching, appears in both sheets as well as in the brilliant, late landscape drawing in the British Museum. The British Museum drawing also has slopes shaded with parallel hatching that sweep the eye across the intersecting planes of land, as they do in the Katalan drawing. The complete absence of cross-hatching in the Katalan drawing is noteworthy; its presence in a Carraccesque landscape, as in other Carracci drawings, may indicate that it is by Agostino.[6] Another distinctive trait in Annibale's landscape sketches is his habit of indicating distant trees with one or two short vertical strokes for the trunk, a few short horizontal lines over the trunk, with a curlicue contour line for

1. Posner (1971, 113) aptly characterizes landscape painting as "a peripheral activity for Annibale," but his description of "a vast and never ceasing production of landscape drawings" exaggerates the surviving evidence considerably. He was writing, however, before recent scholarship began to isolate groups of drawings by other hands then given to Annibale. Surviving landscape drawings by Annibale himself are rare.

2. Two drawings in the Louvre can be connected with the Fête Champêtre *(Marseilles) and the* Landscape Scene with Fishing *(Louvre, Paris); see Posner (1971; 2:cat. nos. 16 and 44, pls. 16b and 44b). If Clovis Whitfield's attribution of the* Fête Champêtre *and its related drawing to Agostino is accepted (see note 4), then only one of these two drawings would be by Annibale. If the Marseilles picture is by Agostino, then the possibility that he painted the* Fishing Scene *and its companion* Hunting Scene *(Posner 1971, 2:cat. no. 43) needs to be considered, and thus whether the other Louvre landscape drawing might be by him. Another study in the Louvre for the fresco in the Palazzo Magnani, showing the wolf suckling Romulus and Remus, which is mainly a landscape drawing, has been attributed to both Annibale and Ludovico since the Carracci exhibition in 1956; see Cavina (1988, 19 f.). Since an attribution to Ludovico is possible, and in my view correct, the drawing cannot be included among Annibale's certain landscape drawings.*

3. The identification of P. P. Bonzi's landscape-drawing style by various scholars, whose discoveries are summarized and expanded by Howard (1988, 227–49), was especially helpful, for many of them had been attributed to Annibale and Agostino Carracci. Another group of landscape studies can probably be attributed to Francesco Brizio. For example, see Ellesmere sale, Sotheby's, London, 11 July 1972, lots 36 (now at the Fitzwilliam Museum, Cambridge) and 37, both given to Agostino. A pen sketch at Chatsworth is given to Annibale. Jaffé (1987–88, cat. no. 16). Another one on a Mariette mount with an attribution to Ludovico Carracci was sold at Christie's, London, 6 July 1993, lot 52. Brizio's Holy Family in a Landscape *(Stuttgart) is the key drawing for establishing his interpretation of the Carracci landscape style, for it has typical Brizio figures on the left and landscape on the right. Thiem (1983–84, cat. no. 13).*

4. Clovis Whitfield has broached the tricky question of Agostino's landscape paintings and drawings in Whitfield (1988, 73–95), arguing that Annibale's fame has resulted in Agostino's work being given to him instead. A key reattribution is the Fête Champêtre *(Marseilles) and the related composition drawing in the Louvre (Posner 1971, 2:pls. 16a and 16c), and the* Vision of St. Eustace *(Capodimonte, Naples; Posner 1971, 2:cat. no. 27), which may be right. The consequences of this hypothesis are, however, much greater than Whitfield seems to realize (cf. note 2), and in emphasizing highly finished landscape composition drawings in his later discussion, several of which are, in my view, copies, Whitfield has missed some more obvious cases of landscape drawings by Agostino being given to Annibale. The question is too complex to be settled in a footnote, but I believe the following examples are by Agostino: Ellesmere sale, Sotheby's, London, 11 July 1972, lots 52, 54, 56, 57, 58, 62;* Landscape with Bathers, *Oppé Collection (Posner 1971, 1:fig. 95); and* Landscape with Two Travelers, *Louvre (Posner 1971, 1:fig. 96). The draw-*

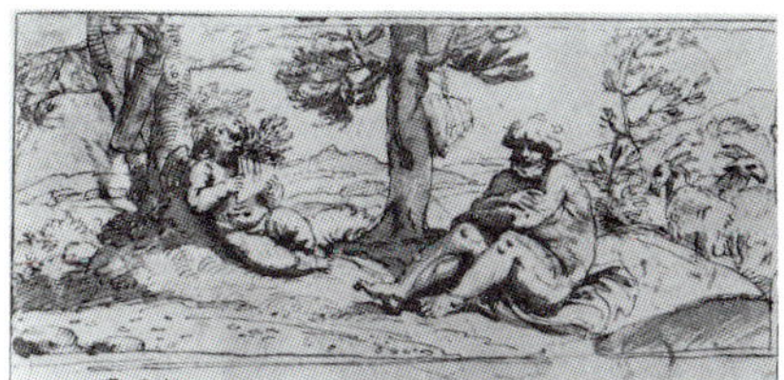

Fig. 5: Annibale Carracci, *Bacchus and Silenus,* Städelsches Kunstinstitut, Frankfurt

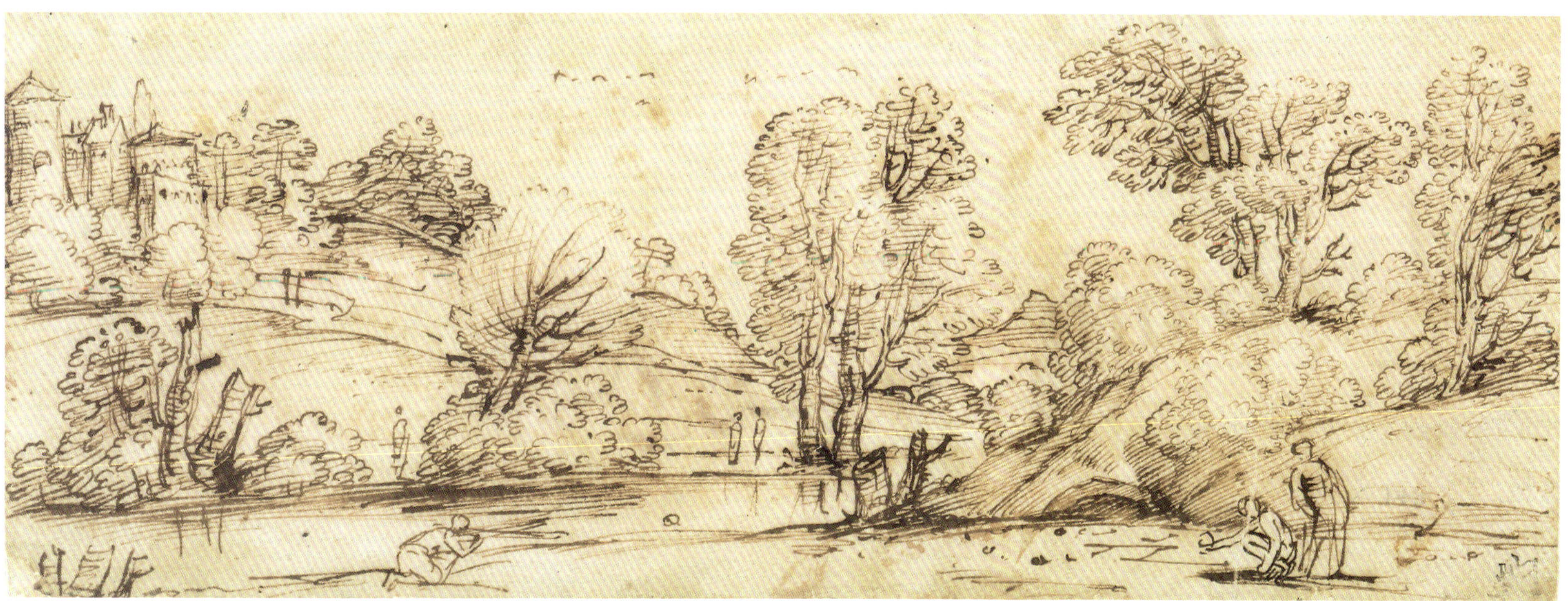

the mass of foliage. The trees on the left of the Katalan drawing, just below the castle wall, are drawn in this characteristic manner and resemble many in the British Museum sheet, in which most of the trees are in the distance instead of in the middle ground. This way of drawing trees is one of many elements of Annibale's (and Agostino's) landscape drawings that G. F. Grimaldi imitated with great skill in his numerous, formulaic repetitions, which are based on first-hand knowledge of original sheets by both of the Carracci.[7]

Since the landscape drawings that most closely resemble the Katalan drawing can be dated around 1600, it must also have been made during Annibale's Roman years. It is not quite as bold as the British Museum drawing, nor as schematic as another late landscape drawing formerly in the Ellesmere collection.[8] Therefore a date before, rather than after, 1600 seems likely. The painted landscape whose structure looks most like the Katalan drawing is that in the lower right of the *Pan and Diana* fresco on the ceiling of the Farnese Gallery in Rome.[9] The right half of the drawing could have served as the artist's guide as he prepared that section of the painting, with only minor changes. A date of 1598–99 thus seems appropriate.

ASH

ing in the Metropolitan Museum related to the double-sided Ellesmere sheet (lot 58) should also be given to Agostino (Bean 1982 , cat. no. 99). The only landscape drawings in the Ellesmere sale by Annibale are lots 43, 71, 72, 73, and 74. The complexity of the situation regarding copies can be summed up by one drawing in Oxford, of which four other versions are known. Macandrew (1980; 257, cat. no. 170). There are many other cases of multiple copies, some very clever, and anyone tackling the Carracci landscape problem needs to be aware of them.

5. *Posner (1971, 2:cat. no. 116). The drawing was first published by Jaffé (1956, 398 and fig. 10).*

6. *To the examples listed in note 4 can be added the* St. Jerome in a Landscape *in Budapest, of which there is a good copy in the Uffizi; see Fenyö (1967, 259 and pls. 8 and 9). The Budapest drawing was already attributed to Annibale by Mariette. Fenyö compares it to the double-sided sheet (Ellesmere sale, cat. no. 58) here given to Agostino. The graphic mannerisms of an engraver, as Agostino was, are especially evident in the Budapest* St. Jerome. The Landscape with Card Players *in the Louvre (Fenyö 1967, 261 and pl. 13), of which there is a sensitive copy in Budapest (pl. 12), is also by Agostino. Both versions—of a landscape drawing with the Baptist preaching published by Fenyö (1967, 260–61, pl. 11)—seem to be copies of a lost original by Annibale.*

7. *Michael Jaffé first explored the relationship between Annibale and G. F. Grimaldi. Jaffé (1964, 87–97 and figs. 62–65).*

8. *Ellesmere sale, 1972, lot 74, now in Stuttgart.*

9. *Posner (1971, 2:pl. 111z).*

Pietro Faccini

Bologna, 1562–Bologna, 1602

35 Recto: *A Standing Male Nude, Seen in Profile, his Left Arm Raised* Verso: *Head Studies* (1590–92)

Black chalk heightened in white chalk (recto); black chalk, pen, and brown ink (verso)

560 x 354 mm (22 x 13 15/16 in)

Provenance: from an album of academy studies from the studio of Giuseppe Ghezzi; [Sotheby's, New York, 13 January 1988, lot 29]

Literature: Llewellyn and Romalli 1992, cat. no. 25; Turner 1992, 539–41; *Financial Times*, exhibition review, 28 July 1992

Exhibitions: *Drawing in Bologna 1500–1600*, Courtauld Institute Galleries, University of London, 18 June–31 August 1992, cat. no. 25

Malvasia already recalled "infiniti [disegni] in tutte le raccolte, tra le quale quella del serenissimo Sig. Principe Cardinal Leopoldo, presso il quale sono ridotte le centinaia, alle volte cosí guizzanti cosí svolozzanti e quel che piú, cosí facili e franchi che sembrano del suo maestro (Annibale Carracci)" [an infinite number (of drawings) in all collections, among them that of the Most Serene Signor Prince Cardinal Leopoldo where around one hundred drawings ended up, which are at times so dashing and fluttering and, what is more, so easy and direct that they seem to be by his master (Annibale Carracci)].[1] More recently, these nude studies have seemed "singolari come accademie, per la vivacitá del segno e l'umore interno inquieto che rivela un'immaginativa indipendente sia dai modelli naturali sia da quelli offertigli dai testi carracceschi contemporanei" [singular studies, for the liveliness of touch and the uneasy interior mood that reveals an imagination independent both of models in nature and of models taken from contemporary Carraccesque examples].[2] There is no doubt that this nude figure, in profile, facing left, documents for Faccini a moment of departure from the teaching of Annibale. While the classic quality of Annibale is still noticeable in *Reclining Nude* (Oxford),[3] previously attributed to Ludovico Carracci, and to a lesser degree in *Mercury* and *Seated Nude*, both in the Uffizi (invs. 17446F, 17447F),[4] the composition of the figure in *Male Nude Seen from the Front* recently shown in London,[5] with the forceful quality of the muscles of the legs, already points to an attitude that is decisively opposed to the Carraccesque academy. We can probe more deeply by looking at the series of nudes in the Uffizi (invs. 17445F, 17448F, 17449F) executed in the same technique as *Study for a Crucified Christ* in the Galleria Estense, Modena (inv. 767 B)[6] and, further, at a sheet in Berlin (inv. 79.D35.4, recto, Kupferstichkabinett, Preussischer Kulturbesitz, Staatliche Museen), which presents strong analogies with the present drawing, such as the strokes of light in white chalk, which give plasticity to the figures, and the unnatural position of the figure in a seemingly undefined space. On the verso of the sheet is a series of sketches of male and female heads drawn quickly in pen. They are shown frontally, in profile or cleverly foreshortened *di sotto in su*, vaguely caricaturelike, which demonstrates Faccini's interest in this genre of anti-academic pictures.

MDG

1. *Malvasia ([1678] 1841, 398).*
2. *Borea (1975; 57, ed. trans.).*
3. *Parker (1956, n. 172); DeGrazia (1984; 404, fig. 128b).*
4. *Di Giampaolo (1989b, 302).*
5. *Llewellyn and Romalli (1992, n. 26).*
6. *Di Giampaolo, (1989b, 216).*

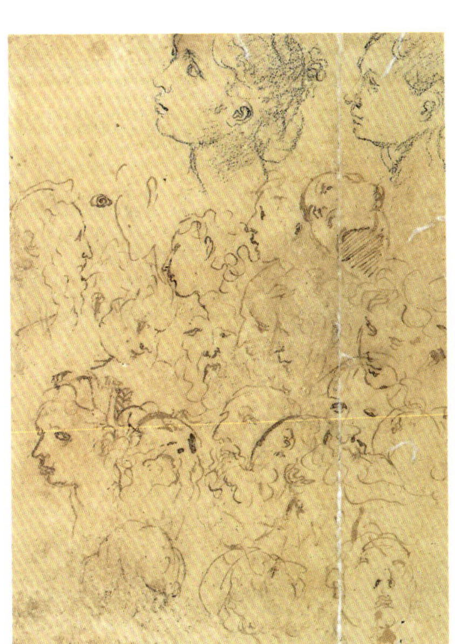

Verso, detail

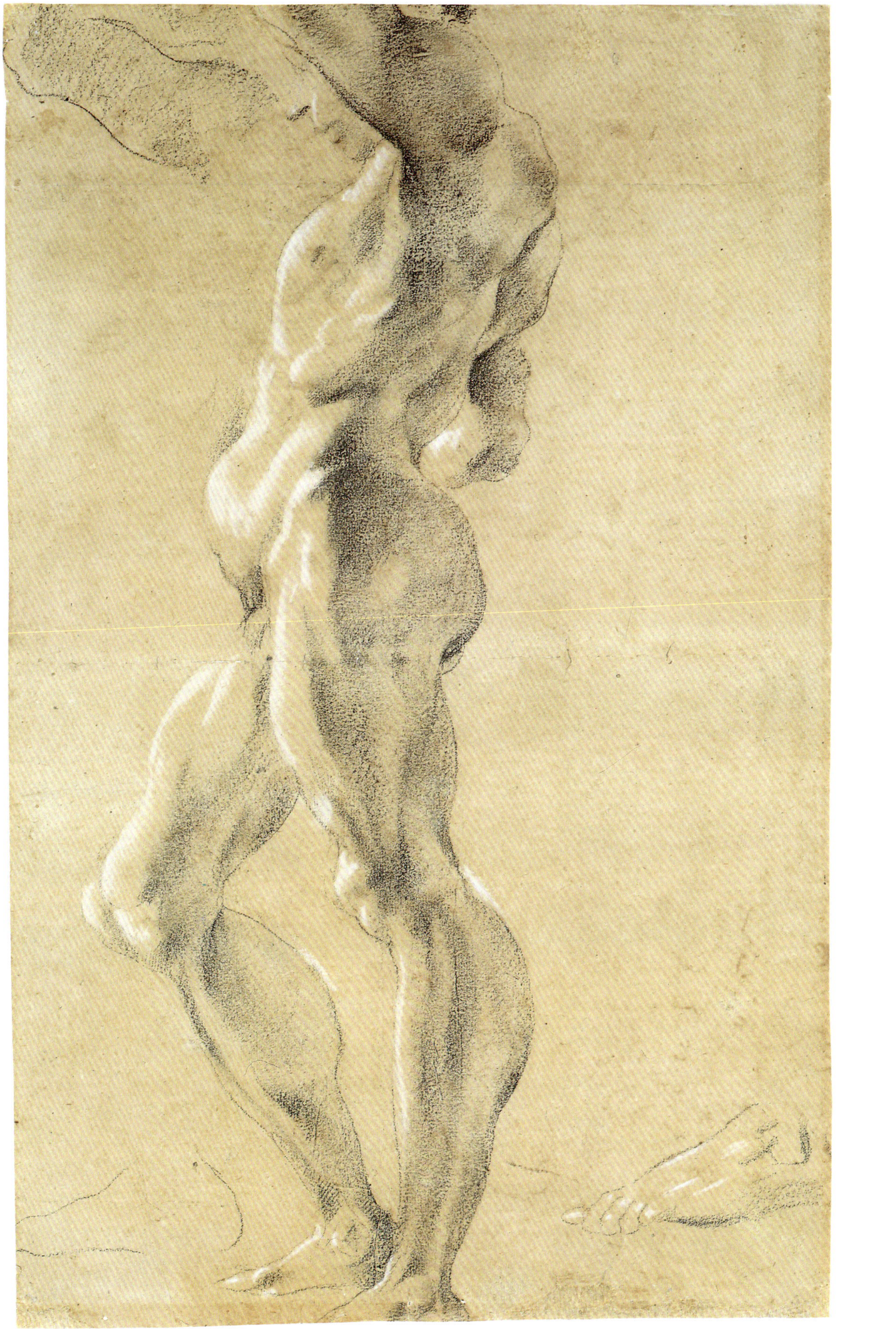

Recto

Giulio Cesare Procaccini
Bologna, 1574–Milan, 1625

36

Studies of Heads

Black and red chalk on cream paper; an old inscription in pen and ink in the lower left, *38 G. C. Procaccino*

168 x 183 mm (6 5/8 x 7 1/4 in)

Provenance: [Jacques Petit Hory, Paris, 1991]

Literature: Galerie La Scala, 1991, cat. no. 18

Exhibitions: *Femmes*, Galerie La Scala, Paris, June 1991, cat. no. 18

Giulio Cesare Procaccini, the son of the sculptor Ercole Procaccini, moved from Bologna, where he was born, to Milan when he was thirteen. He started his career there as a sculptor in the Duomo and at S. Maria presso S. Celso, and also worked in Cremona. He began working as a painter around 1600, and did six paintings of miracles by St. Charles Borromeo for the Duomo in Milan in 1610. He forged a style as a painter that combines brilliant, rhythmic, impasted brushwork and dense, energetic compositions that exploit both *maniera* spatial compression and baroque energy. He was one of the finest painters working in northern Italy in the generation that followed Caravaggio and the Carracci, a key figure—with Daniele Crespi—in the revival of the Milanese painting school after the death of Leonardo's derivative followers and the mundane efforts of the Campi brothers.

The Katalan drawing is typical of sketch sheets by Giulio Cesare in both ink and chalk combining a variety of motifs—head studies, figure studies—that he used, as both Palma il Giovane and Agostino Carracci apparently did, to relax and get the creative juices flowing. The chalk studies are often reminiscent of Parmigianino—as with the principal study on the Katalan sheet, an elegantly coiffed woman seen in profile—a type that can be traced back to Michelangelo's *teste ideale*. Behind this figure in the middle of the upper part of the sheet is a less elaborated study of a similar young woman, and to the right a profile study of an old man with a large nose and the pointed ear of a faun. Three other small, lightly drawn heads appear in the left margin and above the main study; a seated draped figure can just be made out in the lower right. None of these heads can be connected definitively with a known painting, although each head is a Procaccini type and can be found in his paintings. The main sketch of a young woman facing left resembles the mother on the right of *Miracle of Carlino Nava* in Milan Cathedral.[1] The head of the woman facing right behind the main sketch matches in both type and hairstyle the angel in the left background of the artist's *Holy Family with St. John the Baptist* (Nelson-Atkins Museum, Kansas City). It would be unusual for an artist to combine studies for different works of different types on one sheet, so these parallels are probably generic, and the drawings should not be considered preparatory studies for the works cited.

This sheet is appealing in part because of the combination of extreme delicacy in the head of the old faun and the bolder, more energetic drawing of the main study. The faun can be compared with an especially refined example of Procaccini's chalk study for an annunciate angel in the Getty Museum, Malibu.[2] The bolder, more fluid chalk strokes in the main study can be compared instead with a red chalk study for an annunciate angel with two studies for the Virgin in the Ratjen collection.[3] The main study on the Katalan sheet can be imagined as a detail study for the bust of the Virgin in the right hand of the two Ratjen sketches, though her expression with the open lips and hint of a smile does not seem appropriate for this occasion.

ASH

1. Rosci (1993, 69). Jak Katalan, who pointed out these links to me, has noted other connections between similar types among the other, slighter sketches on this sheet and other heads in the artist's canvases in the Duomo, Milan.

2. Goldner (1988, cat. no. 7). This sheet has an old attribution to Correggio.

3. Harprath (1977, cat. no. 21).

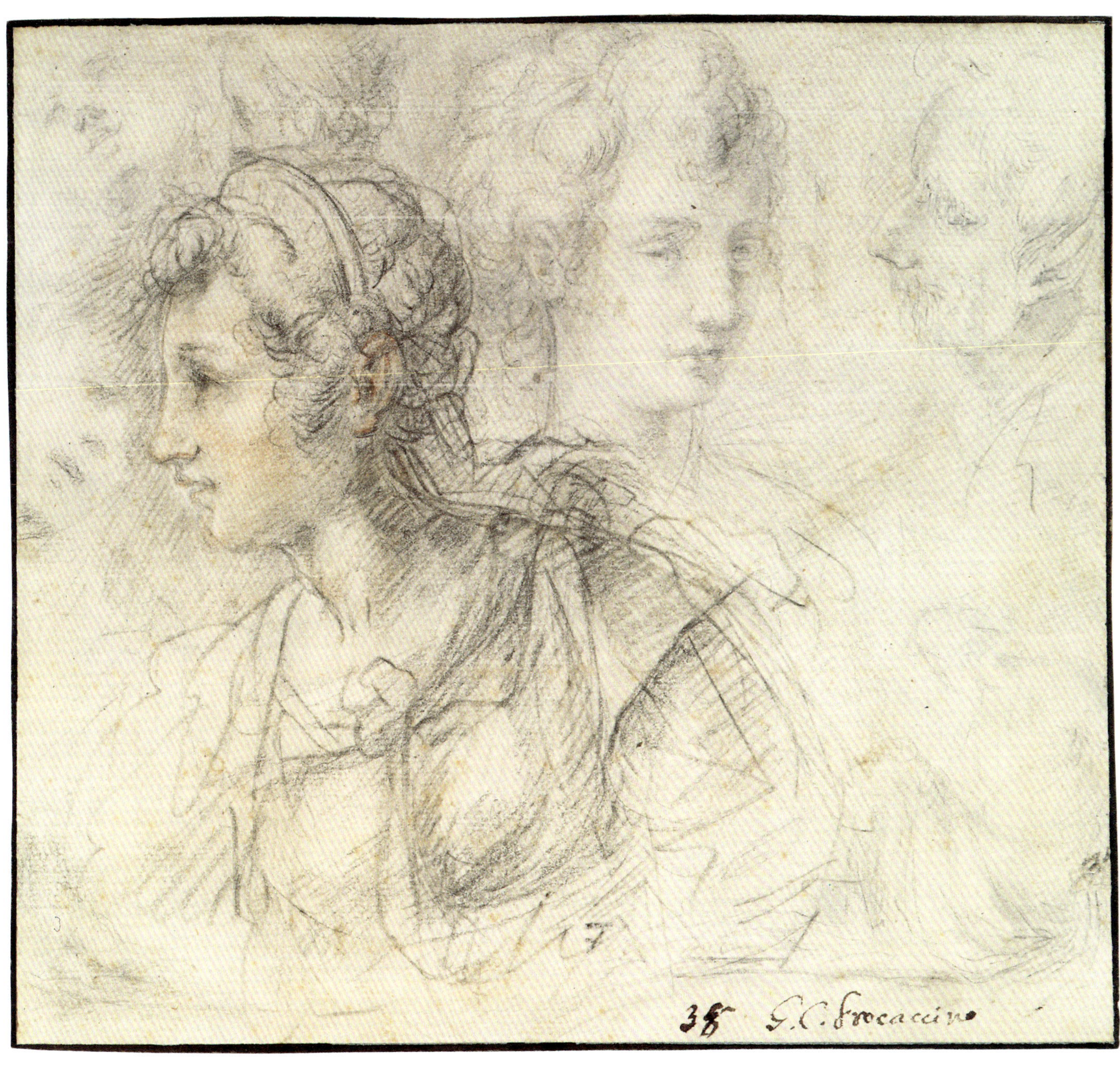
35 G.C. Procaccini

Guido Reni

Bologna, 1575–Bologna, 1642

37 *Head of Seneca* (ca. 1620)

Black and white chalk on buff paper; the top left and right corners cut away

116 x 142 mm (3 9/16 x 4 9/16 in)

Provenance: Giovanni Piancastelli; Mary and Edward Brandegee (?); [Sotheby's, London, 6 July 1992, lot 165, as Lombard School, ca. 1600]

Literature: unpublished

1. Kurz (1955, cat. no. 397).

2. Kurz (1942; 223, fig. 1 A-C).

3. Malvasia [1678] 1841, 2:59).

4. Pepper (1988; cat. no. 150, fig. 140).

5. Pepper (1988; cat. no. 195, fig. 182).

The attribution to Guido Reni was proposed independently by Ann Sutherland Harris and Babette Bohn. Except for some minor variations, the head is identical to that in a drawing in the Royal Library, Windsor Castle, which was identified by Kurz as a Seneca.[1] Kurz attributed the Windsor drawing to a pupil, but identified the prototype as the *Bust of Seneca* in the National Archeological Museum, Madrid, one of Guido Reni's rare ventures into sculpture.[2]

Kurz describes Reni's *Bust* as showing "such stress on the characteristics of extreme old age that its realism borders almost on caricature. But the expression of extreme despair which parts the lips and makes the eyes turn upwards as if they were just breaking has been rendered with a sense of tragedy, far transcending mere realistic representation." The *Bust* is first mentioned in the life of Guido Reni by the Bolognese writer of artists' biographies, Conte Carlo Cesare Malvasia, who cites it as follows: "He also made sculptures as is shown by the famous sculpture called the head of Seneca which has found its way into all the studios. He made it after a Dalmatian whom he found on the embankment in Rome and modeled to represent Seneca."[3]

Reni obviously developed a liking for this tragic-looking, bald-headed, Slavic type, since he crops up in a number of important paintings. He appears as the priest circumcising the Christ Child in the *Circumcision* of 1636, in S. Martino, Siena[4]; and as one of the shepherds in the *Adoration of the Shepherds* of 1640–42, in the National Gallery, London.[5]

The Katalan drawing seems closer to the sculpted model than to its painted derivations and, like its three-dimensional counterpart, is a virtuoso performance in the representation of old age. Here, too, the artist has gone to great lengths to define the furrows of flesh at the brow and in the back of the neck, to describe the wrinkles in the cheeks and at the temples, and has carefully picked out with white chalk the glistening highlights in the various promontories of this aged and irregular face.

NT

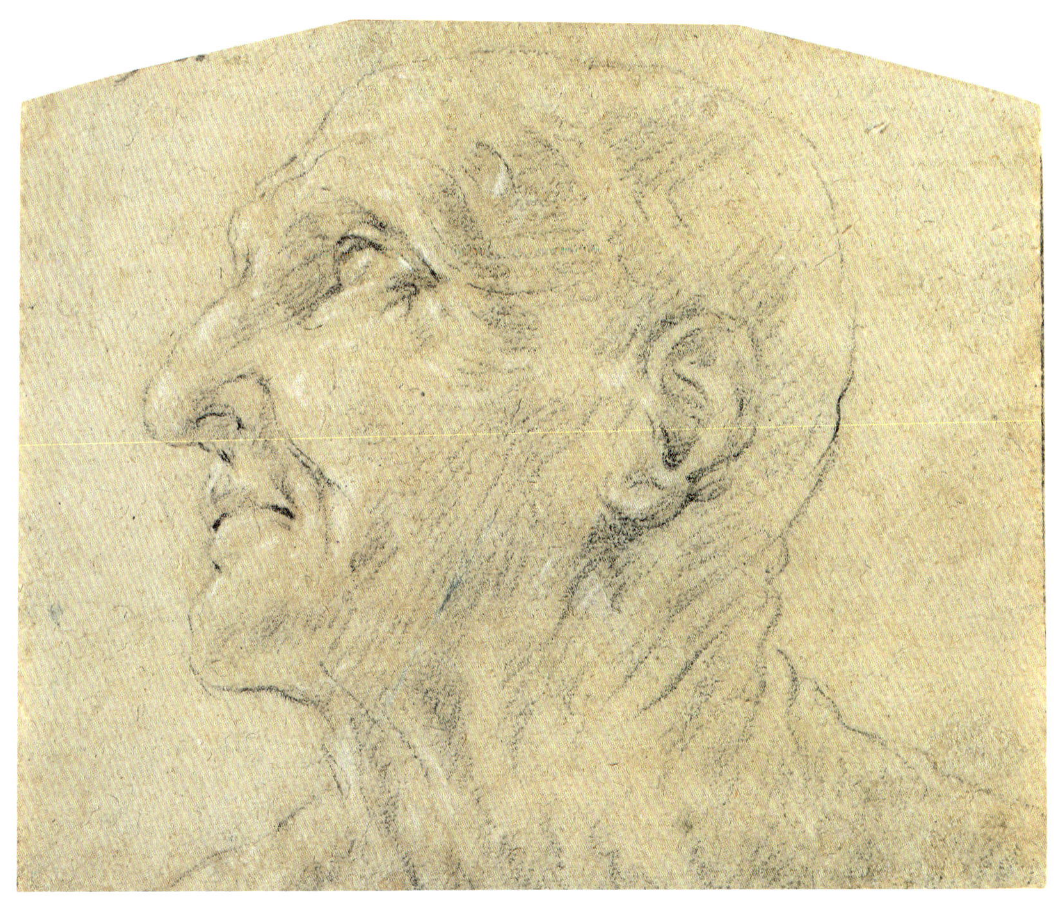

Guido Reni

Bologna, 1575–Bologna, 1642

38 Recto: *Head of a Young Woman Looking Down* Verso: *A Kneeling Woman* (ca. 1638)

Red and white chalk on gray paper (recto and verso)

207 x 172 mm (8 1/8 x 6 3/4 in)

Provenance: G. Vallardi (L. 1223); Carlo Prayer (L. 2044); Juan and Felix Bernasconi; [Christie's, London, 5 July 1988, lot 235, as Bolognese School ca. 1680]

Literature: unpublished

Guido Reni was probably the greatest of the Carraccis' students. A brilliant painter and draftsman as well as an occasional etcher, his clear, pastel coloring and even lighting soon displaced the dramatic chiaroscuro of Caravaggio and the young Guercino as the dominant manner in Italian baroque painting. Although much less prolific as a draftsman than his contemporary, Guercino, Reni produced many preparatory studies for his own paintings.

This sheet, sold by Christie's as an anonymous work of the Bolognese school ca. 1680 and subsequently attributed to Flaminio Torri (1621–61), was first recognized by this writer as an autograph work by Reni. The sketch of a kneeling woman on the verso is strikingly close, stylistically, to a drawing at Windsor that is a preparatory study for a destroyed painting of *Bacchus and Ariadne*, datable to ca. 1637–40.[1] Indeed, the closeness of the two round faces, with similarly high foreheads and prominent noses, suggests that the same model was used for both drawings.

The head on the recto is also analogous to chalk drawings by Reni from the late 1630s. This figure resembles a *St. Margaret of Antioch* on the London market.[2] However, it is even closer to a painting of *St. Catherine Martyr* (City Art Gallery, Manchester) of ca. 1638–39 (Fig. 6) and was probably a preparatory study for the Manchester picture. Both the drawing and painting have similar facial features and share the same tilted pose. Although the drawing lacks the crown that appears in the painting, x-rays indicate that the crown was a later addition to the composition by a hand that, according to Pepper, is not Reni's. The figure originally wore only a veil on her head and may have represented St. Margaret rather than St. Catherine. The original painted image corresponded closely with a *St. Margaret* engraved by P. Vitale in Rome in 1782, according to Pepper.[3]

BB

1. Windsor, inv. 3454, in red chalk; 209 x 108 mm. Kurz (1955, cat. no. 360 and fig. 74). The drawing was a study, with changes, for a painting commissioned by Cardinal Francesco Barberini as a gift to Queen Henrietta Maria of England, wife of Charles I. Cardinal Giulio Sacchetti, who acted as intermediary between Reni and Cardinal Barberini, was papal legate to Bologna from 1637 to 1640, which is also consistent with the probable dates of execution. The composition is known from two somewhat different painted copies (Accademia di S. Luca, Rome and Palazzo di Montecitorio, Rome) and two engravings. See Malvasia ([1678] 1841, 2:51); Pepper (1988, 290–91, cat. no. 166); and Birke in Ebert-Schifferer et al. (1988, 398–99, cat. no. B63 [repr.]).

2. Colnaghi (1994, 14–18).

3. On the Manchester canvas, see Pepper (1988, 293–94, cat. no. 171); and Casali Pedrielli in Schaefer (1988, 162–63, cat. no. 68).

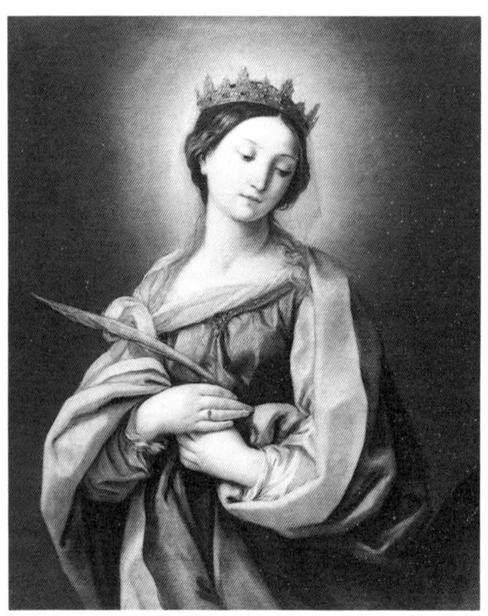

Fig. 6: Guido Reni, *St. Margaret Martyr,* City Art Gallery, Manchester

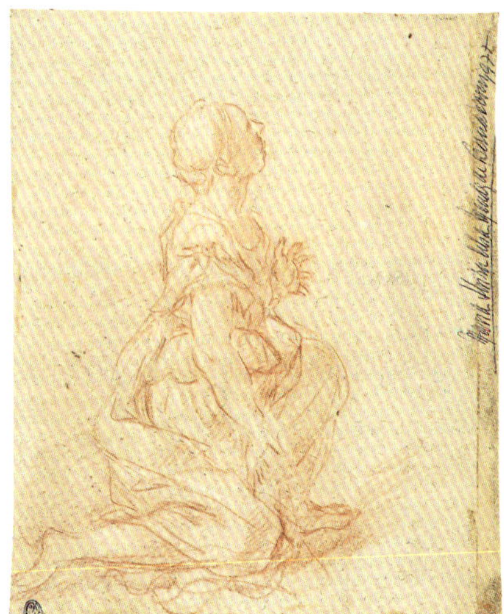

Verso

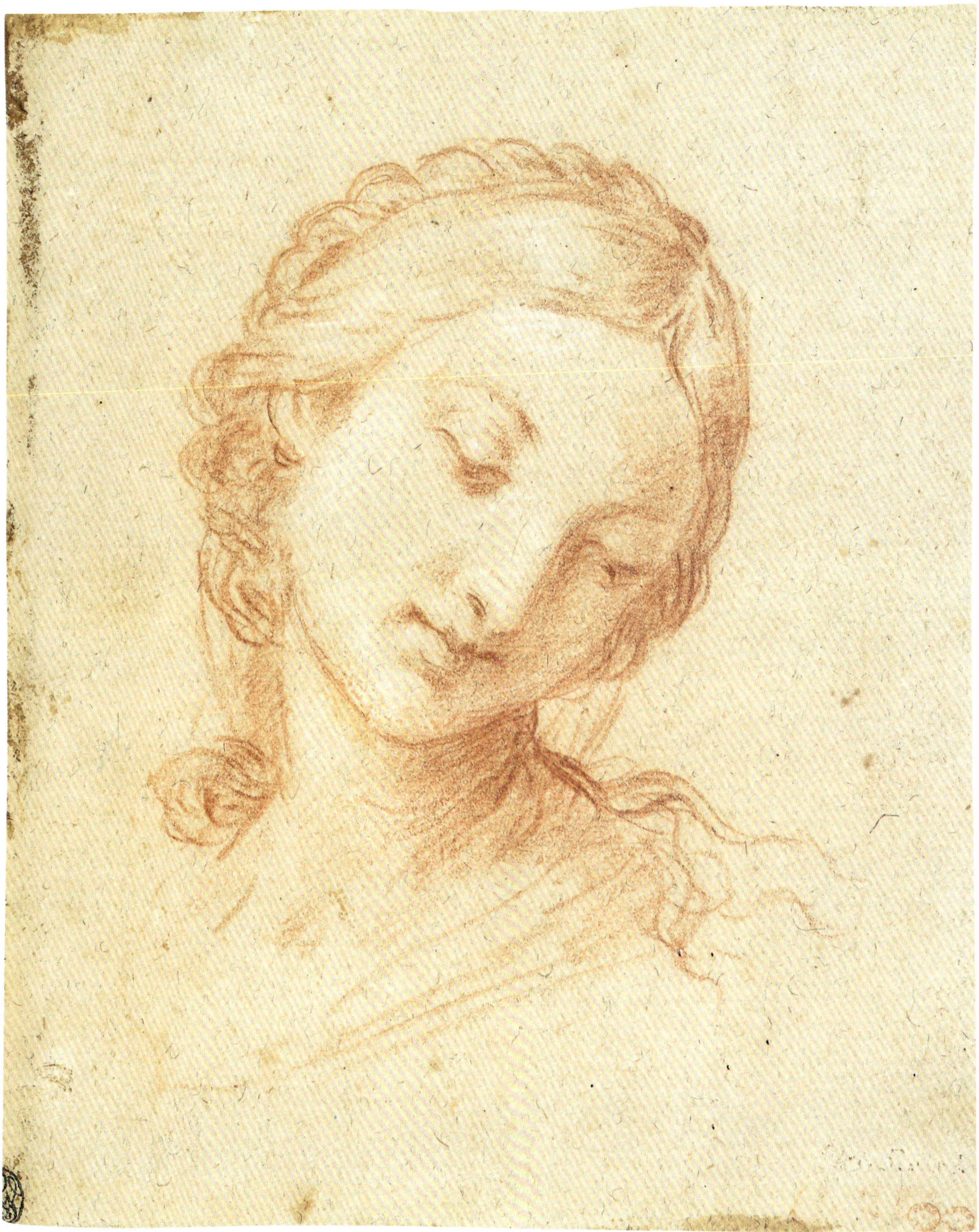

Recto

Domenico Zampieri, called Il Domenichino
Bologna, 1581–Naples, 1641

39 Recto: *A Seated Woman Holding a Bundle in her Lap* Verso: *A Standing Soldier* (ca. 1619)

Black and white chalk (recto); black chalk (verso)

230 x 155 mm (9 x 6 1/16 in)

Provenance: private collection, United States; [Sotheby's, New York, 13 January 1993, lot 80]

Literature: unpublished

The sheet, which was first attributed to Domenichino by Nicholas Turner, shows on the verso a study of a male figure, which was discovered after the recent conservation; it can be reasonably associated with the soldier placed at the far left of *The Martyrdom of St. Agnes* (inv. 473, Pinacoteca Nazionale, Bologna), commissioned from the painter for the high altar of the monastery church of St. Agnese and executed between 1619 and 1622–25.[1] The figure, barely sketched with a touch of black chalk, represents a first idea for the painted composition, reworked in two succeeding drawings, one in Haarlem (inv. 131r, Teylers Stichting),[2] which retraces the upper body of the soldier; the other at Windsor Castle (inv. 1746, Royal Library), which shows the whole figure of the soldier and which was executed close to its transposition into the painting.[3] The Katalan drawing, therefore, should be added to the many drawings at Windsor Castle (a good fifty-five in number) that are related to the altarpiece.[4] *The Seated Woman* drawn on the recto of the sheet, which was not used in the painting, is stylistically close to drawings for *Angel Playing the Violin* and *God the Father*, which appear in the upper part of the altarpiece.[5]

MDG

1. Borea (1965, 176 n. 65); Spear (1982, 216–17).

2. Van Regteren Altena (1966; 144, fig. 94).

3. Pope-Hennessy (1948, 33 n. 45).

4. Pope-Hennessy (1948, 31–34 and nn. 11–65).

5. Pope-Hennessy (1948; 33, nn. 51, 58); more recently, Benati (1991, 81–85).

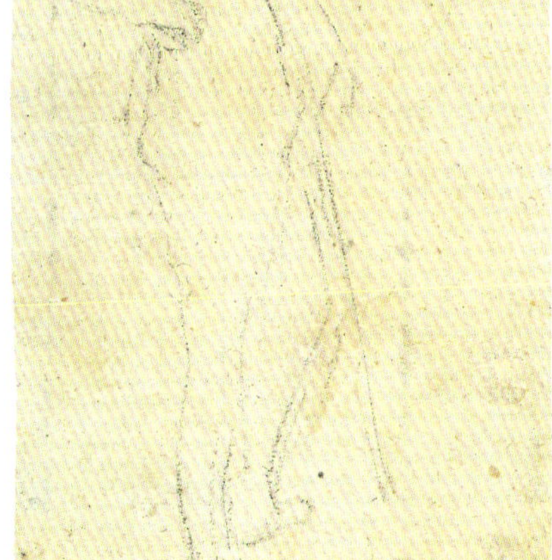

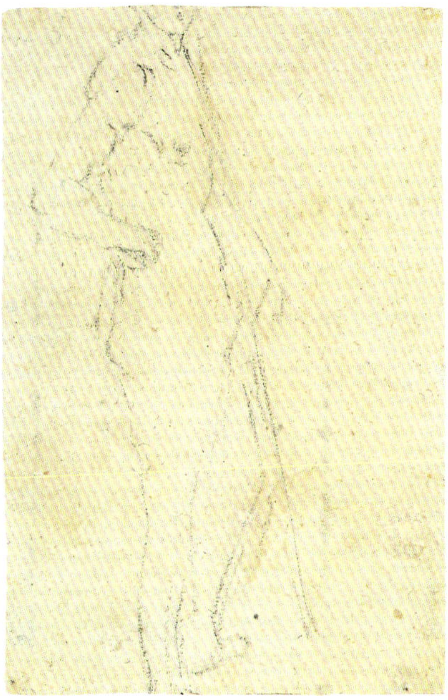

Verso

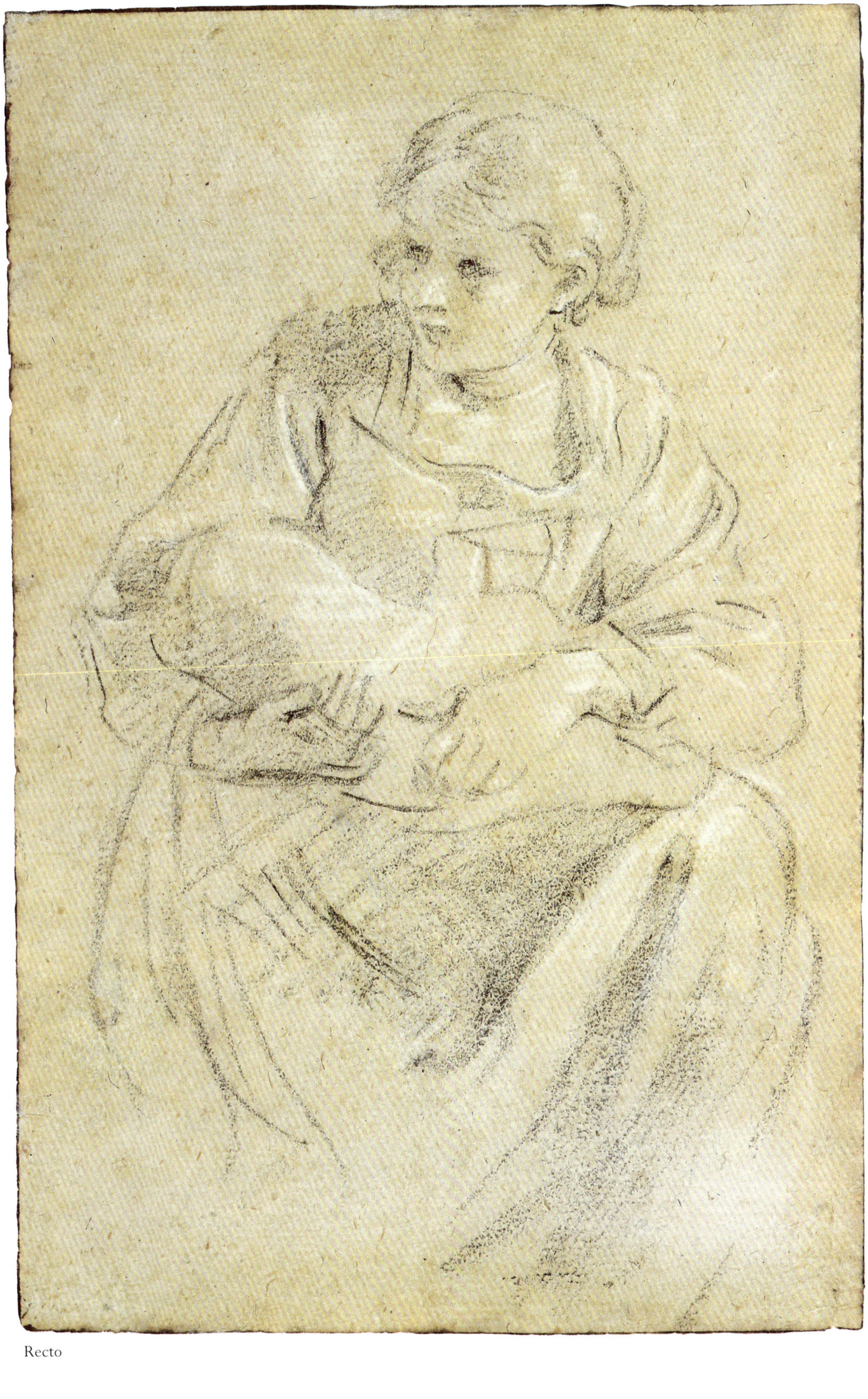

Recto

BARTOLOMEO SCHEDONI

Modena, 1578–Parma, 1615

40 *Woman Seated on the Ground with a Child on her Lap*

Red chalk, with some red wash and stumping; inscribed in brown ink in the lower right, *Baroccio*

58 x 62 mm (2 1/4 x 2 3/8 in)

PROVENANCE: [Guido del Borgo, Rome, 1985, as Burrini]

LITERATURE: unpublished

1. Miller (1985–86; 38, fig. 2).

The old attribution to Federico Barocci (ca. 1535–1612) may have come about because of the drawing's subject-matter rather than its style, since Barocci was well known for the tender treatment of domestic scenes such as this. However the sheet is evidently by an artist of a later generation, and when sold in 1985 it was given to the Bolognese, Giovanni Antonio Burrini (1656–1727). That attribution has now been superseded by the present one to Schedoni, first proposed by this author, a suggestion that is supported by the stylistic parallels with Schedoni's drawings. The variation of the accents are noteworthy: emphatic darks contrast with the untouched areas of the paper that serve as highlights, while the lighter passages of drawing act as midtones. The smudging or stumping was done by hand rather than with a "stump," as the fingerprints over the child's head and in the area of his left arm confirm.

Jak Katalan has since observed a resemblance between the figure group in the drawing and the young woman and child seated in the left foreground of Schedoni's *Charity of St. Elizabeth*, a painting datable to 1612–13 and now in the Palazzo Reale, Naples.[1] But the correspondence is by no means exact: the young woman holds forward her child's right hand to receive alms from a youth, in what is a charming and touching interlude in the picture, whereas in the drawing she holds in her right hand what appears to be a spoon with which she has apparently been feeding the child, and the child's head is turned towards its mother rather than away from her to receive the coin from the passerby. Although it is true that Schedoni may have first conceived of the group in the painting as a woman feeding her child, an alternative purpose cannot be ruled out. The drawing may have been intended, for example, for a *Rest on the Flight into Egypt*, a scene in which the Virgin is often shown seated on the ground feeding the infant Christ.

Schedoni, who was born in Modena, spent much of his career at Parma. He was taught in Rome by Federico Zuccaro (1540/41–1609), though nothing of this artist's influence is detectable in his surviving paintings. It was, rather, the work of the Carracci in Bologna and Rome and that of Correggio in Parma that proved decisive in the formation of Schedoni's style.

NT

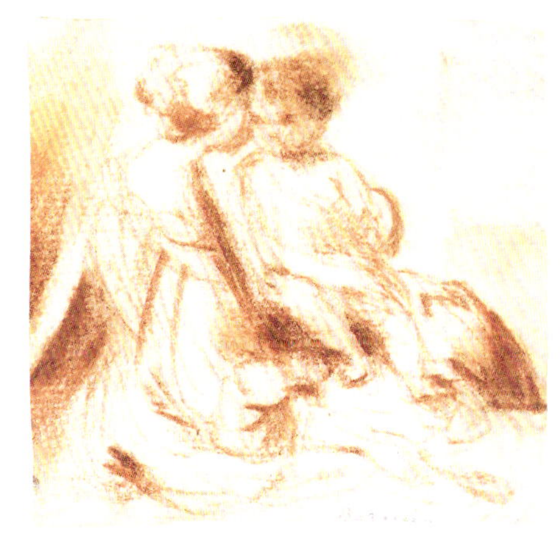

ANTONIO D'ENRICO, called TANZIO DA VARALLO

Riale d' Alagna, ca. 1580–Varallo Sesia, 1632/33

41 *Drapery Study* (ca. 1627)

Red chalk

199 x 124 mm (7 13/16 x 4 7/8 in)

PROVENANCE: G. Vallardi, [Katrin Bellinger, Munich, 1992]

LITERATURE: unpublished

The first attempt at a systematic understanding of the graphic work of Tanzio da Varallo can be traced to the *Disegni* section of an exhibition held in Torino in 1959,[1] followed by subsequent contributions,[2] and leading to the selection of drawings made for the Milan exhibition of 1973,[3] in which the production of drawings by the master was presented in relation to his painted work. In *Drapery Study*, as in other similar drawings by Tanzio, the painter is concerned with the composition of the human figure with a sometimes subtle, sometimes more forceful, touch, leaving the limbs barely sketched in; he does this in order to leave space, in the final rendering, for the movement of the drapery. This drawing, along with the *Draped Figure* and the sheet of sketches, both in the Pinacoteca, Varallo,[4] is related to one of the angels in the frescoes in the Chapel of the Guardian Angel in the church of S. Gaudenzio, Novara (illustrated in Testori 1959, fig. 91), a work that was carried out between 1627 and 1629. The *St. Francis* (ex-Scholz; Pierpont Morgan Library, New York)[5] and the *S. Rocco* in the Galleria dell'Accademia, Venice,[6] executed with the same intent, exhibit a plasticity of the figure that is achieved through strong chiaroscuro contrasts.

MDG

1. Testori (1959, 47–55).

2. Testori (1964, 45–47); Rosenberg (1966, 54–55 n. 199); Andrews (1967, 63–65 n. 207); Neilson (1970, 275–76).

3. Bora (1973, 31–32).

4. Testori (1959; nn. 42, 55, pls. 139, 150).

5. Bora (1973; 32 n. 128, reproduced).

6. Ruggeri (1982, 137 n. 122, with previous bibliography).

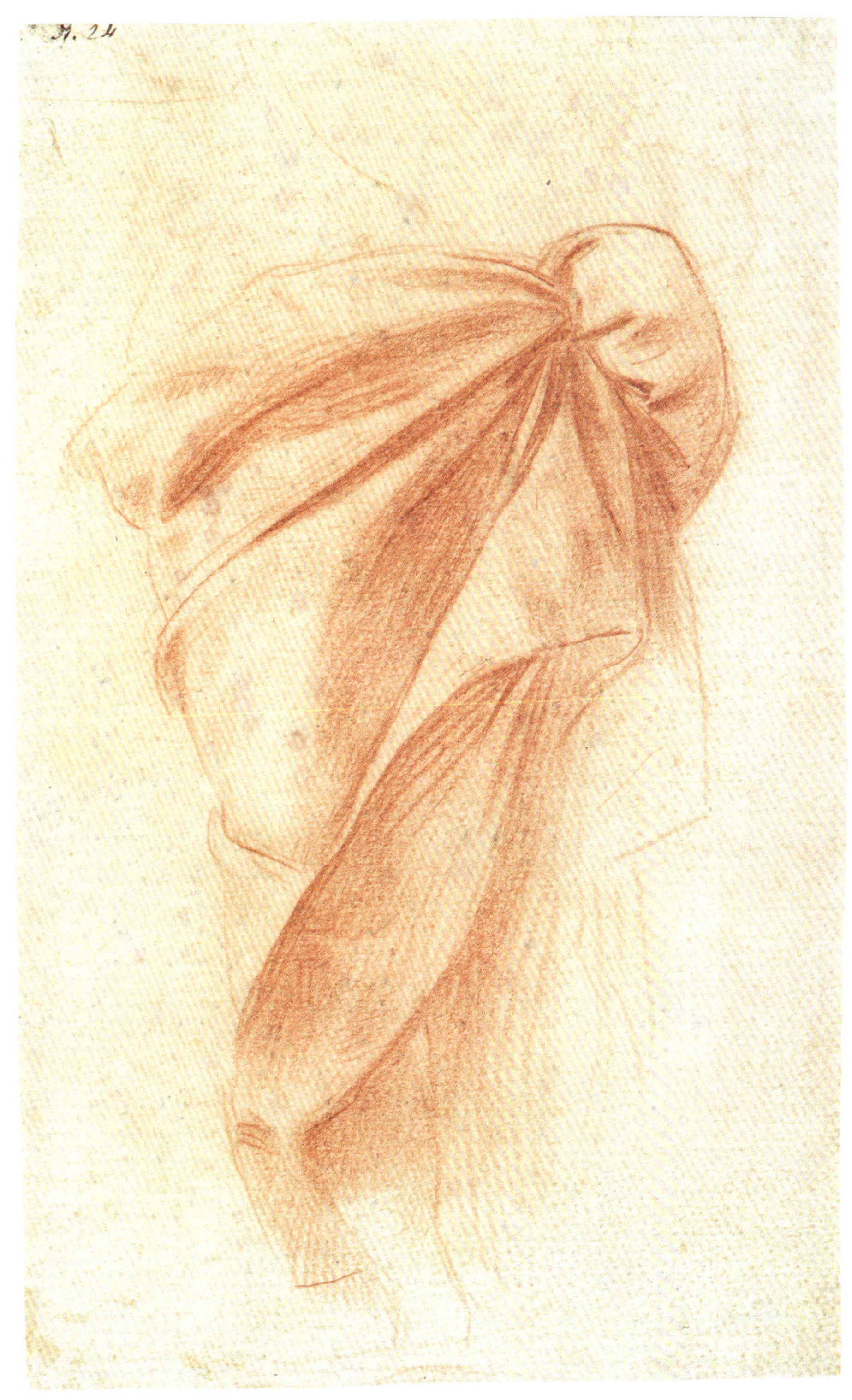

GIOVANNI FRANCESCO BARBIERI, called GUERCINO

Cento, 1591–Bologna, 1666

42 *St. Francis Kneeling in a Landscape Contemplating a Crucifix* (ca. 1641)

Pen and brown ink with dark brown wash

242 x 198 mm (9 1/2 x 7 3/4 in)

PROVENANCE: Guercino's studio and thence by descent to one of the artist's great-nephews, by whom sold to the dealer Francesco Forni of Bologna; John Bouverie (L. 325 and Sup., wrongly as the Hon. Edward Bouverie); his nephew Christopher Hervey; his aunt Elizabeth Bouverie; the earls of Gainsborough; [Jacques Petit Hory, Paris, 1988]

LITERATURE: Stone 1991, cat. no. 44

EXHIBITIONS: *Guercino, Master Draftsman: Works from North American Collections*, Harvard University Art Museums, 1991, cat. no. 44

Traditionally accepted as Guercino (see provenance), the drawing was briefly given to the artist's follower Pier Francesco Mola (1612–66) while in the possession of Jacques Petit Hory (though he later sold it with the correct attribution). There can be no question of Guercino's authorship. His characteristic draftsmanship is seen in the fluent pen-and-wash technique and in the mastery of effects of light and dark. Nevertheless, the particularly somber tones are unusual, as if the artist had deliberately chosen a nocturnal setting for the subject. As with many of Guercino's studies, it is drawn on the other side of a draft of a letter, either in his own handwriting or that of his brother Paolo Antonio Barbieri. The writing shows through from the back onto the recto.

In the catalogue that accompanied the exhibition of drawings by Guercino from North American collections (1991), David Stone recorded this author's view that the drawing could be a study for the *Stigmatization of St. Francis*, painted in 1646 for the church of the Osservanza at Cesena.[1] It now seems more likely to me that it was made for a picture of the same subject painted some four or five years earlier for Padre Giovan Battista d'Este.[2] The d'Este picture was first placed in the church of the Cappuccini at Castelnuovo di Garfagnana, was subsequently transferred to the apartments of the d'Este family in the Ducal Palace at Modena, and was then confiscated by the French in 1796; it is now in the Mittelrheinisches Landesmuseum, Mainz. Two studies, one in the Courtauld Institute of Art, London (inv. 1369) and the other in the Louvre (inv. 6881), were connected with the Mainz picture by Denis Mahon in the catalogue to the exhibition of drawings by Guercino held in Bologna (1991).[3] Both are consistent in style with the present sheet.

Guercino was a leading painter of the Bolognese School and one of the most accomplished draftsman of the Italian baroque. He was born at Cento in Emilia, where he spent his early career, apart from a short period in Rome in 1621–23. He transferred to Bologna in 1642 following the death of Guido Reni and remained there until his own death twenty-four years later.

NT

1. *Stone (1991, 104); Salerno (1988, cat. no. 229).*

2. *Salerno (1988, cat. no. 201).*

3. *Mahon (1991, cat. no. 113).*

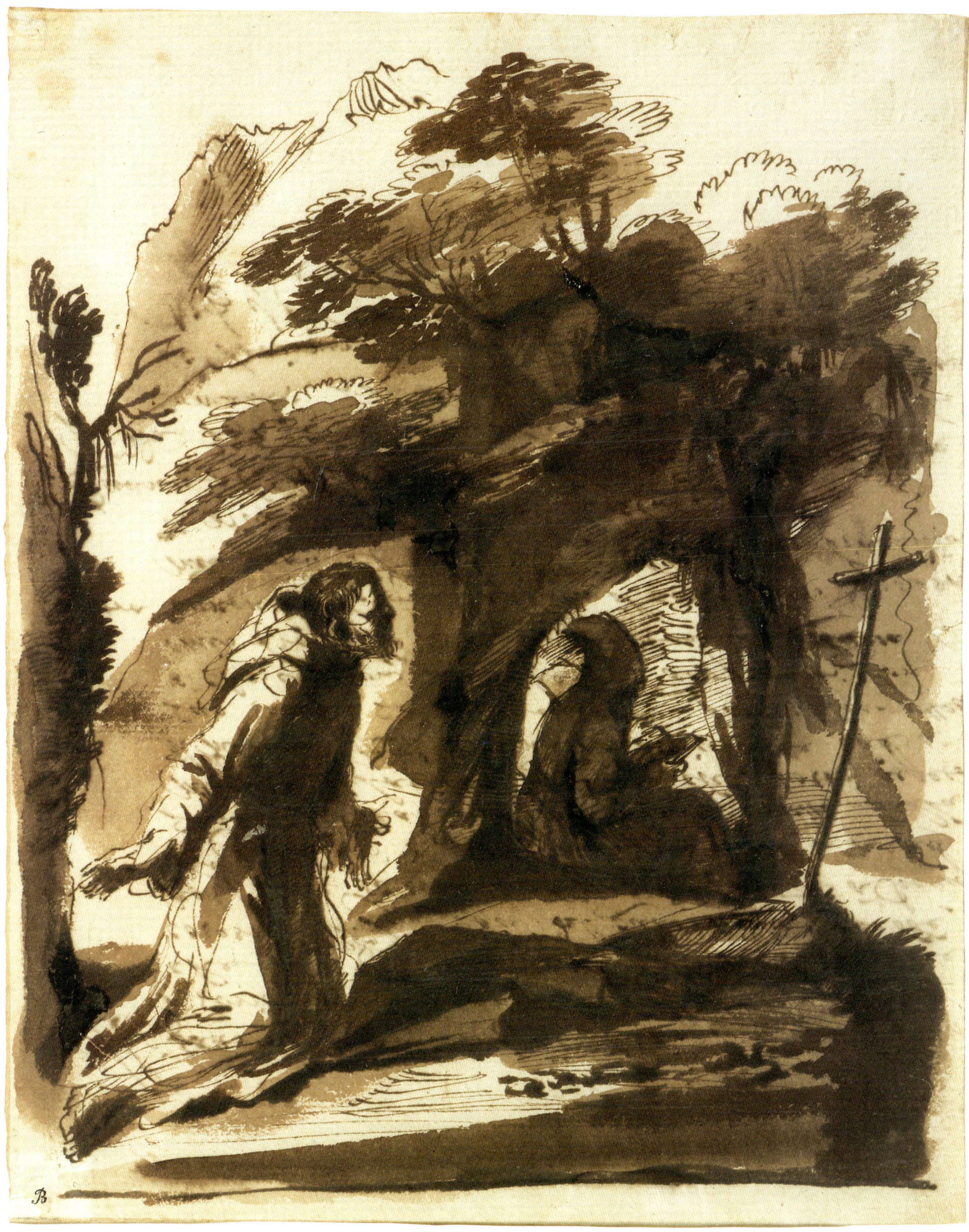

BERNARDO STROZZI

Genoa, 1581–Venice, 1644

43 **Recto:** *Head of St. John the Baptist*
Verso: *Nude Figure Seen from Behind, One Leg Raised and Arms Outstretched* (ca.1625)

Black chalk, heightened with white, on gray paper, with watermark (crossbow within a circle)

292 x 215 mm (11 1/2 x 8 1/2 in)

PROVENANCE: "Borghese" Albums, with an old mount; annotation on recto, *P. G. No. 18*; Michel Gaud; Sotheby's, Monaco, 20 June 1987, lot 120, ill. (recto); private collection, Boston; [Sotheby's, New York, 8 January 1991, lot 132, ill. (recto and verso)]

LITERATURE: unpublished

1. *Mortari (1966, pl. 82).*

2. *Newcome Schleier (1985; cat. no. 49, recto ill.).*

3. *Kozak and Monkiewicz (1993, cat. no. 19).*

4. *On the different versions of* Mercury, *see Avery and Radcliffe (1978–79, 83–87).*

5. *Newcome Schleier (1985, cat. nos. 52 and 50).*

6. *Briquet (1907, 1:49).*

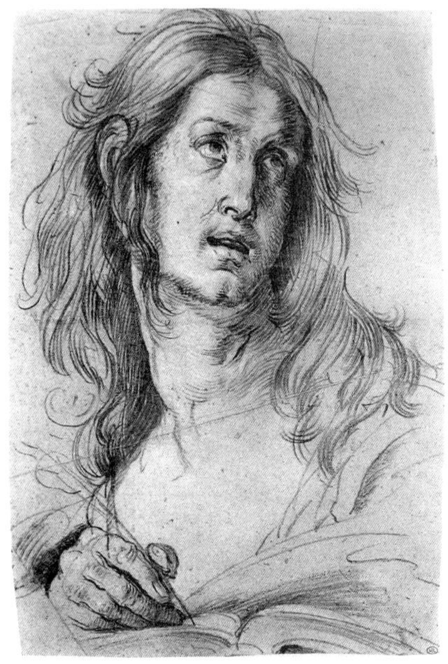

Fig. 7: Bernardo Strozzi, *St. John the Evangelist*, Musée du Louvre, Cabinet des Déssins, Paris

Bernardo Strozzi was trained in the workshop of the Siennese artist Pietro Sorri in Genoa. He entered the convent of the Capuchins of S. Barnaba in 1597, which he left in 1601. His first works are of religious subjects. Later on, after 1630, Strozzi settled in Venice. At the time of the present drawing's execution, the mature artist had given proof of extraordinary draftsmanship. The painting for which this drawing is a study (Landesmuseum, Hanover)[1] represents *St. John the Evangelist Writing the Apocalypse Inspired by the Angel*, and could be dated 1625, at the end of his stay in Genoa. Whereas, in another drawing of the same provenance and similar style, now in the Louvre (inv. RF 38817) (Fig. 7),[2] the saint is studied in half-length, here only his face is the focus of attention. Newcome Schleier describes the Louvre drawing as being mannerist and lyrical.

The present *Head* displays a rich pictorial quality perceived in Flemish models, such as could be seen in Genoa, in the works of Rubens and Van Dyck. Other studies of heads also in black chalk, by Dürer, such as *Head of a Bearded Man* (dated 1510, Ossolinski National Institute of Wroclaw),[3] could likewise be referred to by way of comparison, thus widening the field of possible Northern models to which Strozzi had recourse for his vigorous style. His use of diagonal hatching without stumping to define shadows is very similar in both drawings.

Like many drawings from the Sagredo collection of Venice (long known as the "Borghese" Albums), including the Louvre study previously cited, this sheet is drawn on both sides. Katalan has observed a similarity between the figure on the verso—the Sotheby's sale catalogue of 8 January 1991 questions whether the figure is male or female—and the bronze *Mercury* by Giambologna, one of the most celebrated works by the Florentine sculptor.[4] Such a figure shows the strong influence of the *maniera* and of the *figura serpentinata* on a totally baroque artist. It is not, in any case, a copy after the statue, the fleshy live model employed having nothing to do with the fine elongated figure of the bronze *Mercury*. The nude figure is rarely studied in Strozzi's drawings. Often the figures drawn on the two sides of the sheet are preparatory for different works, which adds to the complexity of dating these sheets.

The study of the paper itself should not be neglected, as has been the case thus far. The watermark of the crossbow, present in this sheet, is found in several others used by Strozzi for studies related to works of the Venetian period (inv. RF 38820, RF 38822; Louvre).[5] According to Briquet the use of the crossbow watermark, typically Italian, can be traced back to the fourteenth century, while the crossbow inscribed in a circle surmounted by a clover (as is the case of the Katalan and Louvre drawings) comes most usually from Ferrara, and is very likely a product of the Venetian paper industry: "The crossbow watermark continued to be used in the states under the Republic up and throughout the XVIIth century."[6] As a result of this, one should perhaps assume that the drawing exhibited here, and others with the same watermark, were executed by Strozzi after he moved to Venice in 1630.

CMG

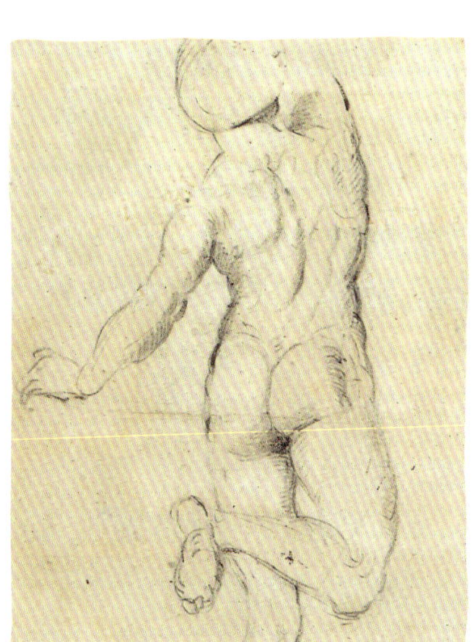

Verso

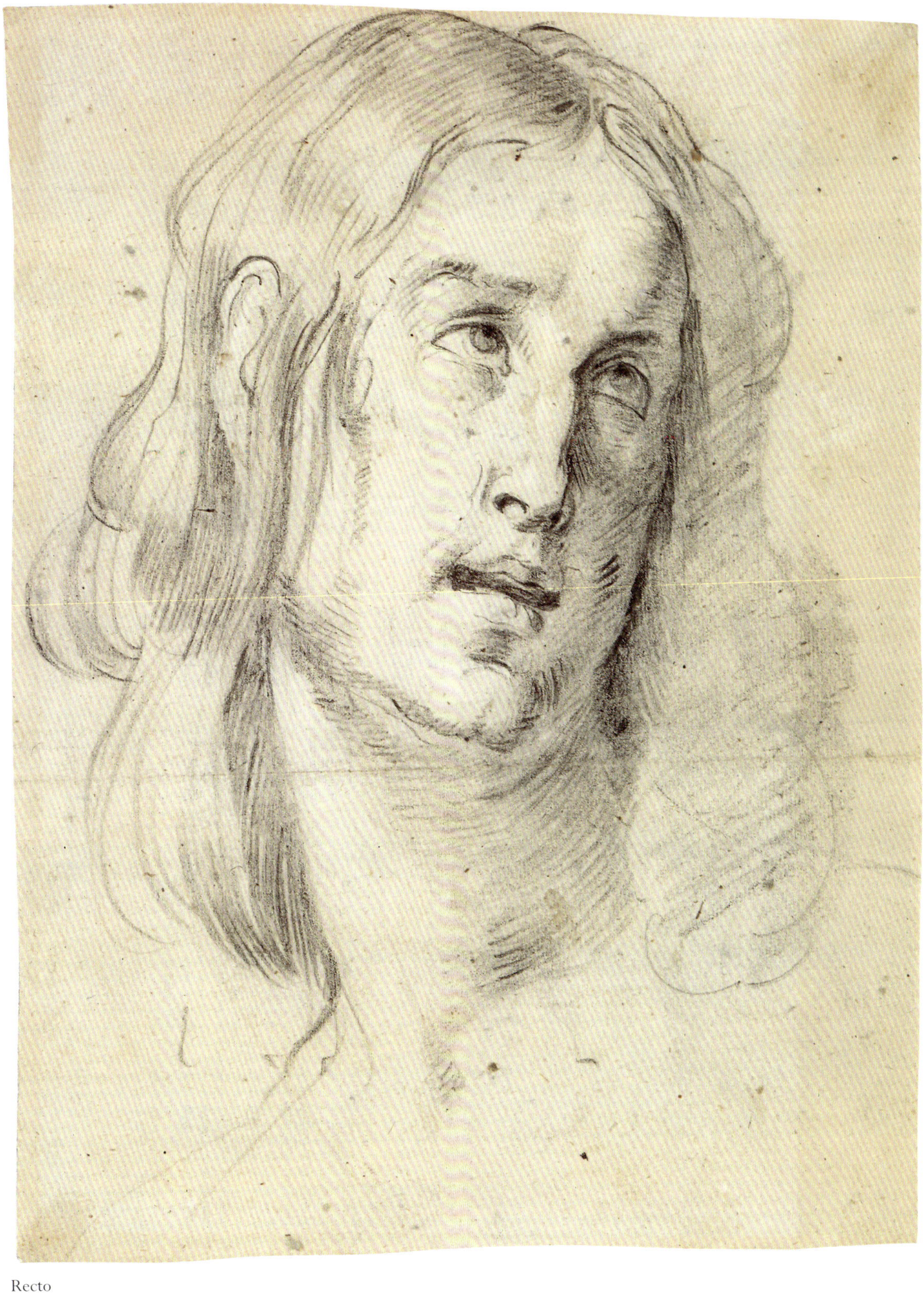

Recto

Gian Lorenzo Bernini

Naples, 1599–Rome, 1680

44 *Virgin in Glory with Two Angels* (1636–39)

Black chalk on buff paper

180 x 248 mm (7 1/4 x 9 1/2 in)

Provenance: Alessandro Viggiano (L. Sup. 191a); [Marcello Aldega, 1991]

Literature: unpublished

1. Dreyer (1981, 161–63). This sheet has some drapery studies on the verso.

2. McTavish (1985–86, cat. no. 46).

3. The significance of this commission was underlined by Lavin (1980; 50–53 and 169–71, for all relevant documents).

4. Lavin (1980, 2:pl. 87). The drawing was then in a private collection.

5. Lavin (1980, 1:171).

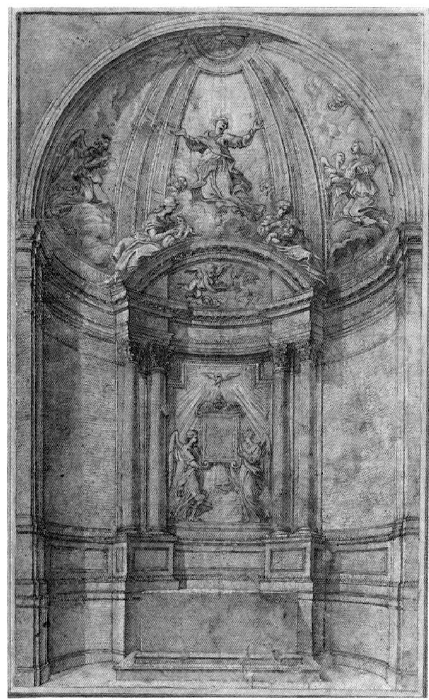

Fig. 8: Workshop of Gian Lorenzo Bernini, *Assumption of the Virgin*, The Pierpont Morgan Library, New York

In the last decade, several drawings executed in black chalk have surfaced by Gian Lorenzo Bernini, all coming from the Viggiano collection. The first of these sheets to emerge in public view was a study in the Mathias Polakovitz collection, now on loan to the Fogg Art Museum, Harvard University, a drawing connected with the dome fresco by G. B. Gaulli in the Gesù painted between 1672 and 1675.[1] Another sheet, now in the Ferretti collection, proves that a school drawing for an unidentified funerary monument in the Victoria and Albert Museum associated with Bernini does depend on some autograph invention of his, although the commission cannot be identified.[2] A few others remain on the art market, two of which can also be connected with the Gesù commission. McTavish associated the style of the Ferretti drawing with other, rough, late, chalk composition studies by Bernini made in the 1670s, an entirely reasonable conclusion on the basis of the surviving evidence. The Katalan drawing, however, is connected with a commission executed in the early 1640s, suggesting that the loss of most of Bernini's earlier preparatory drawings has created a false impression of a stylistic evolution from disciplined control to a late style of painterly expressiveness.

Bernini is known to have designed a work that included the subject of the Virgin's Assumption to heaven only once. The apse and high altar of S. Maria in Via Lata, for which Bernini provided designs by 1639, when work began, has a repainted fresco of this subject in the vault.[3] A workshop drawing in the Morgan Library (Fig. 8) shows a preliminary scheme for the apse and altar, with a figure of the Virgin facing to the left, her arms upraised on a bank of clouds, as she appears in the Katalan drawing.[4] The low arch of the high altar's pediment is also shown with the clouds covering the central area, creating the illusion that this vision is emerging from the top of the high altar instead of floating above it, which the scheme recorded by the Morgan Library drawing indicates. The vault ribs shown in the Morgan Library study do not appear in the Katalan sheet. Instead, a circular band of cherubim heads that radiate streaks of light frames the Virgin and fills the surrounding space. Two music-making angels float on either side of her. The scheme already prefigures the visionary emergence of *The Cathedra Petri* in the apse of St. Peter's, for which Bernini started making plans after 1655 .

The fresco, executed by Andrea Camassei, does not show ribs behind the Virgin either, and the Virgin is also much larger in relation to the overall space of the vault than in the Morgan Library scheme. Thus the design in the Katalan drawing, which is far more innovative than that in the Morgan Library drawing, must have been made after his workshop prepared that careful scheme, which nevertheless records many of the architectural elements actually carried out. Lavin dates Bernini's design to the period 1634–36.[5] Bernini commissions for which a series of composition drawings survive often show how his thoughts continued to develop long after his patrons probably thought the design process was over. The first designs were quite conventional, but they gave Bernini the opportunity to think through the commission carefully before letting his imagination take flight, a process that could be enormously expensive!

If Francesco d'Aste refused to let Bernini carry out the scheme in the Katalan drawing, it may not have been for financial reasons. The patron spared little expense when it came to semiprecious marbles. It is more probable that the priests thought that the design would overwhelm the sacred image of the Virgin attributed to St. Luke that was reinstalled on the new altar in 1643. Among the other changes made were the addition of memorial tabernacles for the parents of Francesco d'Aste on either side of the

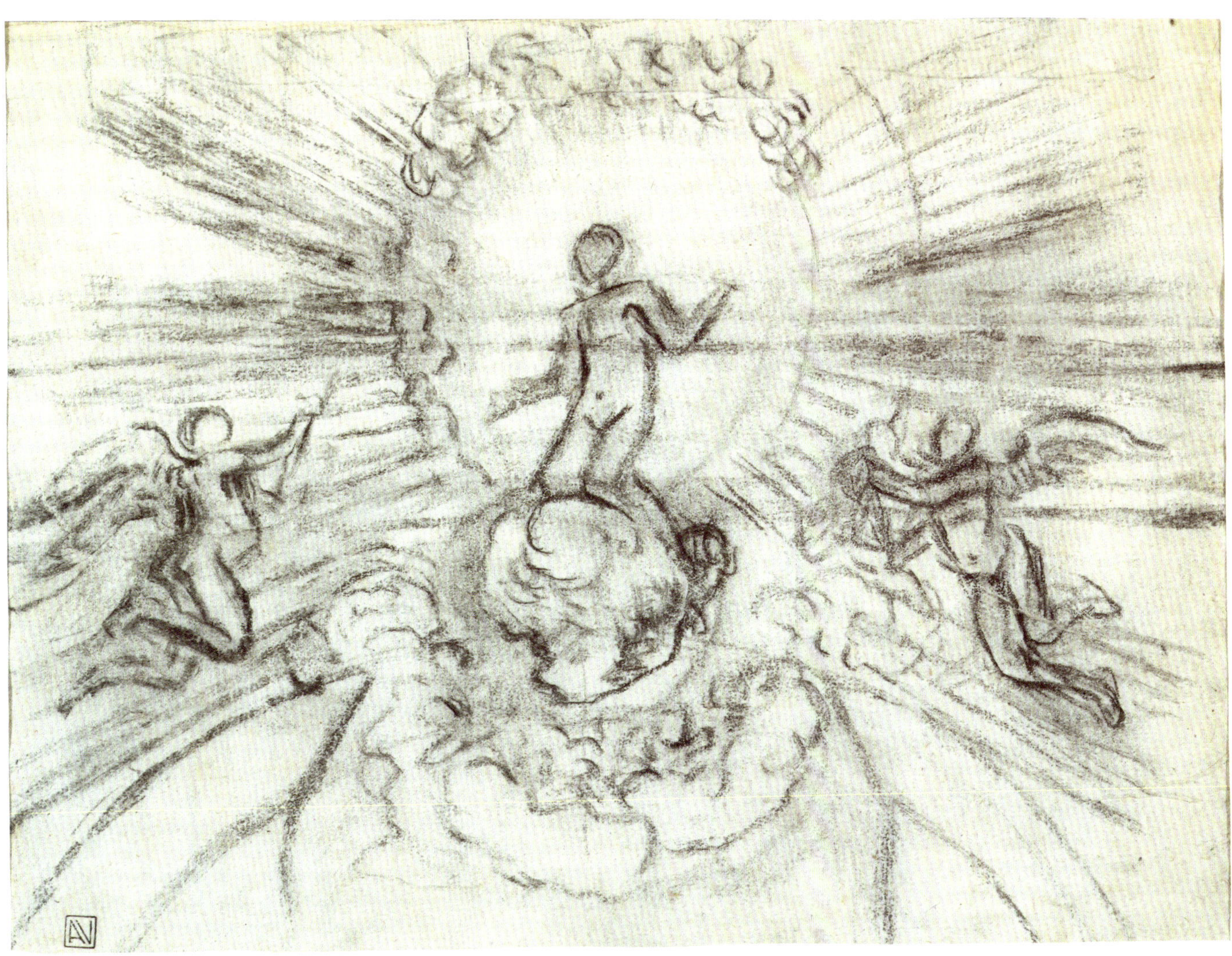

6. *Brauer and Wittkower (1931, 2:80–81).*

7. *Brauer and Wittkower (1931, 1:45–46 and 2:pls. 20 and 22). For the fullest and most recent discussion of these drawings, see Lavin et al. (1981, cat. nos. 14, 17, and 18). The two saints have not been connected with any commission so far, but I argue in my forthcoming catalogue of Bernini's drawings that they were planned for niches to either side of St. Teresa in the Cornaro Chapel. There is no other commission of this period into which the allotted space and proportions of these figures would fit. Bernini probably dropped this scheme in order to keep the focus clearly on the image of St. Teresa.*

altar and a much heavier, more elaborate setting for the miraculous image on the altar, which was given an emphatic triangular pediment of its own set at a slightly higher level than the rounded pediments above the two tombs. All the architectural elements are thicker and bulkier in the executed design than in the daintily proportioned scheme preserved in the Morgan Library drawing.

The vision of light, clouds, and cherubim surrounding holy figures that is the subject of this drawing seems too closely allied stylistically to Bernini's broadly handled charcoal studies for *The Cathedra Petri,* whose later phases were prepared in the early 1660s; thus a date for the Katalan drawing some thirty years earlier may seem implausible.[6] The earliest rough black chalk preparatory studies so far published are those in Leipzig for *Truth Revealed by Time* and for a pair of gesticulating saints that Bernini drew on the verso of the same sheet. Both sides are therefore likely to date from 1645–46, during his brief fall from papal favor after the death of Urban VIII in 1644.[7] While no comparable studies in black chalk by Bernini from the 1630s have been traced so far, so few preparatory studies have been preserved from that decade that we cannot declare that Bernini never used this medium in this manner before the mid-1640s. The Katalan drawing is somewhat sharper and crisper than the blurred black chalk studies of the 1640s and later. Thus it does not seem implausible that the drawing was made in the late 1630s. Finally, there is no other documented commission by Bernini with which it can be connected. It thus becomes a valuable link between the red chalk studies for *St. Longinus* of the late 1620s and the one red chalk study for the *Triton Fountain* of 1642, and it is a reminder of how little we know about Bernini's working drawings before the 1640s.

ASH

ANDREA SACCHI

Rome, 1599–Rome, 1661

45 Recto: *Studies for a Figure of Apollo* Verso: *Studies of Three Figures and Drapery* (1638–40)

Red chalk with some pen and brown ink on buff paper

277 x 400 mm (11 x 16 in)

PROVENANCE: Christie's, London, 12 April 1983, lot 64; [Yvonne Tan Bunzl, 1988]

LITERATURE: Tan Bunzl 1984, cat. no. 30; McTavish 1985–86, cat. no. 34

This drawing combines art historical significance and aesthetic pleasure to an unusual degree. Andrea Sacchi's portrait of the castrato soprano, Marc'Antonio Pasqualini (1614–91) (Fig. 9), to which the recto of this drawing is connected, has attracted more attention from scholars than any other picture in his entire *oeuvre* since 1977.[1] Neither the identity of the original patron nor the date of execution of this ambitious portrait could then be discovered, although a date around 1638–40 could be deduced from stylistic evidence and the approximate age of the sitter. The Katalan drawing helps to substantiate a date of around 1640, for the studies on the verso can be connected with a documented painting, *Urban VIII Visiting the Gesù on October 2, 1639 During the Centenary Celebrations of the Jesuit Order* (Museo di Roma, Rome), for which Sacchi was paid in November 1641.[2] There are other examples of Sacchi reusing the blank sides of study sheets for projects executed within a year or two of each other, thus making it reasonable to assume that the portrait, now in the Metropolitan Museum of Art, New York, was finished a year or two before the Gesù picture.

Although almost two hundred drawings by Sacchi are preserved at Windsor in the Royal Library and in Düsseldorf, these can be but a small percentage of his total output.[3] His drawings are, however, preserved in small numbers in other major European print rooms and are rarely found on the art market. The appearance of three double-sided sheets of red chalk preparatory studies at Christie's in 1983 was therefore a major event for connoisseurs aware of his rarity and familiar with the exceptional subtlety of Sacchi's technique in this medium.[4] Only one other autograph preparatory drawing for the Pasqualini portrait was then known, a study in black chalk with white heightening in Düsseldorf for the sleeve of the singer's costume.[5] Sacchi normally made several composition studies for each work as well as detailed studies from models for all major and many minor figures, so these two sheets represent only a tiny share of the drawings that Sacchi made for this important picture. The details of Apollo's torso observed in the Katalan drawing were used almost without change in the painting: Apollo's left arm at his side supporting his lyre has the same areas shaded, as in the drawing, and the fingers have been adjusted only slightly to give a firmer grip; the shading on the torso and raised right arm were also used, but the upper part of the arm is slightly longer and more forcefully modeled in the painting. The care with which these details were observed is proof of Sacchi's painstaking preparatory procedures.

1. Harris (1977, cat. no. 51). A good synthesis of the subsequent literature is found in Christiansen (1990, cat. no. 18), which also has an excellent color plate of the painting. Later articles have explored the musical iconography of the painting, and argued that the picture was commissioned by the sitter, who was known for his arrogance.

2. Christiansen (1990, 90). Sacchi designed the painting, but the only parts he executed were the figures of Urban VIII and his immediate entourage. The interior of the church and the crowd of unidentifiable figures behind the pope were painted by a perspective specialist, Filippo Gagliardi, while Jan Miel painted the genre figures that fill the foreground.

3. Blunt (1960, cat. nos. 738–865) attributed about 130 drawings (including versos) to Sacchi himself, but only about eighty of these are, in my opinion, autograph, and many corrections were made in my monograph. There are just over a hundred autograph sheets in Düsseldorf. Harris and Schaar (1967, cat. nos. 1–104).

4. Important Old Master Drawings, *Christie's, London, 12 April 1983, lots 64–66. The connection between the studies on the verso of the Katalan sheet with the Gesù painting was first made by Nicholas Turner. One of the other sheets is also in a private collection. McTavish (1985–86, cat. no. 34).*

5. Harris and Schaar (1967, cat. no. 63).

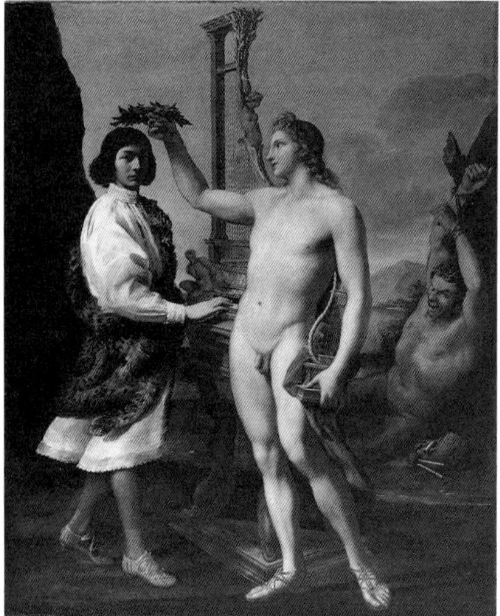

Fig.9: Andrea Sacchi, *Portrait of Marc'Antonio Pasqualini,* Metropolitan Museum of Art, New York

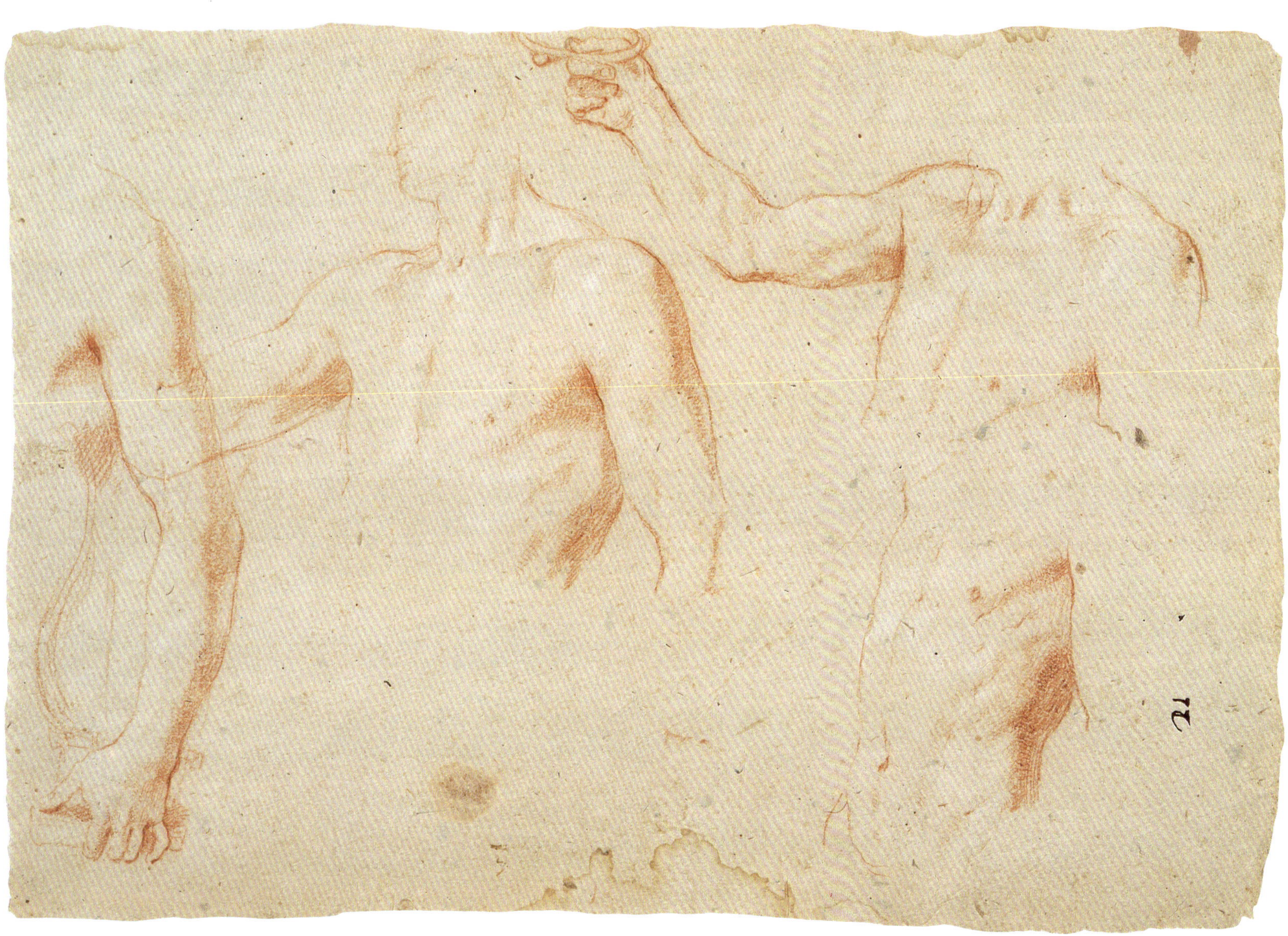

Recto

6. See note 2.

7. Harris (1978, 601). The poses shown here were not followed precisely in the painting.

8. Baldinucci (1680–1728, 4:367).

9. Trezzani (1983; 91f., esp. 110–12).

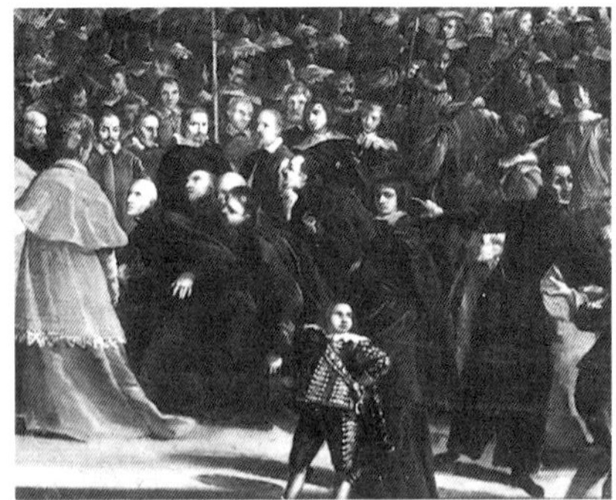

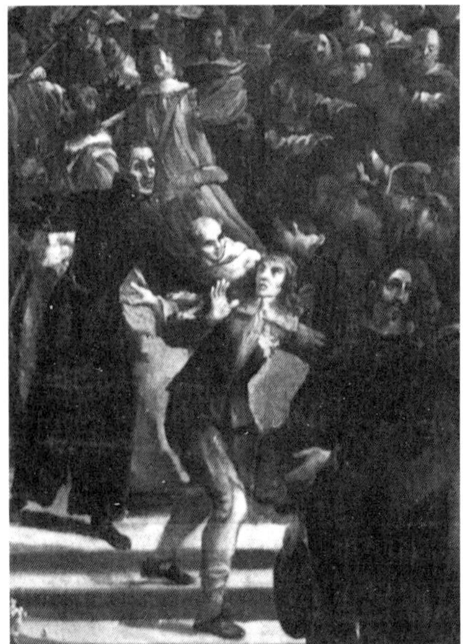

Fig. 10 (top) and Fig. 11 (bottom): Andrea Sacchi, *Urban VIII Visiting the Gesú*, Museo di Roma, Rome (details)

The studies on the verso also have special significance for Sacchi's career since they relate to the large painting documenting Urban VIII's visit to the mother church of the Jesuit order in 1639, for whose execution Sacchi was only partially responsible.[6] A composition drawing by Sacchi using ink and brush tip in a private collection focuses on the most prestigious figures of Urban VIII Barberini and his relatives, the two cardinal nephews, Francesco and Antonio, and the general of the Jesuit Order and five of his associates kneeling behind him (Figs. 10 and 11).[7] This section of the painting is the only part that was executed by Sacchi himself, but it is now clear that he provided drawings for the foreground figures executed by Jan Miel and thus exercised careful control over the whole commission. The verso of the exhibited drawing has two studies for the man walking down the steps to the right of the main group, whose gestures suggest that he has been prevented from entering the church, and for the two most prominently situated Jesuits. The drapery study for a standing figure on the right of the page, whose skirts have been lifted up to prevent him from tripping (the small drapery study at the bottom of the page connects with the lifted section) does not match an executed figure, but presumably connected with a rejected design that showed the pope being assisted in this manner. As McTavish noted, there is another study for the Jesuit general on the Ferretti sheet, which also has a study for the young Maffeo, son of Taddeo Barberini, standing confidently at the top of the steps, and for the young black servant peering from the window of the carriage at the lower left. Thus even a minor figure, whose genre character would seem far from Sacchi's concern, was sketched by him for Miel, who had to follow the planned design closely.

Jan Miel (1599–1664) was the same age as Sacchi and may well have found such a subordinate role humiliating. Baldinucci reported that the two quarreled after Miel, who was a Flemish immigrant and a successful genre painter, joined Sacchi's studio in order to learn how to draw and paint history subjects. Sacchi is supposed to have told Miel that he was too old to learn how to draw, and to go back to painting *Bamboccianti* (low-life scenes).[8] Miel did not begin to receive public commissions for religious or historical subjects, however, until the late 1640s.[9] These do, in fact, reveal some difficulties arranging groups of large figures and architectural settings (Miel's fresco, *St. Cyril's Baptism* of 1651 in S. Martino ai Monti, is an especially clumsy performance), so Sacchi's judgment about Miel's abilities were well founded.

ASH

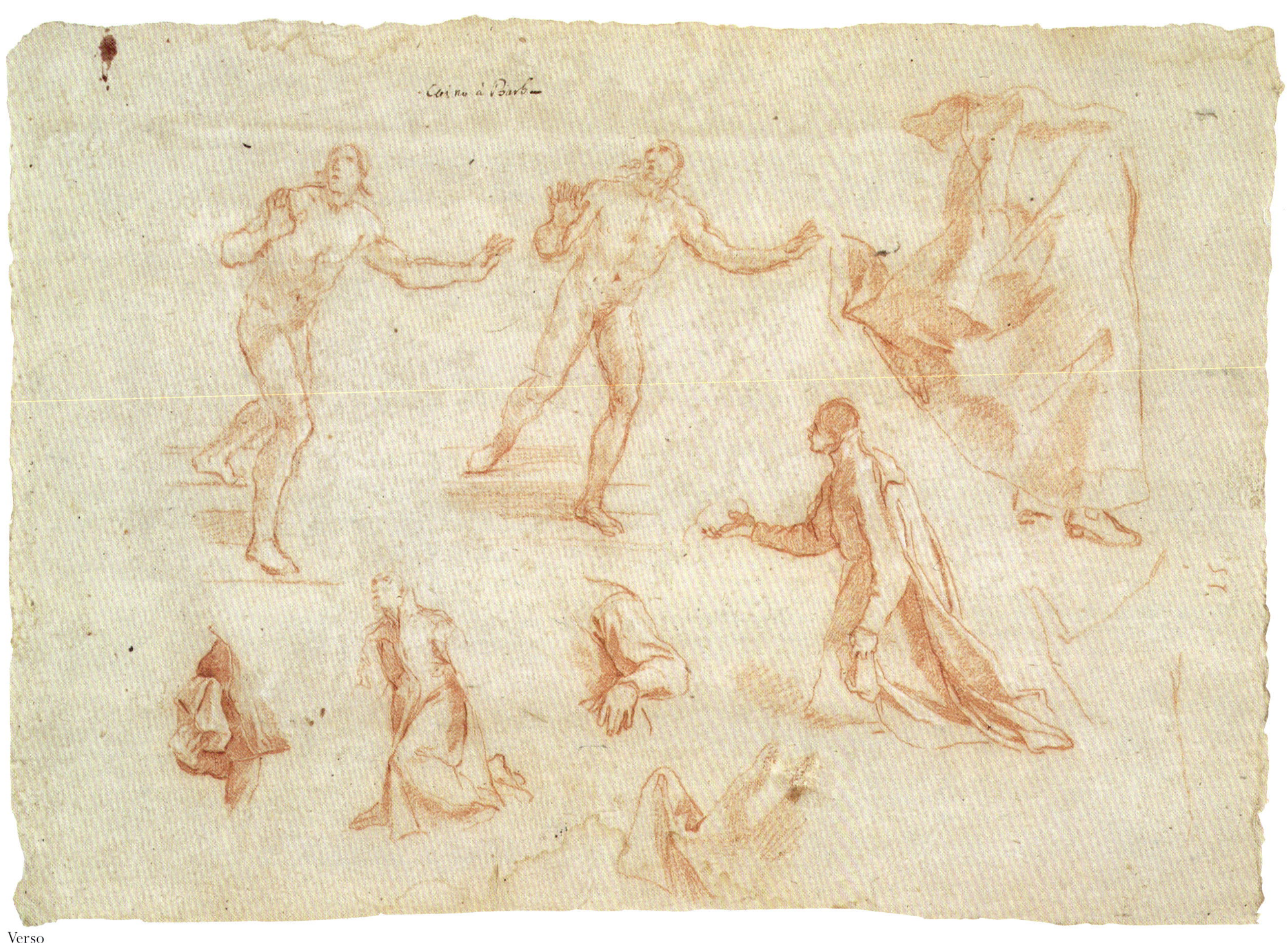

Verso

Francesco Maffei

Vicenza, 1605–Padua, 1660

46

Recto: *Standing Female Figure* Verso: *Two Falling Male Nudes* (ca. 1647)

Pen and brown ink with bistre wash (recto); pen and brown ink with bistre and gray wash (verso); on ivory paper; inscribed at top in pen in a seventeenth-century hand, *Lattantio* (at left), *Gambara* (at right); and in pen in a slightly later hand, *bresciano, Scol. di/Giulio/Campi* (at left); and in pen at lower right, *L. 407*; and along the bottom in pen in the same hand as the uppermost inscription, *era fra li donatimi/ dal s. Pier Antonio della Penna Cavalier/Servittisimo Perugino*

269 x 158 mm (10 5/8 x 5 1/4 in)

Provenance: Pier Antonio della Penna, Perugia; Padre Resta, Milan, before 1714 (L. 2992); Lord Somers, London, before 1716 (L. 2981); Pierre-Jean Mariette, Paris, before 1774 (L. 1852); de Damery, Paris, before 1803 (L. 2862); [Galerie de Bayser, Paris, 1991]

Literature: unpublished

1. Ruggeri (1972, 133–44); Meijer (1984, 303–10); and Rossi (1991, 165–72).

Padre Resta, the preeminent *marchand amateur* of the seventeenth century, ascribed this sheet to the sixteenth-century Brescian master, Lattanzio Gambara, and recorded that it was a gift from Pier Antonio della Penna. Under the clearly erroneous name of Gambara he passed it on to Lord Somers, from whom it went through a series of distinguished collections, to be acquired in 1991 by its, present owner, who attributed it to Francesco Maffei.

Francesco Maffei, the most fluent, painterly master in Vicenza during the seicento, has attracted a widely heterogeneous range of drawing attributions, very few related to his paintings but almost all characterized by a smudged handling of chalk that appears analogous to his tonalist brush stroke. It has become clear that most of these attributions are erroneous, and although recent studies by Ruggeri, Meijer, and Rossi have attributed several new sheets to him, all retain or add drawings of a manifestly diverse character that still present a confused picture of this attractive painter as a draftsman.[1]

Those that present the best claim for inclusion in his corpus are not pictorial in character, but are instead linear and emphatic in contour, in much the same range of pen work that characterizes his master, Giambattista Maganza il Giovane, and Paolo Veronese, the presiding master of an earlier generation. Maffei's early drawing style is pedestrian and academic in its use of pen and wash. *The Presentation of the Virgin* (no. AE 1829, Landesmuseum, Darmstadt) bears an early ascription to Maffei and is evidently by the same hand as *Sacrifice of Zaccharias* (Cod. F 253, inv. 1173, Ambrosiana, Milan). Both depend on the example of Maganza and may be dated to ca. 1625–30. Maffei's later style is more fluent, but remains rather staid, as in the *Two Saints* (Riva 116, Museo Civico, Bassano del Grappa), which is probably preparatory to the *Madonna and Saints* (Madonna dei Prati, Brendola) of 1555–1656. The Katalan sheet helps to fill the intervening gap of a quarter century.

Neither the recto nor verso can be associated directly with a painting by Maffei, but very similar allegorical female figures appear in such works as the *Votive of Podestà Alvise Foscarini* (Museo Civico, Vicenza) of 1655, and the *Glorification of Giovanni Cavalli* (Rotunda, Rovigo). The supplicant woman in the sketch wears highly stylized theatrical garb, a reminder that beginning with the opening of *Oedipus* in 1584, the Maganza family (cf. cat. 20), along with many subsequent Vicentine artists, created costumes for classical dramas presented in Palladio's Teatro Olimpico. In fact, in the Sala dell'Olimpo in the Odeon, adjacent to the theater, Maffei painted a decorative fresco cycle, only partially preserved today, including an elaborately costumed female usually identified as an allegory of the Accademia Olimpica.

Although she differs in pose, the decorative character in the fresco is strongly reminiscent of Maffei's drawing. In the study, highly stylized anatomical details such as hands and feet have the same incoherent structure that may be found in Maffei's paintings, in which intense color often disguises a deficient grasp of natural form. Strong effects of illumination are vividly suggested by the deeply shaded wash, and hands and feet are subjected to an abstracted formula that is even more pronounced on the verso of this sheet. There the clumsy nudes seem, in the incoherent shadows that are but vaguely related

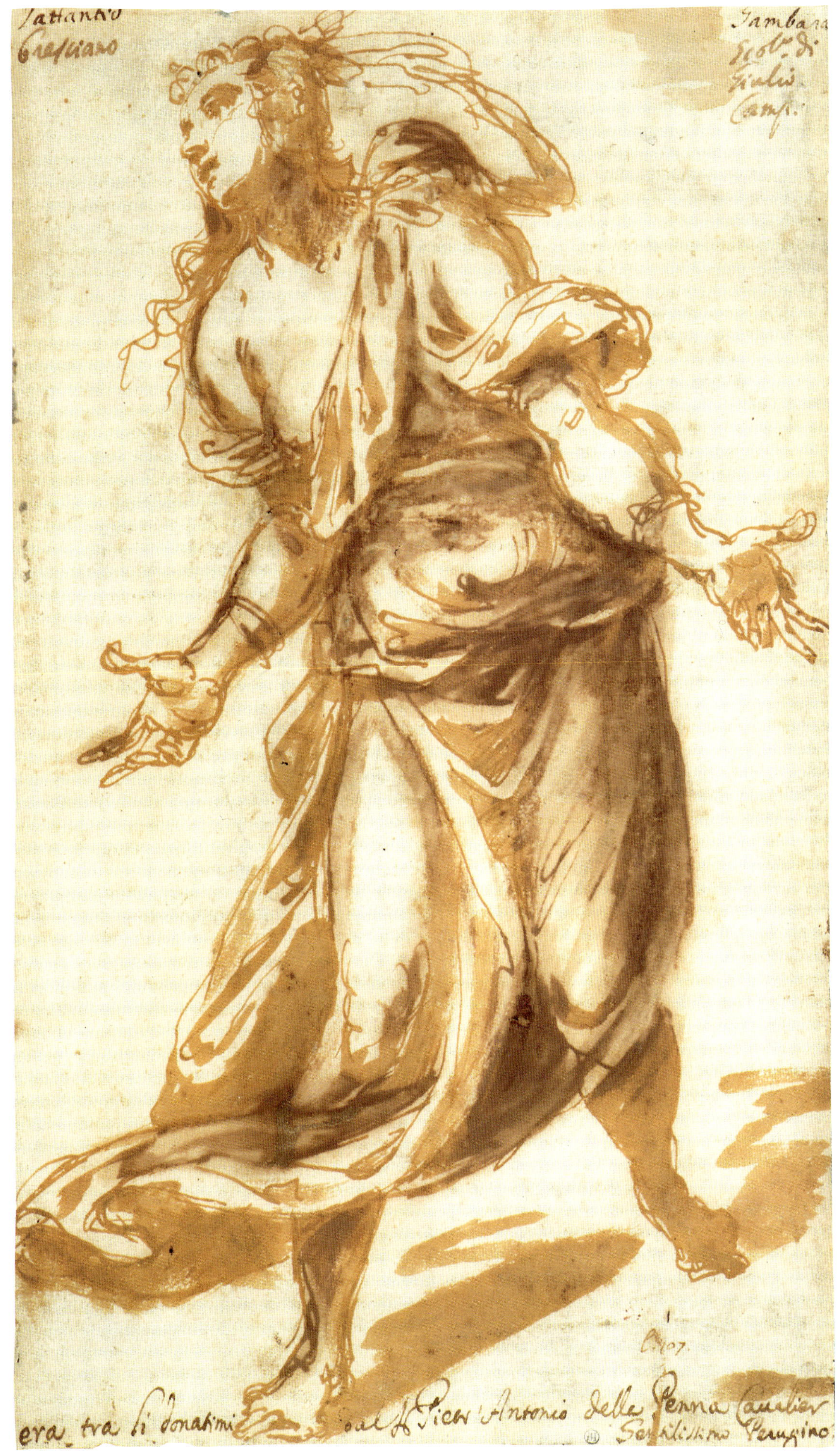

Recto

2. Bjurström (1979, cat. no. 137).

3. Rossi (1991; 128, cat. no. 153).

to the figures on which they depend, more indebted to an academic anatomy manual than to the study of a model. The closest stylistic parallel may be found in *Telemonic Male Nude with Three Graces* on its verso (private collection, Bergamo) published by Ruggeri as Maffei but rejected by Rossi. Related to the *Graces* is *Caritas* (no. NM 35/1973, Nationalmuseum, Stockholm), which is inscribed with Maffei's name.[2] By extension, an analogous handling of pen and wash may be seen in *Male Nude* (no. 1320, Albertina, Vienna), and the use of wash, particularly to suggest shadow behind the feet on the recto, is much like that found in *Three Male Nudes* (no. 5387, Departement des Arts Graphiques, Musée du Louvre, Paris). All of these male nudes might have formed a preliminary stage in the formulation of *Fall of the Rebel Angels* (Seminario Vescovile, Venegono Inferiore), although none of the cascading figures there is identical in pose. Somewhat closer are the drowning soldiers in *Passage of the Red Sea* (Convent of Santa Lucia, Vicenza), which Rossi has convincingly dated to just after 1650.[3] The Bergamo nude in particular shares graphic mannerisms with *Evangelist* (Riva no. 318, Museo Civico, Bassano del Grappa), which, in turn, is related to *Assumption of the Virgin* (Oratorio della Zitelle, Vicenza) of about 1649. Finally, since among the Odeon frescoes the figure of the Olympic Academy is so close to the theatrical woman in the present sketch, and the Bergamo nude might well be for a telemonic figure flanking the inscriptions in the Odeon frieze, we are tempted to see the Katalan sheet as part of Maffei's preparation for the Teatro Olimpico cycle. Commissioned in 1646, begun the following year, and paid for in 1649, these frescoes suggest, along with the evident echoes in just-subsequent works, a dating of ca. 1647 for this sheet.

Although this nervous, wiry sketch at first might seem irreconcilable with the fluid élan of Maffei's paintings, it is, in effect, the near hysteria of his visual fantasy that united them. Once recognized, this type of pen sketch will doubtless open the possibility of identifying still more of his studies, including, one hopes, some directly related to his paintings.

WRR

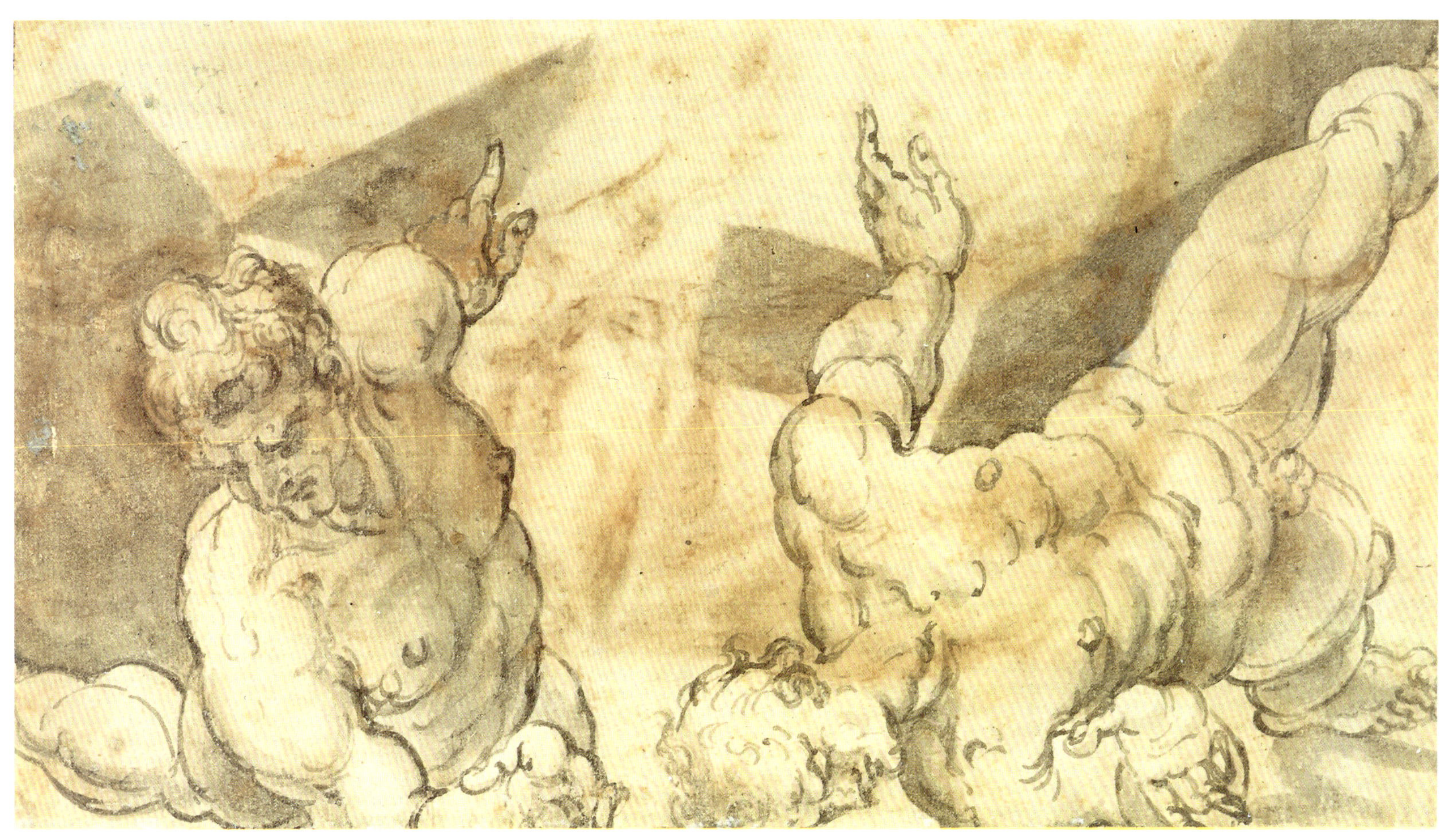

Verso

FRANCESCO MONTELATICI, called CECCO BRAVO

Florence, 1601–Innsbruck, 1661

47 Recto: *A Seated Nude Seen from the Back* Verso: *Studies of a Head and a Foot* (ca. 1653)

Red chalk (recto and verso); laid down (verso); watermark with bunch of grapes; brown stains

208 x 147 mm (8 1/8 x 5 1/2 in)

PROVENANCE: [Christie's, London, 8 April 1986, lot 61]

LITERATURE: unpublished

The pose in this drawing corresponds precisely to that of the man seated in the foreground with his back to the light in a compositional study of the *Circumcision* at the Uffizi (inv. 7148).[1] The Uffizi drawing, one of Cecco Bravo's most complete studies, was undoubtedly a preliminary design for an otherwise undocumented painting, presumably lost. The drawing has been regularly exhibited over the past few years.[2] It was executed in red and black chalk, whereas the Florentine artist's preferred medium for studies of individual figures, like this seated nude, was light-colored red chalk alone.

At least two other individual studies for the *Circumcision* have already been identified: one for the young man seen from behind in the foreground on the left (inv. 10705 F, Uffizi),[3] and the other for the head of the seated young woman holding a baby in the lower right-hand corner (inv. C 71/2110, Graphische Sammlung, Staatsgalerie, Stuttgart).[4] The studies of a head and a foot on the reverse side of this drawing were preparatory sketches for the young man on the left of the Uffizi study. Cecco Bravo painstakingly worked out each part of the composition, and the various studies have the same high-strung, capricious style in common. They also bear the mark of chiaroscuro, particularly emphasized in the Uffizi drawing of the composition in its entirety, in which fluid forms dissolve into an unreal atmosphere. In the individual studies, the draftsman seeks rather to define the structure of these forms, building them up with much more rigor. Cecco Bravo copied drawings by Pontormo (invs. 1020–1023, Louvre, Paris)[5], and his affinity with the Florentine master's mannerist vision shines through here.

The proposed date of 1653 for the Uffizi *Circumcision*,[6] if accepted, would imply that this seated nude is a work of Cecco Bravo's fully mature period, during which his painting was suffused with Venetian color. His work as a draftsman is remarkable both for its quality and its abundance, but it is difficult to trace its evolution. Highly prized by collectors (Francesco Maria Niccolò Gabburri, Filippo Baldinucci), his large sheets of "dreams," whose subject matter remains mysterious for lack of an iconographic key to interpret them, are in a class apart, with no equivalent among the art works of his contemporaries.

CMG

1. Masetti (1962; 110 n. 20, fig. 74).

2. Cantelli (1970; 18, cat. no. 6); Barsanti (1986–87; 2:309–12, cat. no. 2.276).

3. Masetti, op. cit.

4. Thiem (1977, cat. no. 191).

5. Cox-Rearick (1964; 1:405, cat. nos. A 327 to A 330).

6. Barsanti, op. cit., 2:312.

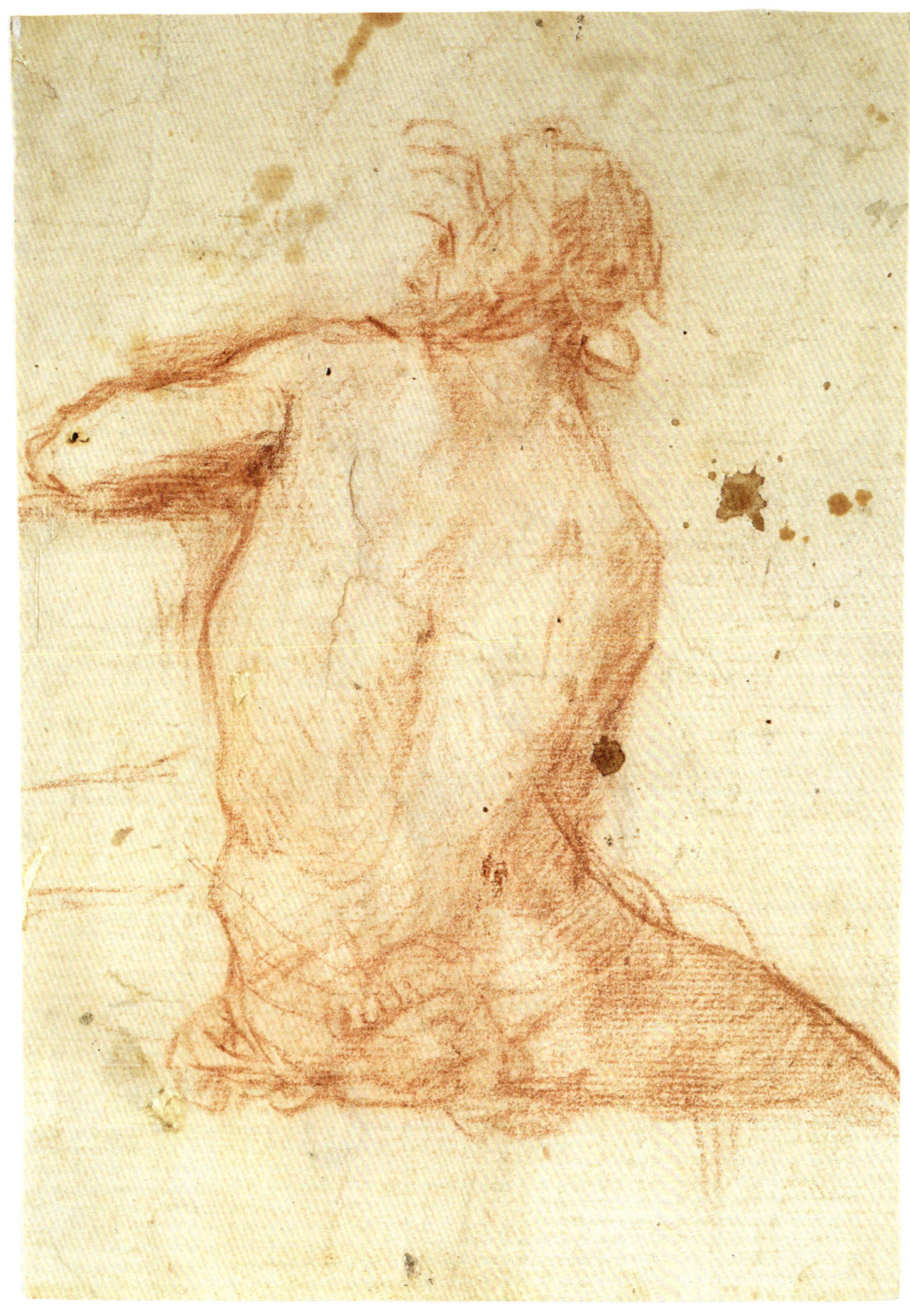

BALDASSARE FRANCHESCHINI, called VOLTERRANO
Volterra, 1611–Florence, 1689

48 Recto: *Study for a Crucifix*
Verso: *Study for a Male Figure and Study for the Drapery over the Left Forearm of a Standing Figure*

Red chalk (recto); black chalk, heightened with white (verso); the recto inscribed at lower right in pen and ink, *Volterrano*, and in graphite, *54*; the verso inscribed at lower left, *21*; some creases; at the lower right of the verso a stain of yellow paint

392 x 240 mm (15 7/16 x 9 7/16 in)

PROVENANCE: [Marcello Aldega and Margot Gordon, 1986]

LITERATURE: unpublished

1. *Stix and Fröhlich-Bum (1932, cat. no. 634).*

2. *Ewald (1973; 282, fig. 21 and 283).*

This drawing has been connected to a drawing in the Albertina, Vienna showing the crucifix being held up to a kneeling cleric for veneration.[1] However, the Albertina drawing was made in preparation for a composition and is not detailed enough to verify if the connection is undoubtedly right. The crucifixes are both seen from the same angle, but while the cross is covered from the knees downward in the Albertina composition, it is fully represented in the Katalan drawing. In a study such as this one, the artist could either draw the whole corpus or limit himself to studying only those parts which would appear in the painting, since the compositional problems would have been solved before work on the studies began.

The upper study on the verso was believed to be preparatory for the painting, *Portrait of a Gentleman*, formerly in the collection of Morris I. Kaplan and sold by Sotheby's on 12 June 1968, lot 45, as seventeenth-century Genoese School. It was attributed to Volterrano by Gerhard Ewald in 1973.[2] The similarities between the drawing and painting, particularly in the posture, are striking. However, the facial character of the more youthful man in the Katalan drawing, and the way the drapery is bound in a big knot over his right shoulder, make him look rather like a Christian warrior saint than like the figure in the Kaplan portrait. The lower study has not been connected thus far.

PD

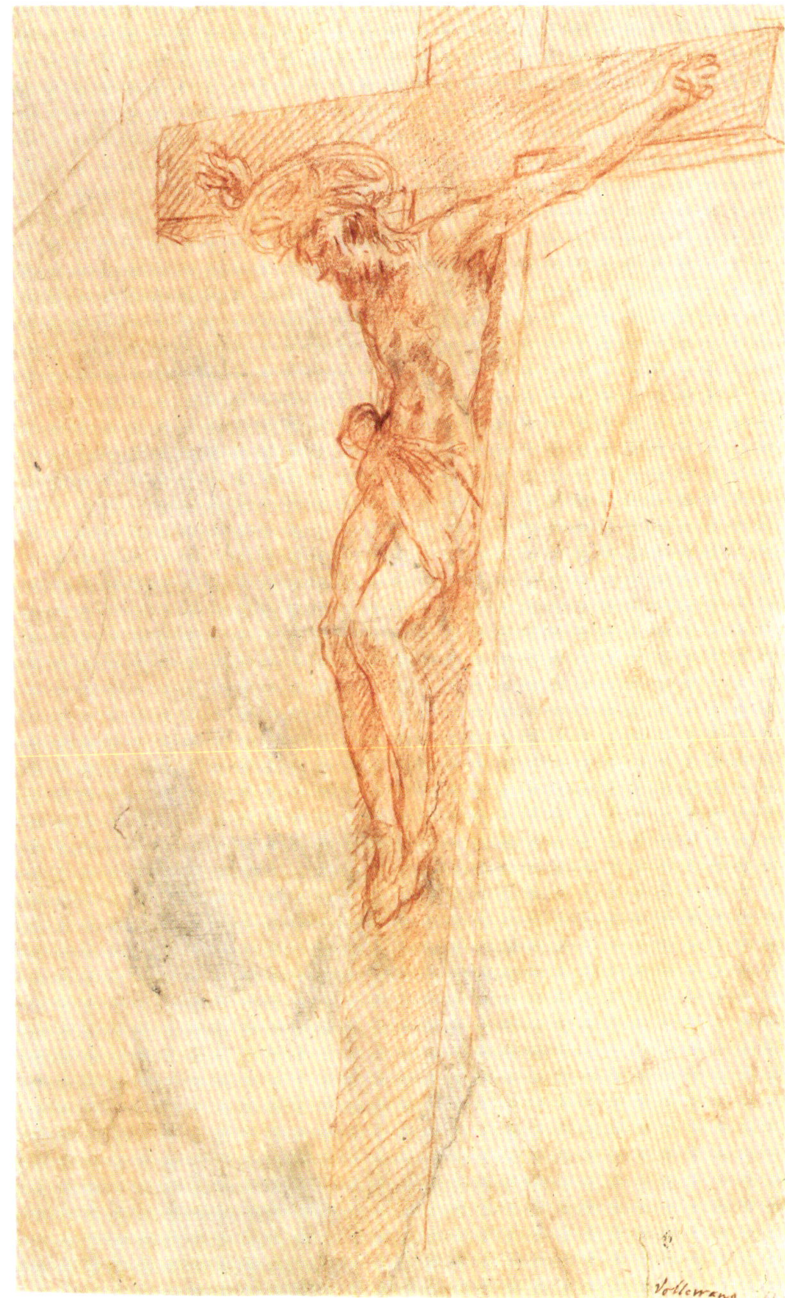

Recto

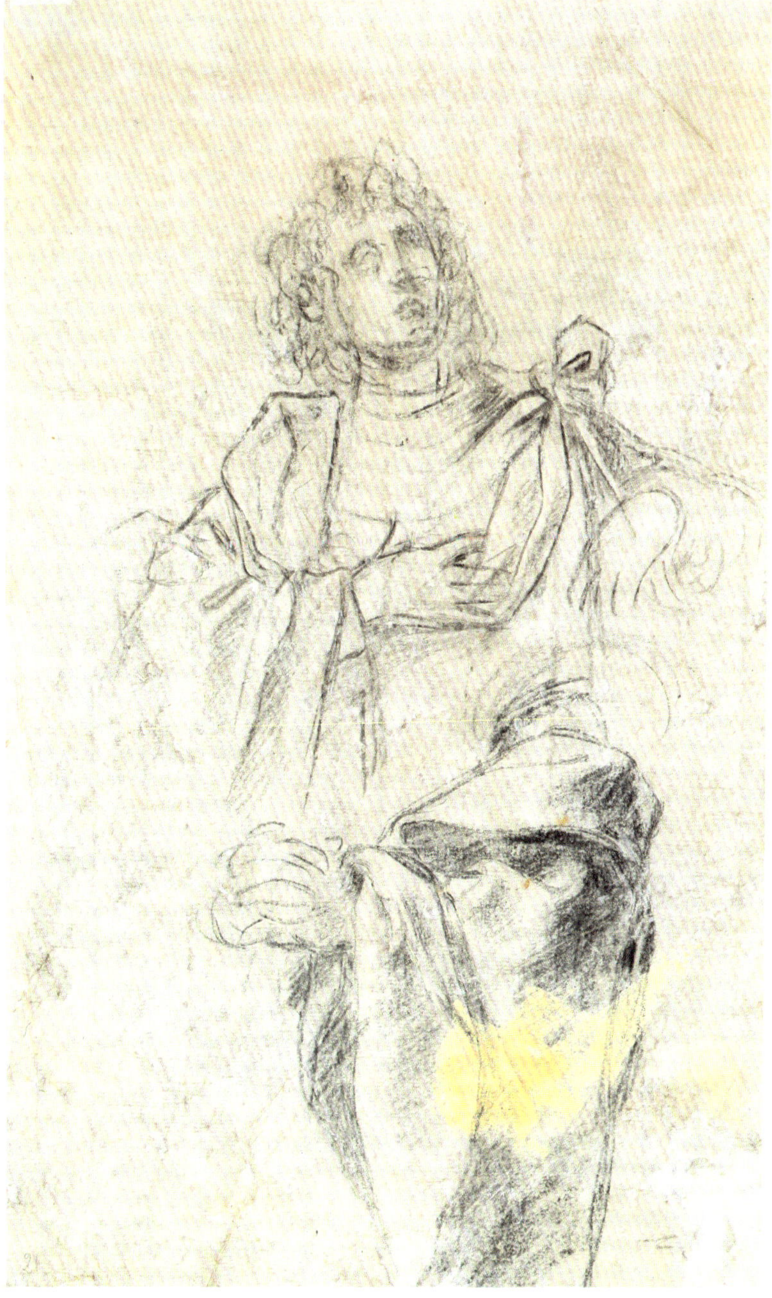
Verso

Salvator Rosa

Arenella, 1615–Rome, 1673

49 a, b

49a Study for the Crucifixion of Polycrates (ca. 1662)

Pen and black ink, with corrections in white, on paper with a grayish patina or a grounding; approximately two-thirds of the lower left margin of paper is a later addition; laid down; a watermark in the form of a small circle could be in the drawing paper or in the backing; some gray foxing

131 x 68 mm (5 5/32 x 2 21/32 in)

49b Study for the Crucifixion of Polycrates (ca. 1662)

Pen and dark brown ink, brown wash on similar paper as described above, in similar condition

176 x 140 mm (6 15/16 x 5 1/2 in); the lower half of the right margin of paper is a later addition; a hole under Polycrates's right foot is repaired

Provenance: [Kate Ganz, London, 1986]

Literature: Ganz 1984, cat. nos. 25 and 26

1. Mahoney (1977, 2:cat. no. 65.1, inv. 6598 S).

2.Wallace (1979, 281).

3. Mahoney (1977, 1:557).

Both drawings are preparatory for Rosa's depictions, both entitled *The Crucifixion of Polycrates*. One of these is the painting in the Art Institute of Chicago, and the other a monumental print (Bartsch 10; Wallace 111) and its *delineatio*—a drawing in mirror image, which served as a *cartoncino* for the engraving—in the Uffizi, Florence.[1]

The smaller drawing (49a) corresponds in many regards with the figure of the crucified tyrant of Samos in its *delineatio*. The structure of the tree to which he is bound and the position of the body are basically the same, the loin cloth moves differently, but its role is of the same importance in the drawing and the printed version.

The larger drawing (49b), on the other hand, is extremely close to the painting. The tree is not growing vertically as in the print, but obliquely, and its structure is richer. Polycrates is crucified with his right knee raised, not his left, as in the drawing for the print. Tree and figure correspond fairly exactly with the painted execution; a major difference is only the lack of the loin cloth in the drawing. The attitudes of the two spectators, which Rosa outlined at the right of the tyrant and on the same level with him, but looking upward and so indicating their intended position beneath the crucified man, represent a stage that could be developed into both the print and the painting. Although drawn full-length in the Katalan sheet, the duo is probably preparatory for the onlookers half overcut by the slope on which the cruel scene takes place. In the painting the two men are separated, but while the one on the right is looking up, the other watches him, as he does in the drawing; in the print, both of them are positioned as in the drawing, but both look up.

Paper, media, and style of both drawings are the same. There is no need to declare one of them to be preparatory for the print, the other for the drawing. Both versions of the tyrant have been developed simultaneously. The question of the priority of the print or painting can therefore not be answered by an analysis of these drawings. The common opinion is that the painting is later than the print.[2] According to Mahoney, late in 1661 and through the first half of 1662, Rosa was working on etchings for which he, in part, returned to themes and compositions of earlier paintings, "refreshing his memory from sketches he had given previously to Ricciardi and which he borrowed back in December 1661."[3] The Uffizi drawing has been identified as one of these, being returned to Ricciardi in March 1662. This assumption is not convincing, because this sheet is made with the engraving in mind, as can be pointed out by the free space at center of the lower margin, destined for the inscription in the print, and by the swords borne at the right side, which would be correct only when reversed. On other drawings for *The Crucifixion of Polycrates*, see Mahoney (1977, 2:cat. nos. 65.2–65.6).

Both the print and the painting belong together with representations (the same size) of *The Death*

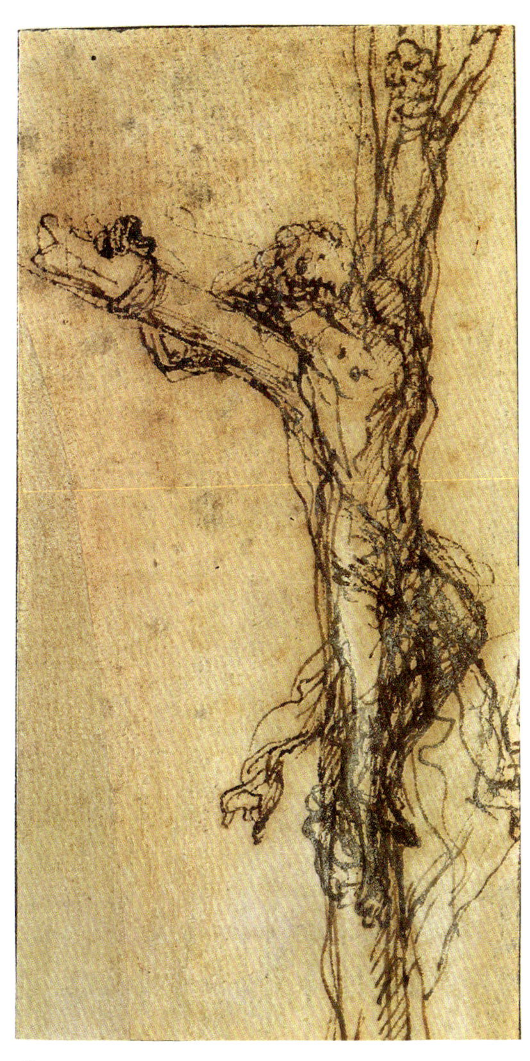

49a

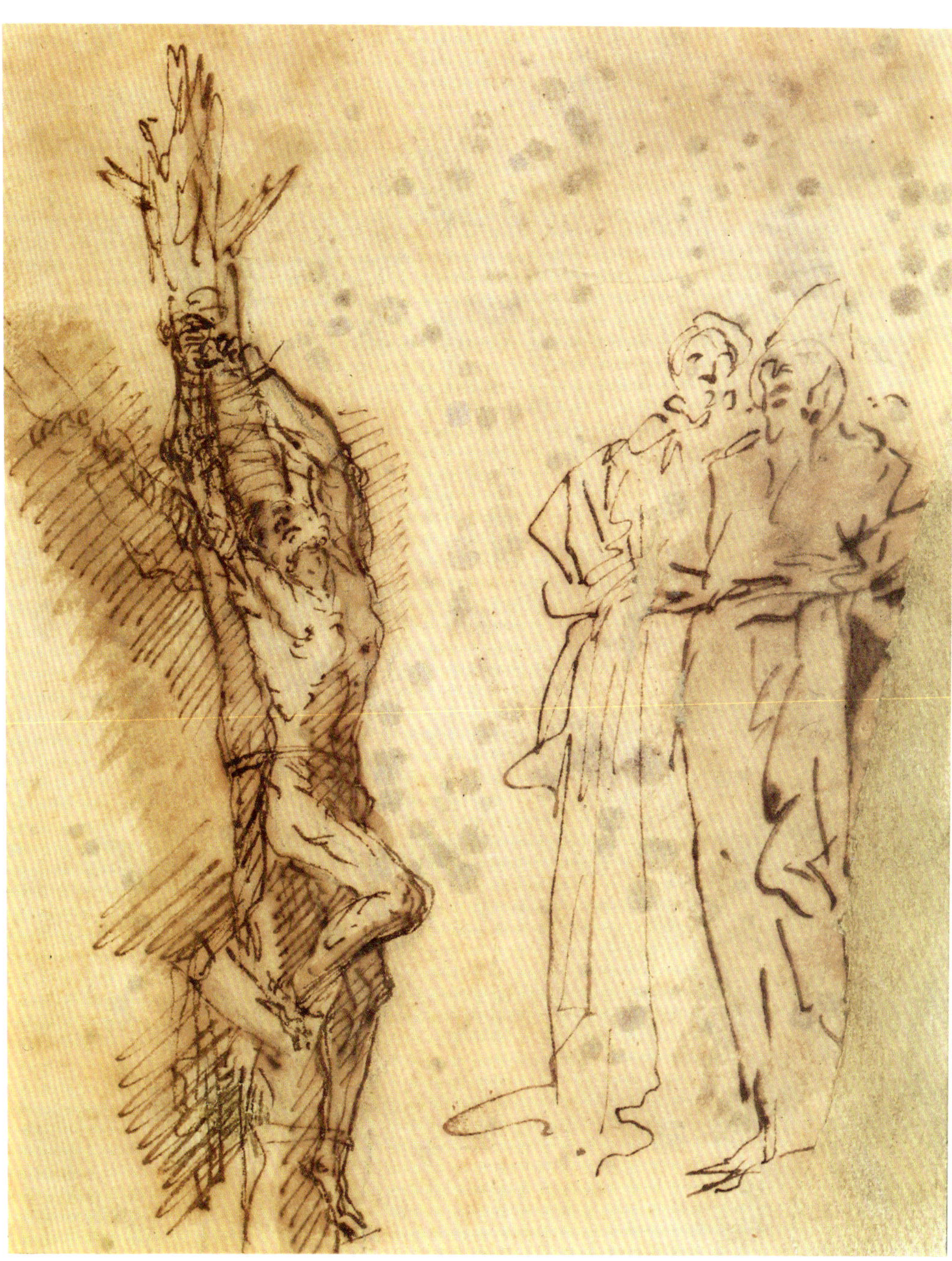

49b

of Regulus. This juxtaposition of the Greek tyrant Polycrates, who was lured to Milet and crucified around 522 B.C., with the heroic Roman general of the First Punic War (consul in 267 and 256 B.C.) who was tortured to death for refusing to break his word to the enemy, may have been made by Salvator Rosa, who was a learned man, as an allusion to Plutarch's *Lives of Greek and Roman Statesmen and Heroes*, in which, however, the lives of neither is described.

PD

GIACINTO GIMIGNANI

Pistoia, 1611–Rome, 1681

50 *Horatius Slaying his Sister Horatia* (ca. 1650)

Black chalk, pen, and brown ink, gray wash heightened with white body color; inscribed by the artist, *Oratio con i curatii*

231 x 368 mm (9 1/4 x 14 1/2 in)

PROVENANCE: first earl of Leicester, his mount with the attribution *Geminianino* in a hand formerly identified as that of William Kent; by descent; Viscount Coke and the Trustees of The Holkham Settled Estates; [Christie's, London, 2 July 1991, lot 41]

LITERATURE: Domenico Cortese 1969, 198–99; Pace 1973, 210, cat. no. 233; Popham and Lloyd 1986, cat. no. 130; Sciolla 1992, 154

EXHIBITIONS: *Old Master Drawings from the Collection of the Earl of Leicester,* Arts Council, London, 1948, cat. no. 14; *Old Master Drawings from Holkham,* Thomas Agnew and Sons, Ltd., London, 1977, cat. no. 35; *Old Master Drawings from Holkham Hall*, Ashmolean Museum, Oxford, 1988 (no catalogue)

1. I am grateful to Dr. Pace for responding to my inquiries.

2. Pace (1973; 159–60, cat. no. 65). Dr. Pace kindly provided me with a photocopy of the ceiling and other comparative material.

3. Briganti (1962, 250–51).

4. Rensi Albums (Band 16, cat. no. 11); pen and brown ink and wash with white body color, 471 x 268 mm (18 7/8 x 10 3/4 in).

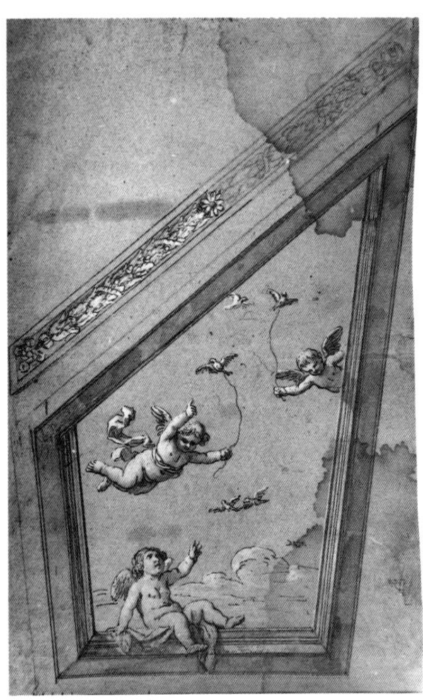

Fig. 12: Giacinto Gimignani, *Putti Playing with Doves*, Museum der Bildenden Künste, Leipzig

This highly finished drawing, with its complex framing elements, has so far not been connected with any of Giacinto Gimignani's recorded commissions. Christopher Lloyd proposed a connection with the Camera delle Donne Illustri in the Palazzo Doria Pamphili in Rome, finished in 1653, but the subjects used there are all from the Old Testament. Furthermore, the slaying of Horatia by Horatius is hardly an example of illustrious female behavior. Ursula Fischer Pace believes that this drawing is connected with a hitherto unidentified decorative commission, perhaps outside Rome, that has escaped the attention of his biographers.[1]

While finished composition drawings using white body color and dark washes with pen and ink on toned paper are typical of Giacinto Gimignani, the complexity of the framing elements in this drawing is unique in his surviving graphic work. These frames would have been much more elaborate than those he painted around his narrative scenes in the Palazzo Pamphili in the Piazza Navona, and are contained within a clean trapezoid unlike his only other known decorative frescoes, the ceiling in the Palazzo Niccolini, Florence, painted in 1653–54.[2] There, cartouches, garlands, shells, and masks embroider the edge of the frame and carry it into the surrounding ceiling area. The Katalan drawing's design is too elaborate and too precise not to have been made with a particular commission in mind. The logical candidate is the Gallery of the Palazzo Pamphili in the Piazza Navona, which Pietro da Cortona painted in 1651–54.[3] Gimignani may have hoped, as he completed his frieze in an adjacent room in 1648, that he might be given the opportunity to decorate the galleria with scenes from Roman history, and prepared this drawing for the Pamphili family to show them what he was capable of doing. A large drawing in Leipzig (Fig. 12) shows an irregular trapezoid in which putti play with doves in the open sky seen through the frame, whose molding matches that just visible in the upper left of the Katalan drawing.[4] Significantly, both frames contain an open flower whose petals are shaped like those of a lily, a Pamphili symbol, as is the dove. Thus a Pamphili connection for both drawings is possible. The galleria seems the only potential commission likely to have inspired Gimignani to such an elaborate scheme combining passages of *quadratura* and illusionistic glimpses of the sky.

The subject (from Livy, 1.23–24) is a grim sequel to the event made famous by J.-L. David's *Oath of the Horatii*. Horatius, the only survivor of the fight for control of Rome between the sons of the Horatii and Curiatii, is slaying his sister, who, he has just learned, was to marry one of the slain Curiatii. He in turn was almost executed for this act of violence, but was given a reprieve after his father pleaded for his life. The unusual subject must have been proposed by the prospective patron. Could this be a reference to Prince Camillo Pamphili, the only nephew of Pope Innocent X, who, after being made a cardinal, resigned to get married, and was exiled from Rome by his uncle (and his manipulative sister-in-law, Donna Olimpia Maida Ichini, who wanted no female rivals at the papal court)? Was the story intended as some kind of warning to a woman who dared to become involved with one of Rome's ruling families? At all events, by the fall of 1651, Cortona was engaged on the project, and the subjects chosen were taken

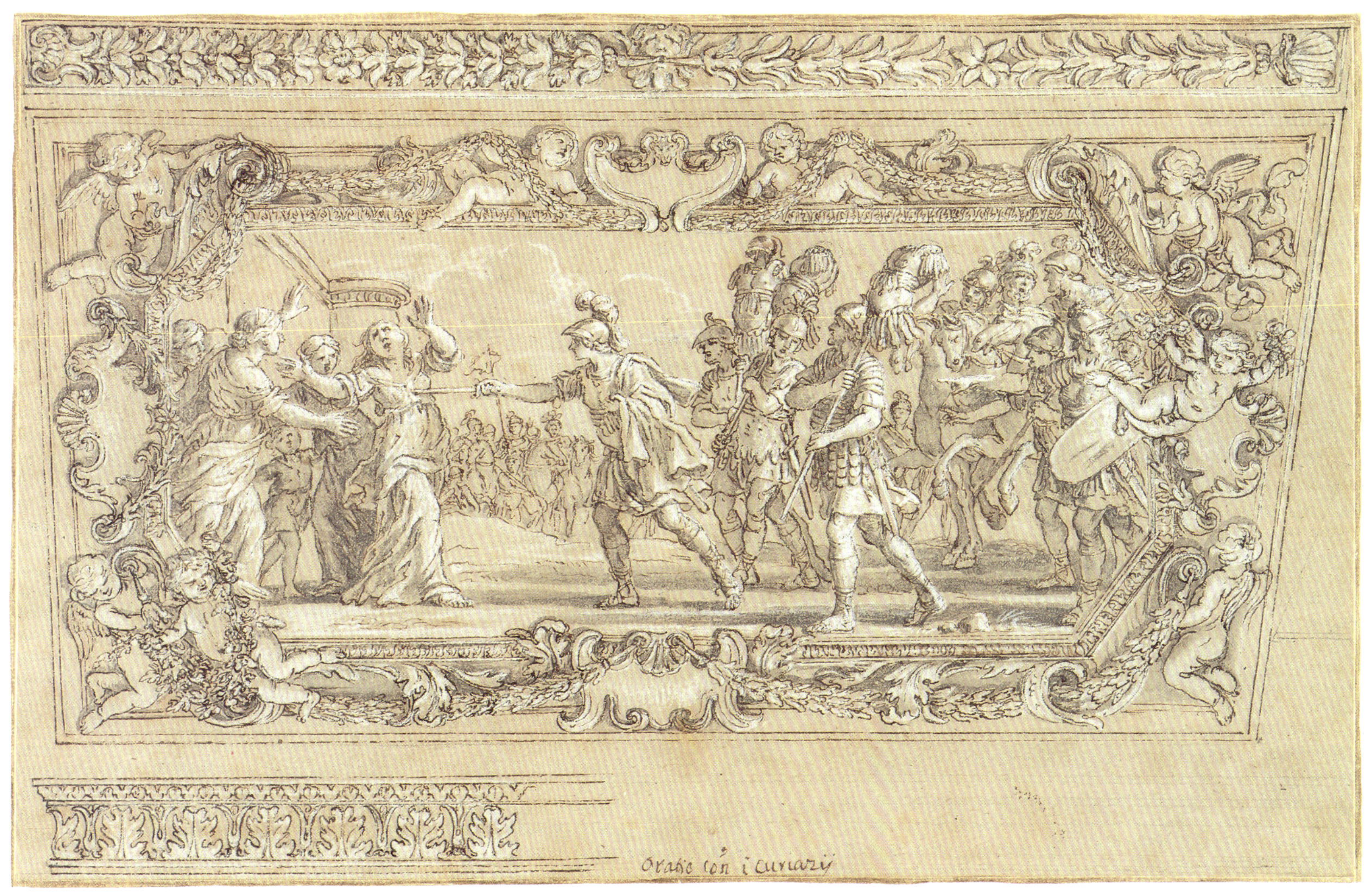

exclusively from Virgil's *Aeneid*. The lower edges of his main narrative scenes have a border whose proportions resemble those of Gimignani's drawing, and rosette-lilies like those in his borders can be found in the decoration of Cortona's scheme as well. This proposal must remain hypothetical, but it will have served its purpose if it provokes someone else to come up with a better explanation.

ASH

Domenico Maria Canuti

Bologna, 1626–Rome, 1684

51 *Head of a Bearded Man Looking Upwards to the Right* (ca. 1677)

Black, red, and white chalk on gray-blue paper

283 x 193 mm (10 1/8 x 6 5/8 in)

Provenance: [Marcello Aldega and Margot Gordon, New York, 1986, as attributed to Giacomo Cavedone]

Literature: unpublished

1. Stagni (1988; 192–93, figs. 40S–V).

2. Stagni (1988, 92ff.).

When this drawing appeared on the New York art market some years ago, it was attributed to the Bolognese painter Giacomo Cavedone (1577–1660). The present attribution to Canuti is due to the resemblance in type to the heads of Canuti's *Fathers of the Church*, painted in monochrome in the library of the Olivetan monastery of S. Michele in Bosco, Bologna,[1] and it seems likely that the drawing was indeed made in that connection. Once pointed out, Canuti's authorship seems obvious. Many technical and stylistic similarities exist between this fine study and his undoubtedly authentic figure studies in chalk, some drawn in three colors, like this example. The echoes of Guercino's manner, seen in the treatment of light and in the rhythmic forms of the fluffy beard and hair, are also consistent with Canuti's hand.

Canuti painted the library of S. Michele in Bosco, together with the *quadratura* painter Enrico Haffner, in 1677–84.[2] The frescoes, the masterpiece of Canuti's late period, occupy all three rooms of the library. The four figures of the *Fathers of the Church*, rendered as feigned sculptures standing on ornamental brackets, appear on the walls of the third and last room, originally planned to house mathematical instruments and other scientific gadgets.

By specializing in large-scale decorative painting of the high baroque style and by spending so much of his career outside his native city, Canuti stands a little apart from his Bolognese contemporaries. Nevertheless, he also worked extensively in Bologna and was patronized by, among others, Taddeo Pepoli, who was abbot-general of the congregation of Olivetans in 1651–54 and 1669–72 and who gained a number of commissions for the painter, including that in S. Michele in Bosco.

NT

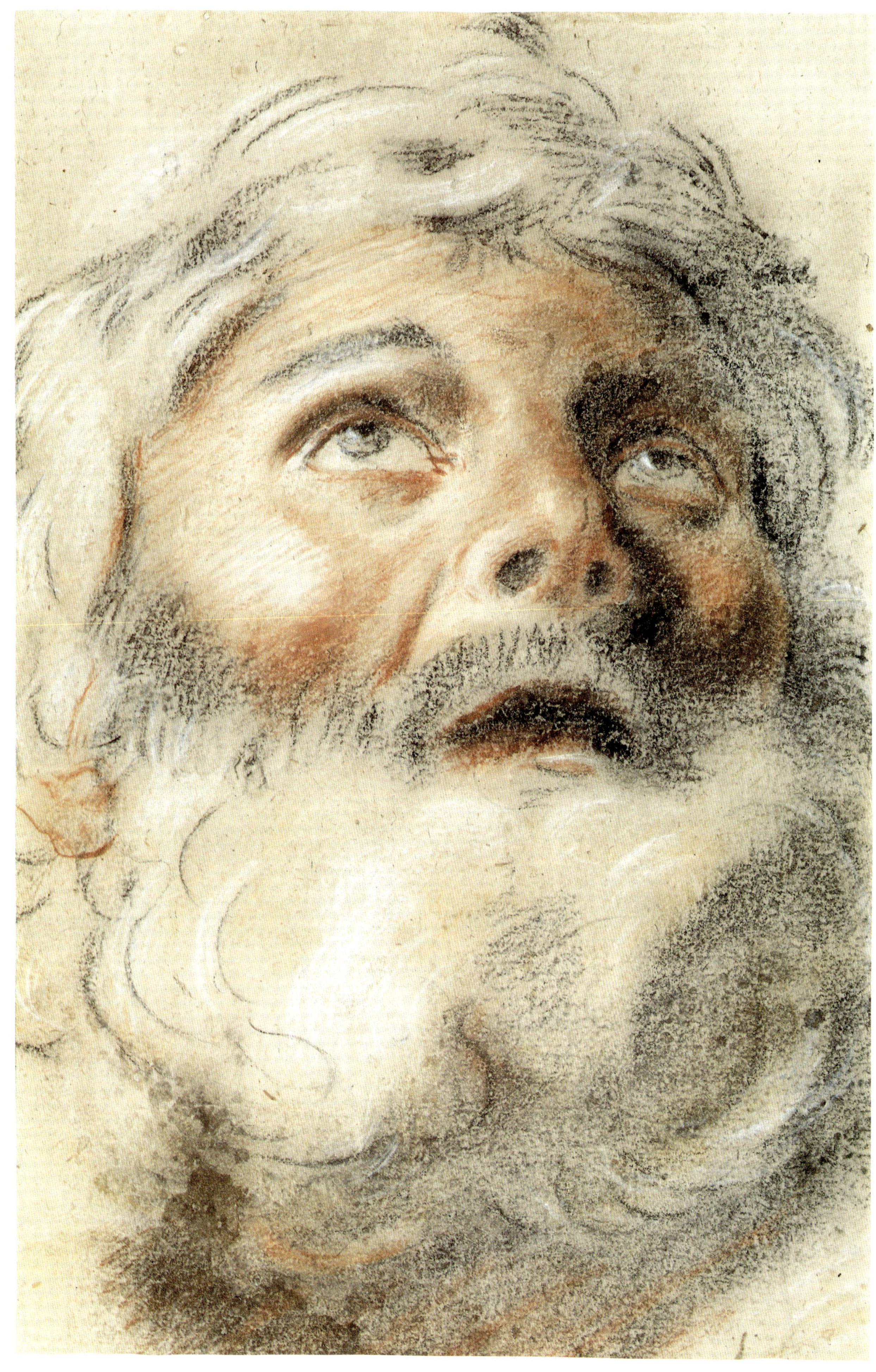

Valerio Castello

Genoa, 1624/25–Genoa, 1659

52 ### Recto: *The Sacking of a Church* Verso: *Head of a Soldier*

Brush drawing in a blue-green and gray wash over black chalk; squared in black chalk; the verso in black chalk

210 x 158 mm (8 1/4 x 5 3/16 in)

Provenance: [Yvonne Tan Bunzl, 1987]

Literature: unpublished

1. Invs. 1950-11-11-55 and 1950-11-11-54. See Newcome (1975; 29–31, 36 n. 12, and fig. 14); and Royalton-Kisch (1982, 132ff.) respectively.

The attribution to Valerio Castello was first proposed by this writer on the strength of the drawing's resemblance to two examples in the British Museum, both of which are studies for his frescoes in the now-almost-completely-destroyed church of S. Maria in Passione, Genoa.[1] The two British Museum drawings were first attributed to the painter by Philip Pouncey, who was, however, unaware of their connection with this decoration, and Pouncey later orally endorsed the attribution to Castello of the present sheet.

The subject remains unclear. A soldier wearing a helmet and armor directs the plundering of a sacred building, presumably a church, while two robed figures on the left of the composition, presumably priests, plead with him. Like the two British Museum drawings, the sheet has been squared for transfer, indicating that the Katalan drawing, too, was probably intended for a painting. The figure types, the placing of a group within an architectural setting, and many other stylistic features are the same as the British Museum drawings.

The short-lived Castello was one of the most talented painters of the Genoese baroque period. His style owed much to the Venetians and to the Flemish painters Rubens and Van Dyck, both of whom had visited Genoa, as well as to the sixteenth-century tradition of Genoese painting. His paintings display a vibrancy of color and a dynamism of composition that are qualities maintained in his drawings.

NT

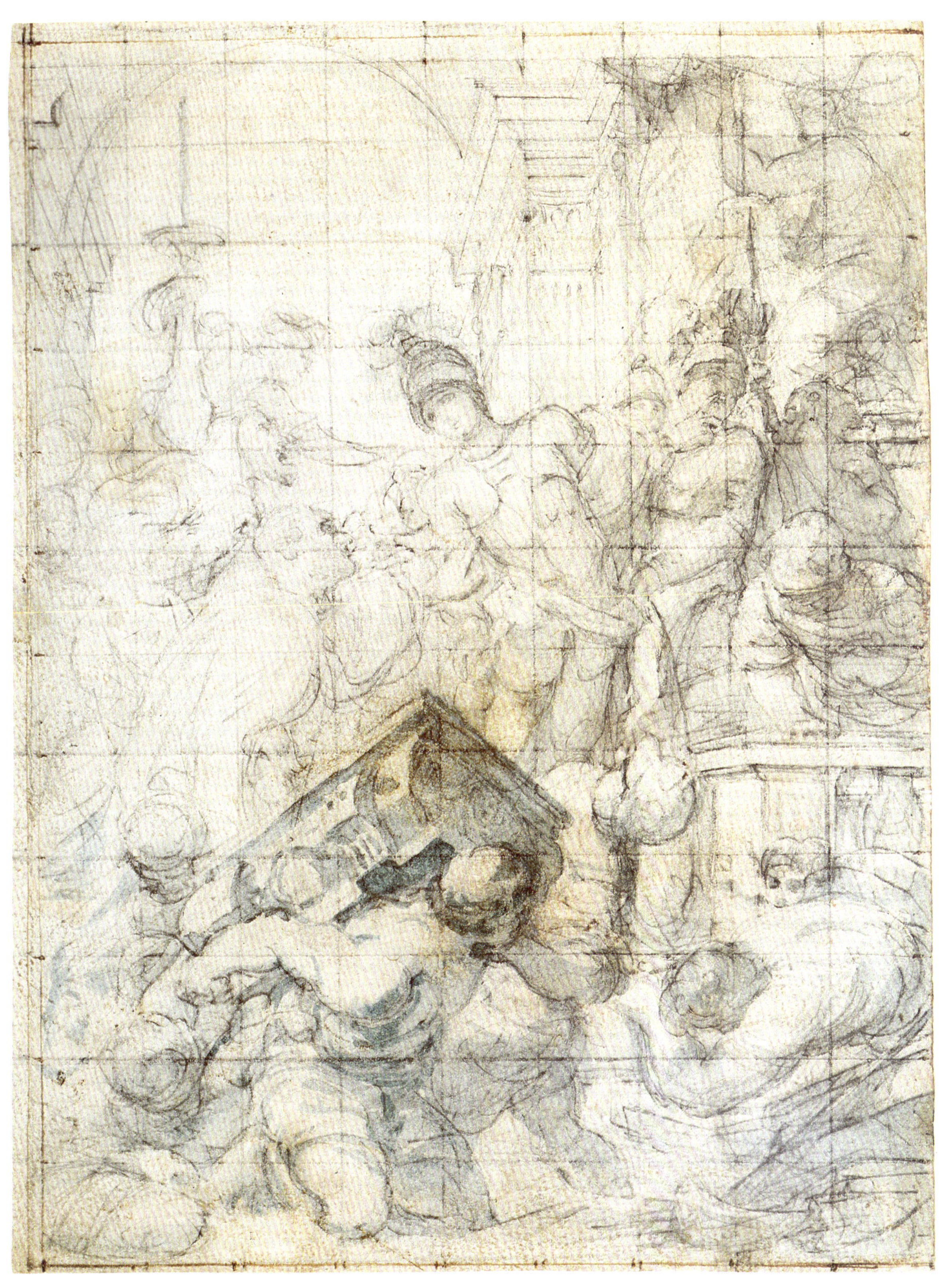

Carlo Maratti

Camerano, 1625–Rome, 1713

53 Recto: *The Emperor Augustus Closing the Doors of the Temple of Janus (The Peace of Augustus)* Verso: *Girl Standing* (ca. 1655)

Red chalk and red wash; the verso in black chalk; inscribed in brown ink in the lower right corner of the recto, *Carlo Maratti*; inscribed in another hand, in the lower center of the verso, *Carlo Marati* [sic] *Z17* (this last is perhaps an early price for the drawing, *17 zecchini*); the collector's mark, *HD*, stamped in the lower right corner is that of the former owner

232 x 152 mm (8 1/8 x 4 15/16 in)

Provenance: Harold A. E. Day; [Sotheby's, London, 6 December 1987, lot 30, as follower of Carlo Maratti]

Literature: unpublished

Although the drawing was sold in 1987 as the work of a follower, the suggestion that it could be by Maratti himself was proposed independently by this writer, Peter Dreyer, and Timothy Clifford. The attribution was confirmed with the subsequent discovery by me[1] that the sheet is a study, with numerous differences, for the picture of the subject in the Musée des Beaux-Arts, Lille.[2] Maratti's *Emperor Augustus Closing the Doors of the Temple Janus (The Peace of Augustus)*, which was painted in Rome in 1655–57 on the commission of Louis-Phélypeaux de La Vrillière, was one of a series of canvases illustrating scenes from Greek and Roman history that was ordered for the decoration of the gallery of the Hôtel de La Vrillière, Paris. Other artists who supplied paintings for this decorative scheme were Guercino (q.v.), Pietro da Cortona (1596–1669), Nicolas Poussin (1594–1665), and Alessandro Turchi (1578–1649); Guido Reni's *Abduction of Helen* (Louvre, Paris), which also formed part of the decoration, but was bought, not commissioned for the gallery.

The subject for the present drawing is taken from the life of Augustus: Peace answers the emperor's sacrifice by descending from the heavens offering an olive branch; she shuts the doors of the Temple of Janus, appeasing War with the spoils of his enemies. In the drawing, Peace appears on a cloud at upper right, holding the branch forward in her extended right hand, while in the left background priests control the forces of War by holding back the military standards; in the painting she appears in the sky at left, while the figures in the left foreground remove the accouterments of War.

In style, the drawing compares especially well with that of Maratti's *Time Ferrying the Four Seasons across the River Styx*, in the Musei Civici e Gallerie d'Arte, Reggio Emilia, similarly executed in red chalk and wash, though with the addition of some white heightening.[3] The Reggio Emilia drawing is a study for the decoration of a night clock that was made by Giuseppe Campini and presented to Louis XIV by Cardinal Antonio Barberini.[4] The clock was shown to Bernini in 1665 on his visit to France, though it must have been made before that date.

Maratti, who was one of the most successful and prolific painters of his day, continued the baroque classicism developed by his master, Andrea Sacchi, and with it his master's disciplined approach to drawing and painting. Indeed, the standing girl seen on the verso of the Katalan drawing agrees in type with the figures of the congregation in Sacchi's *Urban VIII Visiting the Gesù on October 2, 1639* (Museo di Roma, Rome), painted in 1641–42.[5] The roots of this academic approach lay in the work of Annibale Carracci (1560–1609); in his turn, Maratti passed on the same method to his numerous pupils and followers.

NT

1. Letter from Nicholas Turner to Jak Katalan, 14 August 1989.

2. Brejon de Lavergnée and Volle (1988–89, cat. no. 98).

3. Stock and Scrase (1985, cat. no. 33).

4. Gonzales-Palacios and Garstang (1983, cat. no. 20).

5. Harris (1977; cat. no. 63, fig. 130).

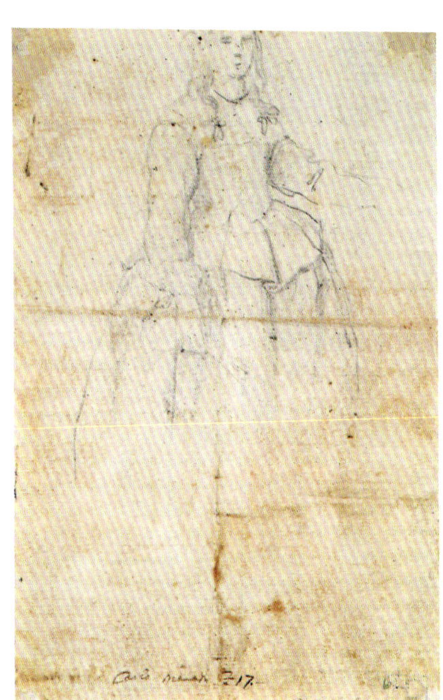

Verso

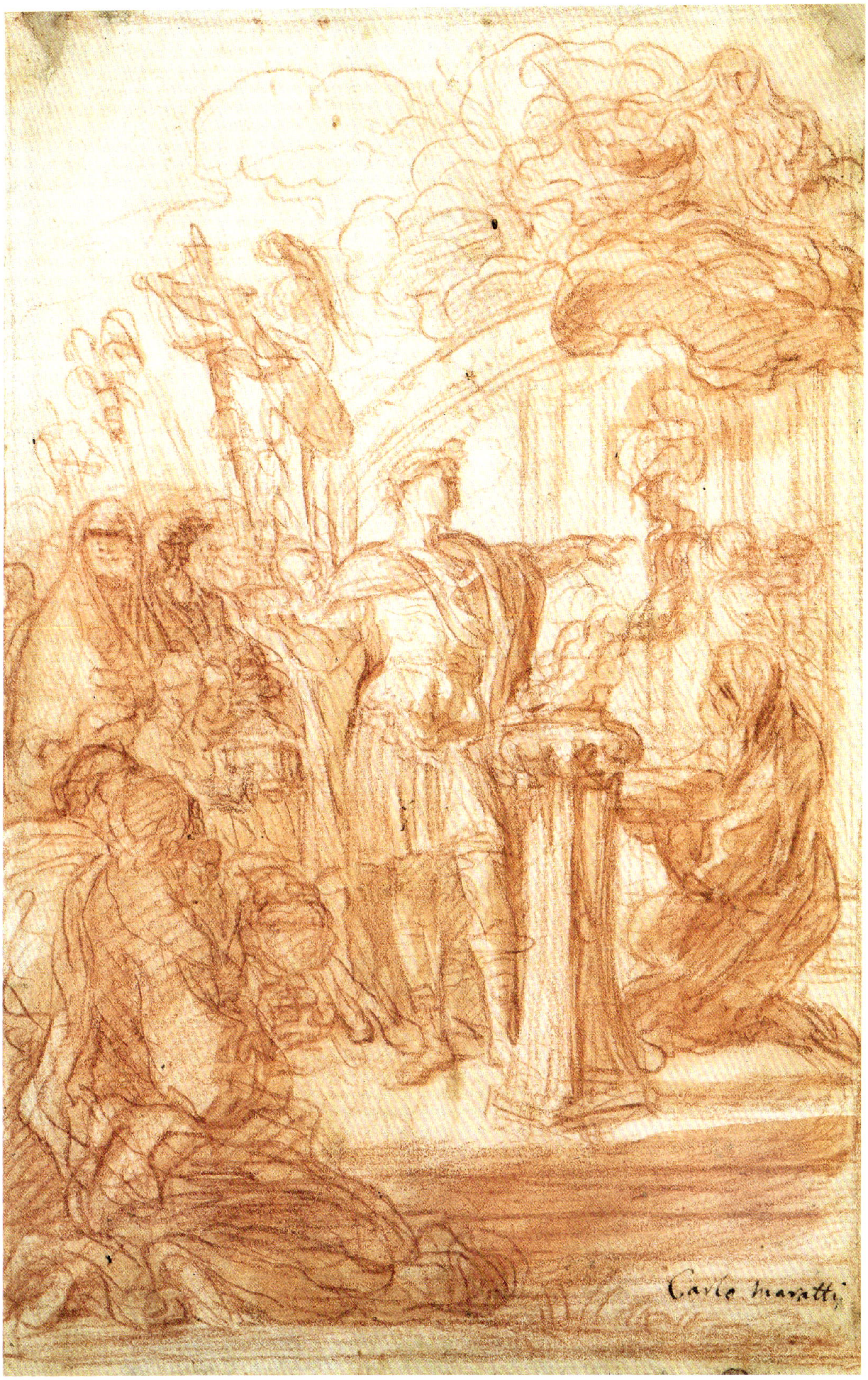

Recto

Guglielmo Cortese

St. Hippolyte, 1628–Rome, 1679

54 *Landscape with St. Eustace* (1650–60)

Pen and brown ink on cream paper

155 x 210 mm (6 1/4 x 8 1/2 in)

Provenance: [Marcello Aldega and Margot Gordon, Rome and New York, 1986, as by Mola]

Literature: Aldega and Gordon 1986, cat. no. 7, as by Mola; Harris 1992, 217, as by Cortese

Most of the more than six hundred drawings by Guglielmo Cortese preserved in Düsseldorf and Rome are red-chalk figure and drapery studies; pen-and-ink composition studies form a small percentage of these holdings.[1] As a result, his pen drawing style still remains hard to grasp and has been confused with that of contemporaries, above all with the drawings of the better-known Pier Francesco Mola (1612–66). In the case of the exhibited drawing, Marcello Aldega compared it with two brush-tip drawings in Düsseldorf attributed to Mola by Dieter Graf.[2] Both are exceptionally bold brush-tip drawings with little pen work; neither connect clearly with a documented or generally accepted painting by Mola. They cannot therefore be used to establish that the *Vision of St. Eustace* is by Mola.

The schematic depiction of the figure with a few short lines and bold blocks of wash can be found in several Cortese ink drawings connected with documented commissions, for example his study for the apostles in his *Assunta* altarpiece in Ariccia.[3] A study in Rome for an *Adoration of the Shepherds* has similar figures and also employs bold patches of dark wash, abrupt pen contours, and bare paper to create a powerful composition.[4] Harder to parallel is the landscape setting, for few of Cortese's surviving drawings contain any landscape elements. Still, the few pen strokes used to block out foliage resemble those in a pen drawing without wash in Rome for a *Holy Family* composition, and the broad, horizontal lines of wash in the foreground and quickly scratched-out tree forms in the distance also occur in a more carefully drawn composition drawing of a *Flight into Egypt* in Düsseldorf.[5] In none of these drawings does Cortese use any red chalk, whereas Mola frequently mixes chalk and ink in his composition drawings. Mola's contour lines are also more fluid and continuous and far less schematic than those of Cortese, and his wash is not so dark.[6] Nevertheless, confusion between them is understandable and will persist until a study of Cortese's ink drawings defines this aspect of his graphic personality with some precision.

St. Eustace's vision of a stag with a shining crucifix between its antlers, which appeared to him while he was hunting near Tivoli, according to the legend in the time of Trajan, is a rare subject in the sixteenth and seventeenth centuries, but it inspired a painting attributed to both Annibale and Agostino Carracci, whose layout is not unlike Cortese's composition.[7] It is the type of subject that attracted Mola, who liked to show people in a landscape setting facing their destiny. Cortese and Mola both worked in S. Marco and in the Quirinale, on adjacent commissions, in the 1650s, as well as at the Pamphili Palace in Valmontone in that decade, as Graf has noted in correspondence with Jak Katalan. Graf has sensibly proposed a date for this drawing in that decade.

ASH

1. Graf (1976) and Rodinò (1979–80).

2. Graf (1973, cat. nos. 105 and 106).

3. Graf (1976, cat. no. 21). Cortese's high-altar fresco in S. Maria dell'Assunzione, Ariccia, was painted between 1664 and 1666. A damaged pen-and-ink composition drawing in Düsseldorf showing the penitent Magdalene in a landscape, also with a horizontal format (FP 11, 489; 79 x 132 mm), offers many technical parallels with the Katalan drawing. Graf, who omitted it in his catalogue, brought it to my attention when I sent him a photograph of the Katalan study.

4. Rodinò (1979–80, cat. no. 121). Cat. nos. 158 and 160 in the catalogue also help to substantiate the attribution of the Katalan drawing to Cortese.

5. Rodinò (1979–80, cat. no. 159) and Graf (1976, cat. no. 107). Rodinò traced four landscape drawings by Cortese in Rome (cat. nos. 262–265) but they are drawn in chalk and thus hard to compare with the pen drawing under discussion. A landscape drawing executed in pen and ink with wash sold as by Mola at Christie's, London, 3 July 1990, lot 41, is, in my opinion, by Cortese. It has the rougher texture and more abrupt tonal contrasts typical of his work.

6. For many characteristic examples, see Turner (1989–90; section 3:13–15, 48, 59, 63, 70, 81, 93, and 103).

7. See Posner (1971, 2:cat. no. 27) with references to print sources. An attribution to Agostino has been suggested by Whitfield (1988, see cat. no. 34 n. 4 in this catalogue).

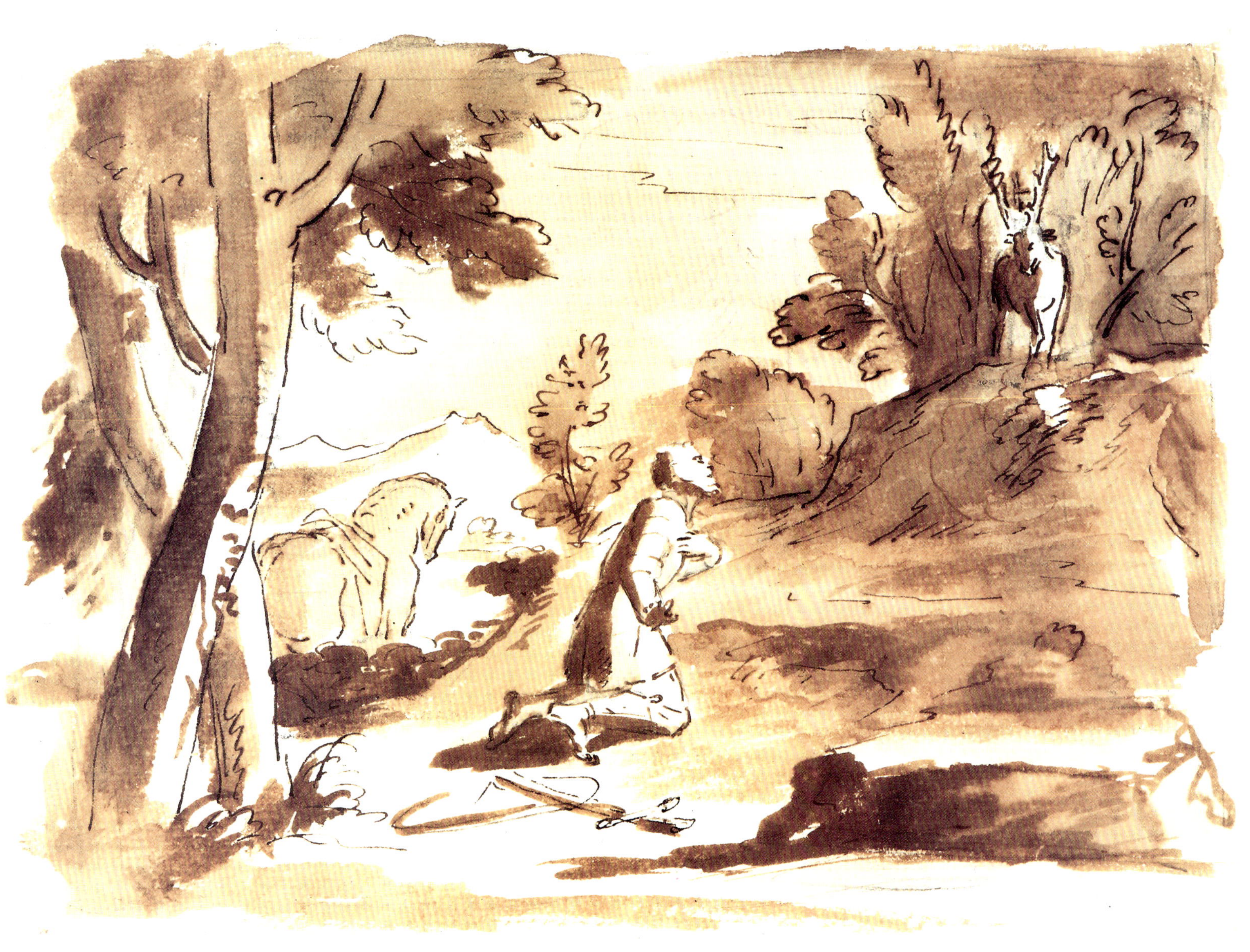

Ciro Ferri

Rome, 1628/34–Rome, 1689

55 *Two Victories Holding the Arms of Pope Innocent XI Odescalchi* (1676–81)

Black chalk, the image of the arms in red chalk; watermark: fleur-de-lis in a circle crowned with a fleur-de-lis; on the verso at the center of the upper margin inscribed in pen and ink, *Ciro Ferri*

251 x 367 mm (9 29/32 x 14 7/16 in)

Provenance: Kate de Rothschild; [Sotheby's, London, 7 December 1987, lot 148]

Literature: unpublished

According to file notes in the Katalan collection, this drawing is preparatory for Ercole Ferrata's sculpture above the high altar of the Roman church of Sta. Agnese in the Piazza Navona. Ferri indeed made drawings for sculpture in Sta. Agnese, and drawings for reliefs of angels above the altars on the piers of the dome are preserved in old copies.[1] There is a certain correspondence in the general position of the right angel over the high altar and the right angel of the Katalan drawing. Nonetheless, the connection is incorrect. Instead of the Dove of the Holy Spirit in the church, a papal coat of arms appears in the drawing. The arms are those of Innocent XI Odescalchi, who was elected on 21 September 1676 and died in 1689, and who had no connection with the Pamphili church in the Piazza Navona.

The trophies appearing behind the right wing of the figure with the trumpet and the armor, between the shield and the figure, as well as the indication of a palm, make their interpretation as Victories more likely than as angels. The left one, in addition, may likewise be interpreted as an allegory of Fame, through the attribute of the trumpet. All this may suggest that the drawing was made for the decoration of ephemeral architecture, such as a triumphal arch erected on the occasion of a victory, or that it is preparatory for an engraving commemorating such an event. One of the latter, celebrating Emperor Leopold I's victory over the Turks, was engraved by Jean Louis Roullet after Ferri's design; and a fireworks machine made on the occasion of the liberation of Buda from the Turks in 1686, based on Ferri's invention, was engraved by Nicolo Dorigny.[2] Both of these commissions date, like the Katalan drawing, from the years of the pontificate of Innocent XI, which covered approximately the last decade of Ciro Ferri's life.

PD

1. Davis (1986, figs. 97–100).

2. Dreyer (1967; 250, Abb. 25 and 267, Abb. 51).

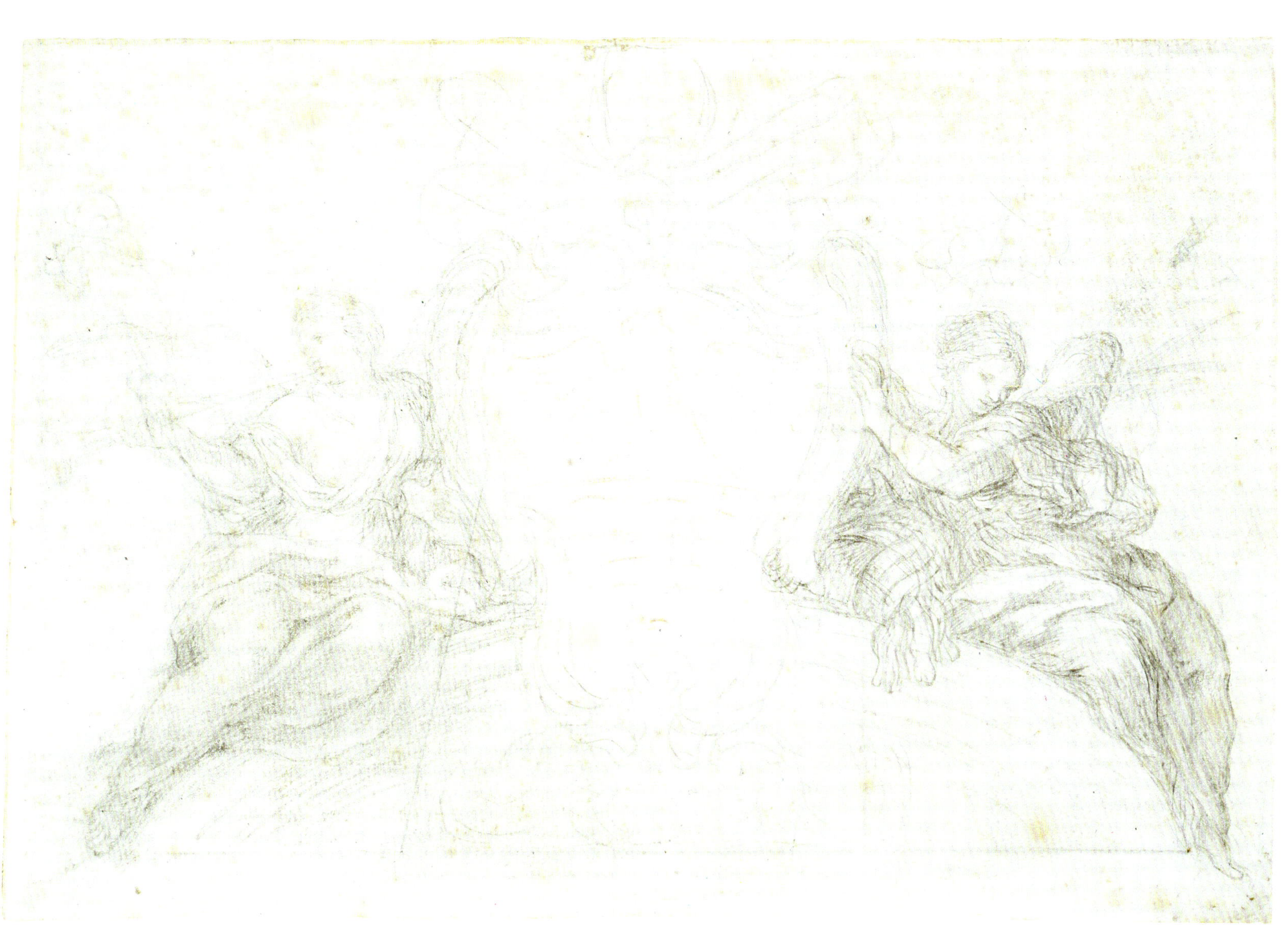

Bibliography

Abromson 1978
Abromson, Morton C. "Clement VIII's Patronage of the Brothers Alberti." *Art Bulletin* 60 (1978): 531–47.

Aldega 1980
Aldega, Marcello. *Disegni Italiani dal XVI al XVIII Sec.* Exh. cat., Rome: De Luca 1980.

Aldega and Gordon 1986
Aldega, Marcello, and Margot Gordon. *Drawings of the Roman Baroque.* Exh. cat., Rome and New York: Aldega and Gordon, 1986.

Aldega and Gordon 1987
Aldega, Marcello, and Margot Gordon. *Italian Drawings of the Sixteenth Century.* Exh. cat., Rome and New York: Aldega and Gordon, 1987.

Aldega and Gordon 1988
Aldega, Marcello, and Margot Gordon. *Italian Drawings, Sixteenth to the Eighteenth Centuries.* Exh. Cat., Rome and New York: Aldega and Gordon, 1988.

Allegri and Cecchi 1980
Allegri, Ettore, and Alessandro Cecchi. *Palazzo Vecchio e i Medici.* Florence: S.P.E.S., 1980.

Andrews 1967
Andrews, Keith. "Two Newly Discovered Drawings by Tanzio da Varallo." *Paragone* 18, no. 207 (1967): 63–65.

Andrews 1969
Andrews, Keith. *Italian Sixteenth-Century Drawings from British Private Collections.* Exh. cat., Edinburgh: Scottish Arts Council, 1969.

Angelini 1986
Angelini, Alessandro. "Compte-rendu du catalogue de l'exposition: 'Andrea del Sarto 1486–1530. Dipinti e disegni a Firenze.'" *Prospettiva* 45 (April 1986): 85–91.

Angelini 1990
Angelini, Alessandro. *Domenico Beccafumi e il suo tempo.* Exh. cat., Siena: Edam, 1990.

Arcangeli 1956
Arcangeli, Francesco. P. 106ff. in *Mostra dei Carracci.* Exh. cat., Bologna: Edizioni Alta, 1956.

Arcangeli 1959
Arcangeli, Francesco. P. 54 in *Maestri della pittura del Seicento emiliano.* Exh. cat., Bologna: Edizioni Alta, 1959.

Arcangeli 1970
Arcangeli, Francesco. *Natura ed espressione nell'arte bolognese-emiliana.* Exh. cat., Bologna: Edizioni Alta, 1970.

Armani 1986
Armani, Elena Parma. *Perino del Vaga: L'anello mancante.* Genoa: Sagep, 1986.

Arslan 1960
Arslan, Edouardo. Vol. 1 in *I Bassano.* Milan: Ceschima, 1960.

Avery and Radcliffe 1978–79
Avery, Charles, and Anthony Radcliffe. *Giambologna 1529 –1608 Sculptor to the Medici.* Exh. Cat., London: Victoria and Albert Museum, 1978–79.

Baccheschi 1977
Baccheschi, Edi. *L'opera completa di Beccafumi.* Milan: Rizzoli, 1977.

Baglione 1642
Baglione, Giovanni. *Le vite de' pittori, scultori et architetti dal . . . 1572. In sino á. . . 1642.* Rome: Andrea Fei, 1642.

Bagnoli 1978
Bagnoli, Alessandro. "Aggiornamento di Rutilio Manetti." *Prospettiva* 4, no. 13 (1978): 23–42.

Baldinucci 1680–1728
Baldinucci, Filippo. *Notizie de Professori del Disegno da Cimabue in qua.* Florence: Santi Franchi, 1680–1728.

Baldinucci 1846
Baldinucci, Filippo. *Notizie dei professori del Disegno, Florence.* Ed. F. Ranalli. Florence: V. Ratelli, 1846.

Barocchi 1965
Barocchi, Paola. "Itinerario di Giovambattista Naldini." *Arte Antica e Moderna*, no. 31 (1965): 3–47.

Barsanti 1986–87
Barsanti, Anna. *Il Seicento Fiorentino.* Exh. cat., Florence: Cantini, 1986–87.

Bean 1982
Bean, Jacob. *15th and 16th Century Italian Drawings in the Metropolitan Museum of Art.* New York: Metropolitan Museum of Art, 1982.

Bellinger 1988
Bellinger, Katrin. *Italian Drawings.* Exh. Cat., London: n.p., 1988.

Bellinger 1991
Bellinger, Katrin. *Die Ziechnung in Florenz: Drawing in Florence 1500–1650.* Exh. cat., London and Munich: n.p., 1991.

Benati 1991
Benati, Daniele. *Disegni emiliani del Sei-Settecento, Come nascono i dipinti.* Milan: Silvana, 1991.

Bertelà 1980
Bertelà, G. Gaeta. *Il Primato del Disegno.* Exh. cat., Florence: Palazzo Strozzi, 1980.

Bisogni 1981
Bisogni, Fabio. "Le opere di Domenico Beccafumi nelle collezioni Galgano Saracini." *Prospettiva*, no. 26 (July 1981): 25–47.

Bjurström 1979
Bjurström, Per. *Italian Drawings.* Stockholm: Liber Förlag, 1979.

Blunt 1960
Blunt, Anthony F. *Roman Drawings at Windsor Castle.* London: Phaidon, 1960.

Bohn 1992a
Bohn, Babette. "Malvasia and the Study of Carracci Drawings." *Master Drawings* 30, no. 4 (1992): 396–414.

Bohn 1992b
Bohn, Babette. "Problems in Carracci Connoisseurship: Drawings by Agostino Carracci." *Drawing* 13, no. 6 (1992): 125–28.

Bohn 1993
Bohn, Babette. "I disegni giovanili in penna di Ludovico Carracci." *Atti e Memorie dell'Accademia Clementina* 29 (1993): 229–54.

Bohn 1994
Bohn, Babette. *Agostino Carracci.* Vol. 39, part 1 in The Illustrated Bartsch. New York: Abaris, 1994.

Bora 1973
Bora, Giulio. Pp. 31–32 in *Seicento lombardo. Catalogo dei disegni, libri, stampe.* Exh. cat., Milan: Electa, 1973.

Borea 1965
Borea, Evalina. *Domenichino.* Milan: G. Barbèra, 1965.

Borea 1975
Borea, Evalina. *Pittori bolognesi del Seicento nelle Gallerie di Firenze.* Exh. cat., Florence: Sansoni, 1975.

Brauer and Wittkower 1931
Brauer, Heinrich, and Rudolf Wittkower. *Die Zeichnungen von Gianlorenzo Bernini.* Berlin: Heinrich Keller, 1931.

Brejon de Lavergnée and Volle 1988–89
Brejon de Lavergnée, Arnauld, and Nathalie Volle. *Le siècle de Caravage dans les collections françaises.* Exh. cat., Paris: Grand Palais; 1988–89.

Briganti 1962
Briganti, Giuliano. *Pietro da Cortona.* Florence: Sansoni, 1962.

Briquet 1907
Briquet, C. M. *Dictionnaire des marques de papier.* Geneva: n.p., 1907.

Byam Shaw 1976
Byam Shaw, James. *Drawings by Old Masters at Christ Church, Oxford.* Oxford: Clarendon Press, 1976.

Byam Shaw 1983
Byam Shaw, James. *Italian Drawings in the Lugt Collection.* Paris: Institute Neerlandais, 1983.

Cantelli 1970
Cantelli, Giuseppe. *Disegni di Cecco Bravo.* Exh. cat., Florence: Unione Fiorentina, 1970.

Carroll 1976
Carroll, Eugene A. *The Drawings of Rosso Fiorentino.* New York: Garland, 1976

Cassirer 1920
Cassirer, K. "Zeichnungen Polidoro da Caravaggio in den Berliner Museen." In *Jahrbuch der Preussischen Kunstsammlungen.* Berlin: n.p., 1920.

Cavina 1988
Cavina, Anna Ottani. "Annibale Carracci e la lupa del fregio Magnani." Pp. 19–38 in *Les Carrache et les Décors Profanes.* Ed. François-Charles Uginet. Rome: École française and Décors de Rome, 1988.

Chappell et al. 1979
Chappell, Miles, et al. *Disegni dei Toscani a Roma (1580-1620).* Exh. Cat., Florence: Leo S. Olschki, 1979.

Chappell 1992
Chappell, Miles L. *Disegni di Ludovico Cigoli, 1556–1613.* Exh. Cat., Florence: Leo S. Olschki, 1992.

Christiansen 1990
Christiansen, Keith. *A Caravaggio Rediscovered: The Lute Player.* New York: Metropolitan Museum of Art, 1990.

Clerici Bagozzi, Pirondini, and Frisoni 1987
Clerici Bagozzi, Nora, Massimo Pirondini, and Fiorella Frisoni. *Lelio Orsi.* Exh. cat., Reggio Emilia: Silvana, 1987.

Colnaghi 1994
Colnaghi. *Master Paintings.* Exh. cat., London: Colnaghi Gallery, 1994.

Conigliello et al. 1989
Conigliello, Lucilla, et al. *Il Chiostro di Ognissanti a Firenze. Gli affreschi del ciclo francescano.* Florence: Centro Di, 1989.

Cordellier 1987
Cordellier, Dominique. "Guido Reni's Separation of Day and Night." *Burlington Magazine* 129, no. 1007 (February 1987): 81–82.

Corti 1989
Corti, Laura. *Vasari. Catalogo completo dei dipinti.* Florence: Cantini, 1989.

Costamagna and Fabre 1991
Costamagna, Philippe, and Anne Fabre. "Di alcuni problemi della bottega di Andrea del Sarto." *Paragone* 491 (1991): 15–28.

Cox-Rearick 1964
Cox-Rearick, Janet. *The Drawings of Pontormo.* First ed., Cambridge: Harvard University Press; 2d ed., New York: Hacker Art Books, 1964.

Davidson 1969
Davidson, Bernice. "Perino del Vaga e la sua Cerchia: Addenda and Corrigenda." *Master Drawings* 7, no. 4 (1969): 404–9.

Davis 1986
Davis, Bruce. *The Drawings of Ciro Ferri.* New York and London: Garland, 1986.

Davis 1979
Davis, Charles. "Per l'attività romana del Vasari nel 1553: incisioni negli affreschi di Villa Altoviti e la Fontanalia di Villa Giulia." *Mitteilungen des Kunsthistorischen Institutes in Florenz* 23 (1979): 197–224.

Davis 1981
Davis, Charles. *Giorgio Vasari.* Exh. cat., Arezzo: Edam, 1981.

DeGrazia Bohlin 1979
DeGrazia Bohlin, Diane. *Prints and Related Drawings by the Carracci Family.* Exh. cat., Washington, D.C.: National Gallery of Art, 1979.

DeGrazia 1984
DeGrazia, Diane. *Le Stampe dei Carracci.* Exh. cat., Bologna: Pinacoteca Nazionale, 1984.

De Marchi 1990
De Marchi, Andrea. "Beccafumi e la sua 'maniera': difficoltà del disegno senese." Pp. 412–25 in *Domenico Beccafumi.* Exh. cat., Siena: Edam, 1990.

Di Giampaolo 1988
Di Giampaolo, Mario. "Bartolomeo Cesi." Pp. 92–171 in *Bartolomeo Cesi.* Ed. Francesco Abbate, Mario Di Giampaolo, and Alberto Graziani. Milan: Angelo Dalerba, 1988.

Di Giampaolo 1989a
Di Giampaolo, Mario. P. 200 in *Disegni della Galleria Estense di Modena.* Exh. cat., Modena: Panini, 1989.

Di Giampaolo 1989b
Di Giampaolo, Mario. *Disegni emiliani del Rinascimento.* Milan: Silvana, 1989.

Di Giampaolo 1990
Di Giampaolo, Mario. *Disegni emiliani del Sei-Settecento. I grandi cicli di affrechi.* Milan: Silvana, 1990.

Di Giampaolo 1991
Di Giampaolo, Mario. *Parmigianino.* Florence: Cantini, 1991.

Di Giampaolo 1993
Di Giampaolo, Mario. *Disegni emiliani.* Exh. cat., Venice: Electa, 1993.

Domenico Cortese 1969
Domenico Cortese, Gemma. "Percorso di Giacinto Gimignani." *Commentari* 17 (1969): 186–206.

Dreyer 1967
Dreyer, Peter. "Pietro Lucatelli." *Jahrbuch der Berliner Museen* 9 (1967): 232–73.

Dreyer 1981
Dreyer, Peter. "Eine unbekannte Zeichnung von Gianlorenzo Bernini." Pp. 161–63 in *Per A. E. Popham*. Ed. Igino and Adrianna Consigli. Parma: Consigli Arte, 1981.

Ebert-Schifferer et al. 1988
Ebert-Schifferer, Sybille, et al. *Guido Reni e l'Europa: Fama e Fortuna*. Exh. cat., Frankfurt: Kunsthalle, 1988.

Edinburgh Festival Society 1972
Edinburgh Festival Society. *Italian Seventeenth-Century Drawings from British Private Collections.* Exh. cat., Edinburgh: Edinburgh Festival Society Limited, 1972.

Ekserdjian 1993
Ekserdjian, David. "Parmigianino and Michelangelo." *Master Drawings* 31, no. 4 (1993): 390–94.

Ekserdjian 1994
Ekserdjian, David. Review of *Sixteenth-Century Italian Drawings in New York Collections* by William M. Griswold and Linda Wolk-Simon, exh. cat., New York, 1994. In *Burlington Magazine* 136, no. 1092 (1994): 203.

Ewald 1973
Ewald, Gerhard. "Unknown Works by Baldassare Franceschini called Il Volterrano (1611–1689)." *Burlington Magazine* 115 (May 1973): 272–83.

Ewald 1981
Ewald, Gerhard. Pp. 74–75 in *Giorgio Vasari*. Ed. Charles Davis. Exh. cat., Arezzo: Edam, 1981.

Falletti et al. 1992
Falletti, Franca, et al. *Chiostri Seicenteschi a Pistoia.* Florence: Cassa di Risparmio di Pistoia e Pescia, 1992.

Faranda 1986
Faranda, Franco. *Ludovico Cardi detto il Cigoli.* Rome: De Luca, 1986.

Feigenbaum 1992
Feigenbaum, Gail. "When the Subject was Art: The Carracci as Copyists." Pp. 297–308 in *Atti del Colloquio C.I.H.A. 1990*. Bologna: n.p., 1992.

Feigenbaum 1993
Feigenbaum, Gail. *Ludovico Carracci.* Exh. cat., Bologna: Nuova Alta, 1993.

Fenyö 1958
Fenyö, Ivan. "Dessins italiens inconnus." *Bulletin Du Musée National Hongrois Des Beaux Arts* 13 (1958): 59–86.

Fenyö 1967
Fenyö, Ivan. "Drawings by Annibale Carracci in Budapest." *Master Drawings* 5, no. 3 (1967): 255–64.

Fischer 1994
Fischer, Chris. *Fra Bartolommeo et son atelier.* Exh. cat., Paris: Réunion des Musées Nationaux, 1994.

Forlani 1959
Forlani, Anna. *Mostra di disegni di Andrea Boscoli.* Exh. Cat., Florence: Leo S. Olschki, 1959.

Forlani Tempesti 1977
Forlani Tempesti, Anna. "Trentotto disegni del Cesi comprati da Leopoldo dei Medici." Vol. 2, pp. 486–98 in idem, *Scritti di Storia dell'Arte in onore di Ugo Procacci.* Milan: Electa, 1977.

Fortunati Pietrantonio 1986
Fortunati Pietrantonio, Vera. "Prospero Fontana." Vol. 1, pp. 339–414 in idem, *Pittura bolognese del '500.* Bologna: Gratis Edizioni, 1986.

Fröhlich-Bum 1931–32
Fröhlich-Bum, Lili. "Zeichnungen des Jacopo Bassano." *Zeitschrift für bildener kunst* 65 (1931–32): 121–28.

Frommel 1990
Frommel, Christoph Luitpold. "Peruzziana: Ab-un Zuschreibungsprobleme in Baldassare Peruzzis figuralen Oeuvre." P. 72 in *Studien zur Kunstlerzeichnung: Essays in Honor of Klaus Schwager*. Ed. Stephan Kummer and Georg Satzinger. Stuttgart: Hatje, 1990.

Fuhring 1989
Fuhring, Peter. Vol. 1 in *Design into Art: Drawings for Architecture and Ornament, The Lodewijk Houthakker Collection.* London: Philip Wilson, 1989.

Galerie La Scala
Galerie La Scala. *Femmes*. Exh. cat., Paris: n.p., 1991.

Ganz 1984
Ganz, Kate. *Old Master Drawings.* Exh. cat., London: Kate Ganz Ltd., 1984.

Gere 1965
Gere, John A. "The Decoration of the Villa Giulia." *Burlington Magazine* 107 (1965): 109–206.

Gere 1969
Gere, John A. *Taddeo Zuccaro: His Development Studied in His Drawings.* Chicago: University of Chicago Press, 1969.

Gere 1970
Gere, John A. "The Lawrence-Phillipps-Rosenbach 'Zuccaro Album.'" *Master Drawings* 8, no. 2 (1970): 123–40.

Gere 1986
Gere, John A. Review of *Polidoro Caldara da Caravaggio* by Lanfranco Ravelli, Bergamo, 1978. In *Master Drawings* 23–24, no.1 (1986): 61–74.

Gere and Pouncey 1983
Gere, John A., and Philip Pouncey. *Italian Drawings in the Department of Prints and Drawings in the British Museum: Artists working in Rome c. 1550 to c. 1640.* London: British Museum, 1983.

Goldner 1988
Goldner, George R. *Catalogue of the Collections, European Drawings, 1.* Malibu: J. Paul Getty Museum, 1988.

Goldner and Hendrix 1992
Goldner, George, and Lee Hendrix. *Catalogue of the Collections, European Drawings 2*. Malibu: J. Paul Getty Museum, 1992.

Gonzales-Palacios and Garstang 1983
Gonzales-Palacios, Alvar, and Donald Garstang. *The Adjectives of History, Furniture and Works of Art 1550–1870.* Exh. cat., London: Colnaghi Gallery, 1983.

Graf 1973
Graf, Dieter. *Master Drawings of the Roman Baroque from the Kunstmuseum, Düsseldorf.* Exh. cat., London: Victoria and Albert Museum, 1973.

Graf 1976
Graf, Dieter. *Die Handzeichnungen von Guglielmo Cortese und Giovanni Battista Gaulli.* Exh. cat., Düsseldorf: Kunstmuseum Düsseldorf, 1976.

Graziani 1939
Graziani, Alberto. "Bartolomeo Cesi." *La Critica d'Arte* 20–22, nos. 2–4 (1939): 54–95.

Griswold and Wolk-Simon 1994
Griswold, William M., and Linda Wolk-Simon. *Sixteenth-Century Italian Drawings in New York Collections.* New York: Metropolitan Museum of Art, 1994.

Hamilton 1980
Hamilton, Paul C. *Disegni di Bernardino Poccetti.* Florence: Leo S. Olschki, 1980.

Harprath 1977
Harprath, Richard, ed. *Stiftung Ratjen, Italienische Zeichnungen des 16.–18. Jahrhunderts.* Exh. cat., Munich: Prestel, 1977.

Harris 1977
Harris, Ann Sutherland. *Andrea Sacchi, Complete Edition of the Paintings, with a Critical Catalogue.* Oxford: Phaidon, 1977.

Harris 1978
Harris, Ann Sutherland. "Drawings by Andrea Sacchi: *Addenda.*" *Burlington Magazine* 120 (1978): 601–2.

Harris 1992
Harris, Ann Sutherland. Review of *Pier Francesco Mola, 1612–1666* by Nicholas Turner, exh. cat., Lugano and Rome, 1989–90. In *Master Drawings* 30, no. 2 (1992): 216–23.

Harris and Schaar 1967
Harris, Ann Sutherland, and Ekhard Schaar. *Die Handzeichnungen von Andrea Sacchi und Carlo Maratta.* Exh. cat., Düsseldorf: Kunstmuseum Düsseldorf, 1967.

Hayward 1962
Hayward, J. F. "The Mannerist Goldsmith and Some Drawings and Designs." *The Connoisseur* 155 (1962): 157–64.

Hayward 1965
Hayward, J. F. "The Mannerist Goldsmith: 3." *The Connoisseur* 158 (1965): 144–49.

Hermann-Fiore 1980
Hermann-Fiore, Kristina. "Studi sui disegni di Giovanni e Cherubino Alberti." *Bollettino d'arte* 5 (1980): 39ff.

Hermann-Fiore 1983
Hermann-Fiore, Kristina. *Disegni degli Alberti.* Exh. cat., Rome: Gabinetto Nazionale di Stampe, 1983.

Howard 1988
Howard, Seymour. "Carraccesque Landscapes by Bonzi." *Gazette des Beaux Arts* 112 (December 1988): 227–49.

Jaffé 1956
Jaffé, Michael. "The Carracci Exhibition at Bologna." *Burlington Magazine* 97 (1956): 392–401.

Jaffé 1964
Jaffé, Michael. "Some pen drawings of landscape with figures by Annibale Carracci." *Bulletin du Museé Hongrois des Beaux Arts* 25 (1964): 87–97.

Jaffé 1977
Jaffé, Michael. *European Drawings in the Fitzwilliam Museum.* Exh. cat., New York: Pierpont Morgan Library, 1977.

Jaffé 1987–88
Jaffé, Michael. *Old Master Drawings from Chatsworth, A Loan Exhibition from the Devonshire Collection.* Exh. cat., Pittsburgh: International Exhibitions Foundation, 1987–88.

Johnston 1973
Johnston, Catherine. *Mostra di disegni bolognesi dal XVI al XVIII secolo.* Exh. cat., Florence: Leo S. Olschki, 1973.

Kaufman Collection 1969
The Kaufman Collection of Art and Design. Exh. cat., Portsmouth: n.p., 1969.

Knackfuss 1896
Knackfuss, Hermann. *Michelangelo.* Bielfeld and Leipzig: Verlag von Delhagen and Klafing, 1896.

Kollewijn 1985
Kollewijn, Roeland D. Introduction to *Wanden en Plafonds*. Nijmengen: n.p., 1985.

Kozak and Monkiewicz 1993
Kozak, Anna, and Macieg Monkiewicz. *European Drawings from Polish Collections.* Exh. cat., Washington, D.C.: National Gallery of Art, 1993.

Kurz 1942
Kurz, Otto. "A Sculpture by Guido Reni." *Burlington Magazine* 81 (1942): 222–26.

Kurz 1955
Kurz, Otto. *Bolognese Drawings of the XVII and XVIII Centuries in the Collection of Her Majesty the Queen at Windsor Castle.* London: Phaidon, 1955.

Lavin 1980
Lavin, Irving. *Bernini and the Unity of the Visual Arts.* New York: Oxford University Press, 1980.

Lavin et al. 1981
Lavin, Irving, et al. *Drawings by Gianlorenzo Bernini from the Museum der Bildenden Kunste Leipzig, German Democratic Republic.* Exh. cat., Princeton: Princeton University Art Museum, 1981.

Liphart Rathshoff 1935
Liphart Rathshoff, Rode. "Un libro di schizzi di Domenico Beccafumi." *Rivista d'Arte* 17 (1935): 33–70, 162–200.

Llewellyn and Romalli 1992
Llewellyn, Elizabeth, and Christiana Romalli. *Drawing in Bologna 1500–1600.* Exh. cat., London: Courtauld Institute of Art, 1992.

Lloyd 1986
Lloyd, Christopher. "Drawings Attributable to Tribolo." *Master Drawings* 6, no. 3 (1986): 243–46.

Macandrew 1980
Macandrew, Hugh. *Catalogue of the Collection of Drawings, III Italian Schools: Supplement.* Oxford: Ashmolean Museum, 1980.

Mahoney 1977
Mahoney, S. Michael. *The Drawings of Salvator Rosa.* New York and London: Garland, 1977.

Mahon 1957
Mahon, Denis. "Afterthoughts on the Carracci Exhibition." *Gazette des Beaux-Arts* 49 (1957): 193–207, 267–98.

Mahon 1991
Mahon, Denis. *Giovanni Francesco Barbieri il Guercino: Disegni.* Exh. cat., Bologna: Museo Civico Archeologico, 1991.

Maiskaia 1986
Maiskaia, Marina. *The Famous Drawings at the Pushkin Museum in Moscow.* Milan: Amilcare Pizzi, 1986.

Malvasia [1678] 1841
Malvasia, Carlo Cesare. *Felsina Pittrice, Vite de' pittori bolognesi.* First ed., Bologna: n.p., 1678; 2d ed. edited by G. P. Zanotti. Bologna: Tipografia Guidi all'Ancora, 1841.

Marabottini 1969
Marabottini, Alessandro. *Polidoro da Caravaggio.* Rome: Edizioni dell'Elefante, 1969.

Markova 1992
Markova, Vittoria. "Un 'Baccanale' ritrovato di Giorgio Vasari, proveniente dalla Galleria Gerini." Vol. 17, pp. 237–41 in *Kunst des Cinquecento in der Toskana.* Munich: Kunsthistorischen Institut in Florenz, 1992.

Masetti 1962
Masetti, Anna Rosa. *Cecco Bravo pittore toscano del Seicento.* Venice: N. Pozza, 1962.

Mason Rinaldi 1984
Mason Rinaldi, Stefania. *Palma il Giovane.* Milan: Electa, 1984.

Masseri 1993
Masseri, Stefania. *Giulio Romano pinxit et delineavit. Opere grafiche autografe di collaborazione e bottega.* Exh. cat., Rome: Fratelli Palombi, 1993.

McTavish 1985–86
McTavish, David. *Italian Drawings from the Collection of Duke Roberto Ferretti.* Exh. cat., Toronto: Art Gallery of Ontario, 1985–86.

Meijer 1984
Meijer, Bert. "Drawings by Francesco Maffei." *Master Drawings* 22 (1984): 303–10.

Miller 1985-86
Miller, Dwight C. "The Drawings of Bartolomeo Schedoni: Toward a Firmer Definition of his Drawing Style and its Chronology." *Master Drawings* 23–24 (1985–86): 36–45.

Monbeig Goguel 1970
Monbeig Goguel, Catherine. *Il Manierismo fiorentino.* Vol. 16 in Maestri del disegno. Milan: Fratelli Fabbri, 1970.

Monbeig Goguel 1972
Monbeig Goguel, Catherine. *Vasari et son temps.* Exh. cat., Paris: Réunion des Musées Nationaux, 1972.

Monbeig Goguel 1979
Monbeig Goguel, Catherine. *Maestri Toscani del Cinquecento.* Vol. 22 in Biblioteca dei Disegni. Florence: Alinari, 1979.

Monbeig Goguel 1990
Monbeig Goguel, Catherine. "Da Francesco Salviati a Cristofano Gherardi e Battista Franco." Pp. 121–30 in *Nuove ricerche in margine alla mostra: Da Leonardo a Rembrandt.* Turin: Disegni della Biblioteca Reale, 1990.

Monbeig Goguel 1991
Monbeig Goguel, Catherine. Review of *Fra Bartolommeo: Master of the High Renaissance* by Chris Fischer, exh. cat., Rotterdam, 1990. In *Burlington Magazine* 133 (July 1991): 453–54.

Mortari 1966
Mortari, Luisa. *Bernardo Strozzi.* Rome: n.p., 1966.

Mortari 1992
Mortari, Luisa. *Francesco Salviati.* Rome: De Luca, 1992.

Moscadelli and Zarrilli 1990
Moscadelli, Stefano, and Carla Zarrilli. "Domenico Beccafumi e altri artisti nelle fonti documentarie senesi del primo Cinquecento." Pp. 678–715 in idem, *Domenico Beccafumi e il suo tempo.* Exh. cat., Siena: Edam, 1990.

Moschini 1931
Moschini, Vittorio. "Disegni del tardo '500 e del '600 all'Accademia di Venezia." *Bollettino d'Arte* 25, no. 2 (1931): 70–83.

Neilson 1970
Neilson, Nancy Ward. "A Drawing by Tanzio da Varallo." *Master Drawings* 8, no. 3 (1970): 275–76.

Neilson 1979
Neilson, Nancy Ward. *Camillo Procaccini: Paintings and Drawings.* New York: Garland, 1979.

Neilson 1989
Neilson, Nancy Ward. *Pinoteca di Brera: Scuole lombarda, ligure e piemontese 1535–1796.* Milan: Electa, 1989.

Newcome 1975
Newcome, Mary. "The Drawings of Valerio Castello." *Master Drawings* 13 (1975): 26–40.

Newcome Schleier 1985
Newcome Schleier, Mary. *Le dessin à Gênes du XVI au XVIII siècle.* Exh. cat., Paris: Réunion des Musées Nationaux, 1985.

Nicholson 1965
Nicholson, Benedict. Review of the exhibition at Thomas Agnew. In *Burlington Magazine* 107, no. 753 (1965): 641.

Nissman, Abromson & Co. 1989
Nissman, Abromson & Co. *Italian Drawings 1500 –1800*. Exh. cat., New York: Nissman, Abromson & Co., 1989.

Pace 1973
Pace, Ursula Fischer. *Giacinto Gimignani (1606–1681), Eine Studie zur römischen Malerei des Seicento.* Freiburg: Albert-Ludwig Universität in Freiburg, 1973.

Parker 1956
Parker, Karl T. *Catalogue of the Collection of Drawings in the Ashmolean Museum, II, Italian Schools.* Oxford: Oxford University Press, 1956.

Pepper 1971
Pepper, D. Stephen. "Augustin Carrache, Maître et Dessinateur." *Revue de l'Art* 14 (1971): 39–44.

Pepper 1988
Pepper, D. Stephen. *Guido Reni: L'opera completa*. Second ed., Novara: Istituto Geografico De Agostini, 1988.

Petrioli Tofani 1985
Petrioli Tofani, Annamaria. *Dieci anni di acquisizioni 1974–1984.* Exh. cat., Florence: Leo S. Olschki, 1985.

Petrioli Tofani 1988
Petrioli Tofani, Annamaria. *Sixteenth Century Tuscan Drawings from the Uffizi.* Exh. cat., Detroit: Detroit Institute of Arts, 1988.

Pillsbury 1976
Pillsbury, Edmund. "The Sala Grande Drawings by Vasari and his Workshop: Some Documents and New Attributions." *Master Drawings* 14, no. 3 (1976): 127–46.

Pinelli 1988
Pinelli, Antonio. "Vivere 'alla filosofica' o vestire di velluto? Storia di Jacone fiorentino e della sua 'masnada' antivasariana." *Ricerche di Storia dell'Arte,* no. 34 (1988): 5–34.

Pope-Hennessy 1948
Pope-Hennessy, John. *The Drawings of Domenichino.... at Windsor Castle.* London: Phaidon, 1948.

Popham 1971
Popham, Arthur E. *Catalogue of the Drawings of Parmigianino.* New Haven and London: Yale University Press, 1971.

Popham and Wilde 1949
Popham, Arthur E., and Johannes Wilde. *The Italian Drawings of the XV and XVI century in the Collections of His Majesty the King at Windsor Castle.* London: Phaidon, 1949.

Popham and Lloyd 1986
Popham, Arthur E., and Christopher Lloyd. *Old Master Drawings at Holkham Hall.* Chicago: University of Chicago Press, 1986.

Posner 1971
Posner, Donald. *Annibale Carracci, A Study in the Reform of Italian Painting around 1590.* London: Phaidon, 1971.

Pouncey and Gere 1962
Pouncey, Philip, and John A. Gere. *Italian Drawings in the Department of Prints and Drawings in the British Museum: Raphael and his Circle.* London: British Museum, 1962.

Ravelli 1978
Ravelli, Lanfranco. *Polidoro Caldara da Caravaggio.* Bergamo: Edizioni Monumenta Bergomensia, 1978.

Ravelli 1988
Ravelli, Lanfranco. *Un Fregiondi Polidoro a Palazzo Baldassini in Roma.* Bergamo: Edizioni dell'Ateneo di Scienze Lettere ed Arti, 1988.

Rensi Albums n.d.
Rensi Albums. Leipzig: Museum der bildenden Kunste, n.d.

Richardson the Younger 1722
Richardson the Younger, Jonathan. *An Account of Some of the Statues, Bas-Reliefs, Drawings and Pictures in Italy, &c. with Remarks.* London: privately printed, 1722.

Rodinò 1979–80
Rodinò, Simonetta Prosperi Valenti. *Disegni di Guglielmo Cortese (Guillaume Courtois) detto il Borgognone nelle collezioni del Gabinetto Nazionale delle Stampe.* Exh. cat., Rome: Villa alla Farnesina alla Lungara, 1979–80.

Romani 1984
Romani, Vittoria. *Lelio Orsi.* Exh. cat., Modena: Silvana, 1984.

Rosci 1993
Rosci, Marco. *Giulio Cesare Procaccini.* Soncino: Edizioni dei Soncino, 1993.

Rosenberg 1965
Rosenberg, Pierre. "Ludovico Carracci." Pp. 54–56 in *Le XVI siècle européan: Peintures et dessins dans les collections publiques française.* Exh. cat., Paris: Réunion des Musées Nationaux, 1965.

Rosenberg 1966
Rosenberg, Pierre. "Un dessin de Tanzio da Varallo au Muse de Copenhague." *Paragone* 17, no. 199 (1966): 54–55.

Rossi 1991
Rossi, Paola. *Francesco Maffei.* Milan: Electa, 1991.

Royalton-Kisch 1982
Royalton-Kisch, Martin. "New Works by Valerio Castello." *Master Drawings* 20 (1982): 132–35.

Ruggeri 1972
Ruggeri, Ugo. "Disegni di Francesco Maffei." *Arte Veneta* 26 (1972): 133–44.

Ruggeri 1982
Ruggeri, Ugo. *Disegni lombardi.* Exh. cat., Venice: Electa, 1982.

Salerno 1988
Salerno, Luigi. *I dipinti del Guercino.* Rome: Ugo Bozzi, 1988.

Sanminiatelli 1957
Sanminiatelli, Donato. "The Beginnings of Domenico Beccafumi." *Burlington Magazine* 99, no. 657 (December 1957): 401–10.

Sanminiatelli 1967
Sanminiatelli, Donato. *Domenico Beccafumi.* Milan: Bramanti, 1967.

Sapori 1982
Sapori, Giovanna. "Artisti e committenti sul lago Trasimeno." *Paragone* 33, no. 393 (1982): 27–61.

Scarpa 1978
Scarpa, Pietro. *Dessins Anciens.* Paris: Grand Palais, 1978.

Schaefer 1988
Schaefer, Scott. *Guido Reni 1575–1642.* Exh. cat., Bologna: Pinacoteca Nazionale, 1988.

Scholz 1959
Scholz, Janos. *Venetian Drawings from the Scholz Collection.* Oakland, Ca.: Mills College, 1959.

Sciolla 1992
Sciolla, Gianni Carlo, ed. *Il Disegno, I grandi collezionisti.* Turin: Istituto Bancario San Paolo di Torino, 1992.

Sisi 1992
Sisi, Carlo. *Il Disegno Fiorentino del tempo di Lorenzo il Magnifico.* Exh. cat., Florence: Silvana, 1992.

Spear 1982
Spear, Richard E. *Domenichino.* New Haven and London: Yale University Press, 1982.

Stagni 1988
Stagni, Simonetta. *Domenico Maria Canuti Pittore (1626–1684).* Rimini: Luise, 1988.

Stix and Fröhlich-Bum 1932
Stix, Alfred, and Lili Fröhlich-Bum. *Die Zeichnungen der Toskanischen, Umbrischen und Römischen Schulen. Beschreibender Katalog der Handzeichnungen in der Graphischen Sammlung Albertina.* Vienna: A. Schroll, 1932.

Stock and Scrase 1985
Stock, Julien, and David Scrase. *The Achievement of a Connoisseur, Philip Pouncey.* Exh. cat., Cambridge, Mass.: Fitzwilliam Museum, 1985.

Stone 1991
Stone, David M. *Guercino Master Draftsman: Works from North American Collections.* Exh. cat., Cambridge, Mass.: Arthur M. Sackler Museum, Harvard University, 1991.

Tan Bunzl 1984
Tan Bunzl, Yvonne. *Old Master Drawings.* Exh. Cat., London: Yvone Tan Bunzl, 1984.

Testori 1959
Testori, Giovanni. *Tanzio da Varallo.* Exh. cat., Torino: Foligrafiche Riunite, 1959.

Testori 1964
Testori, Giovanni. "Tre disegni del Tanzio." *Paragone* 15, no. 173 (1964): 45–47.

Thiem 1977
Thiem, Christel. *Florentiner Zeichner des Frühbarock.* Munich: Bruckmann, 1977.

Thiem 1983–84
Thiem, Christel. *Disegni di Artisti Bolognesi dal Seicento all'Ottocento della Collezione Schloss Fachsenfeld e della Graphische Sammlung Staatsgalerie Stuttgart.* Exh. cat., Bologna: Palazzo Pepoli Campogrande, 1983–84.

Tietze and Tietze-Conrat 1944
Tietze, Hans, and Erica Tietze-Conrat. *Drawings of the Venetian Painters of the 15th and 16th Centuries.* New York: J. J. Augustin, 1944.

Trezzani 1983
Trezzani, Ludovico. "Jan Miel." Pp. 90–131 in Giovanni Briganti et al., *The Bamboccianti, The Painters of Everyday Life in Seventeenth Century Rome*. Rome: Ugo Bozzi, 1983.

Turčić 1983
Turčić, Lawrence. "Niccolò Circignani, called il Pomarancio: Drawings for some Roman Projects." *Master Drawings* 21, no. 3 (1983): 271–74.

Turner 1989–90
Turner, Nicholas. "Pier Francesco Mola: i disegni." Pp. 103–20 and 220–98 in idem, *Pier Francesco Mola, 1612–1666*. Exh. cat., Lugano and Rome: Electa, 1989–90.

Turner 1992
Turner, Nicholas. Review of *Drawing in Bologna 1500–1600* by Elizabeth Llewellyn and Christiana Romalli, exh. cat., London, 1992. In *Burlington Magazine* 134 (1992): 539–41.

Van Regteren Altena 1966
Van Regteren Altena, I. Q. *Les dessins italiens de la reine Christine de Suède*. Stockholm: A. B. Agnellska Boktrycheriet, 1966.

Vasari 1906
Vasari, Giorgio. *Le Vite de' piu eccelenti pittori scultori ed architettori... con nuovo annotazioni e commenti di Gaetano Milanesi*. Florence: Sansoni, 1906.

Vasari 1963–64
Vasari, Giorgio. *Le Vite....* Milan: Club del Libro, 1963–64 (1st ed., Florence: Giunti, 1568).

Viatte 1981–82
Viatte, Françoise. *Dessins baroques florentins du musée du Louvre, LXXIV*. Exh. cat., Paris: Cabinet des dessins, Musée du Louvre, 1981–82.

Voss and Planiscig n.d.
Voss, Hermann, and Leo Planiscig. *Drawings from the Collection of Benno Geiger*. Vienna: Amalthea Verlag, n.d.

Wallace 1979
Wallace, Richard W. *The Etchings of Salvator Rosa*. Princeton: Princeton University Press, 1979.

Ward-Jackson 1979
Ward-Jackson, Peter. *Italian Drawings: Volume One, 14th-16th Century*. London: Her Majesty's Stationery Office, 1979.

Whitfield 1988
Whitfield, Clovis. "The landscapes of Agostino Carracci." Pp. 73–95 in *Les Carrache et les Decors Profanes*. Ed. François-Charles Uginet. Rome: École française and Décors de Rome, 1988.

Wilson 1987
Wilson, Timothy. *Ceramic Art of the Italian Renaissance*. London: British Museum, 1987.

Zacchi 1991
Zacchi, Alessandro. "Bartolomeo Cesi fra tarda maniera e riforma carraccesca: nuove proposte per il catalogo dei disegni." Pp. 111–25 in *Arte cristiana*. Milan: Istituto di Storia dell'Arte dell' Università catolica, 1991.